# Three Days In August

## ABOUT THE COVER

**A U.S. flag waves in the breeze as the sun sets over a U.S. military camp in Iraq August 3, 2007. U.S. Navy photo by Mass Communication Specialist 2nd Class Christopher Perez.**

# Three Days In August

## A U.S. Army Special Forces Soldier's Fight for Military Justice

Bob McCarty, L.L.C.

By Bob McCarty

ISBN-13: 978-1466407923

Bob McCarty, L.L.C.
Typeset by Heather Justesen

First Edition

Printed in the United States of America.

**"You always hope that**

**somebody's got your back."**

-- Neal Riley, U.S. Army Special Forces, Ret.

CONTENTS

# Foreword

In recent years, America's fighting men and women have faced an ever-increasing barrage of legal battles stemming from their actions on battlefields and in combat zones around the world. Perhaps most notable is the case of Army Ranger First Lieutenant Michael Behenna.

On July 31, 2008, Lieutenant Behenna was charged with the premeditated murder of Ali Mansur, a known Al-Qaeda agent operating near Albu Toma, an area north of Baghdad. Seven months later, the leader of the 18-member Delta Company, 5th platoon of the U.S. Army's 101st Airborne Infantry Division was convicted of unpremeditated murder and sentenced to 25 years confinement—later reduced to 15—at the U.S. Military Disciplinary Barracks at Fort Leavenworth, Kansas.

One expert called to testify during Lieutenant Behenna's court-martial contends to this day that Army prosecutors committed a Brady violation when they suppressed evidence favorable to the lieutenant's defense and, in doing so, violated due process and his right to a fair and impartial proceeding. The real "kicker" in the case lies in the identity of the person from whom the allegation of prosecutorial misconduct came. Surprisingly, it wasn't someone on the defense side of the courtroom. Instead, it was the Army's own witness, a renowned forensics expert.

Prosecutors flew Dr. Herbert Leon MacDonell from Corning, New York, to Fort Campbell, Kentucky, for the trial, but never allowed him to testify. Why? Because, during the trial, he had the opportunity to examine key pieces of evidence prosecutors had not shared with him prior to his arrival at the proceedings. When he told prosecutors that his examination of that evidence had caused him to change his mind and believe Lieutenant Behenna was telling the truth, they opted against having the court hear his testimony—words that likely would have resulted in a favorable outcome for the young officer.

As this book went to press, the lieutenant, his friends and members of his family were awaiting the final ruling in his appeal process. Worst-case scenario: He'll be released from prison March 19, 2024—at age 40.

Sadly, Lieutenant Behenna is not alone when it comes to unjust prosecution of men and women in uniform.

Another case involved a group of men who came to be known as the "Haditha Marines."

Lieutenant Colonel Jeffery Chessani, commander of 3rd Battalion, 1st Marines, was responsible for approximately 2,000 American and Iraqi forces. At about 7:15 in the morning November 19, 2005, a squad of Colonel Chessani's Marines was leading a convoy when it was ambushed by an enemy using a roadside bomb and small arms fire from nearby houses. The bomb detonated under a Humvee, killing one Marine and injuring two others. An ensuing house-to-house battle between insurgents and an outnumbered Marine "fire team" resulted in the deaths of 24 Iraqis, including 15 civilians.

After Colonel Chessani and seven Marines in his unit were charged with murder, U.S. Rep. John Murtha (D-Pa.)—a now-deceased former Marine—proclaimed the Marines overreacted and killed 24 Iraqi civilians "in cold blood." A costly, yearlong legal battle followed.

On March 26, 2008, Richard Thompson, president and chief counsel of the Thomas More Law Center, an Ann Arbor, Michigan-based nonprofit group that represented Colonel Chessani, summed up the environment within which the Haditha Marines were caught:

> "The hysteria and media firestorm over Abu Ghraib and the Pat Tillman investigations lead to fear of a similar media reaction to the Haditha incident,

> causing the military's civilian bosses to set up this shadow oversight body," Thompson said in a news release. "This extraordinary action politicized the military justice system and was a clear signal to top generals that they were expected to hold individuals criminally responsible. The investigation turned into a quest for a prosecution—not justice."

Eighty-three days later, a military court found Colonel Chessani not guilty on all charges. Charges against six others were dropped, and the outcome of proceedings against one remaining Marine remained uncertain as this book went to press. The Marines and members of their families paid a heavy emotional price—not to mention being out hundreds of thousands of dollars in legal fees—for service to their country.

More recently, three U.S. Navy SEALs—Julio A. Huertas, Jonathan E. Keefe and Matthew V. McCabe—faced assault charges related to their capture of Ahmed Hashim Abed, the alleged planner of the March 2004 ambush, killing and mutilation of four Blackwater contractors in Fallujah, Iraq. Abed alleged he was punched in the gut and received a fat lip while being apprehended.

Offered administrative punishment, all three warriors refused that option. Instead, they chose—at great cost to themselves and their families—to face court-martial proceedings. It was the only way to clear their names entirely of the charges against them.

Fortunately, all three were found not guilty on all counts during courts-martial in the spring of 2010.

There are, of course, many more cases of U.S. service members facing charges stemming from their actions on the battlefield. Three Army noncommissioned officers—Master Sergeant John Hatley, Sergeant First Class Joseph Mayo and Sergeant Michael Leahy—stand as but a handful of those now serving time in military prisons. Convicted of war crimes. For killing enemy combatants. On battlefields awash with bureaucratic rules of engagement.

In this book, however, I share the appalling details of another wrongful-conviction case in which an Army Special Forces soldier was convicted of alleged crimes that took place far from the combat zones of the Middle East where he had already witnessed firsthand the horrors of war. I share the travesty of military justice embodied in the case, United States vs. Kelly A. Stewart, a case decided during three days in August.

* * *

In an effort to provide readers thorough and complete knowledge of the facts of this case, I relied upon the official Record of Trial as well as other documents and observations obtained from individuals close to the case. In addition, I reached out to both the accused and the accuser in this case.

The accused soldier, U.S. Army Sergeant First Class Kelly A. Stewart, spent hours and hours with me on the phone and via email, answering every question I threw at him. Conversely, his accuser refused to discuss the case.

Responding to my email sent July 15, 2010, German attorney Hans-Peter Schmitt told me he was "not authorized to answer my questions" by order of his client, Stewart's accuser.

Because this case is less about the accuser than it is about the military justice system that convicted Stewart, the name that appears in this book as that of the accuser—including instances where it appears in the Record of Trial—has been changed. Aside from instances where the name of the accused has been replaced with a fictitious name, all other excerpts from the Record of Trial—misspellings included—that appear in this book have not been altered except for the occasional formatting or spacing alteration. Aside from the accuser and the name of the woman who she befriended while both were inpatients at a mental institution, all other names appearing in this book are the actual names of the individuals involved in this case as shown in the Record of Trial.

* * *

## WARNING: GRAPHIC CONTENT

**This book includes often-graphic language and descriptions of a sexual nature taken directly from the official Record of Trial; hence, this book is not recommended for young readers.**

# Longing To Do Something Extraordinary

Kelly Antonio Stewart was born in Landstuhl, Germany, in 1973, the son of John and Renate (pronounced "Ree-naw-tuh") Stewart.

He was the second of two children born to this multinational couple—an American dad and a German mother who kept the household humming while her husband was away. His sister, Sylvia "Diana" was born in Bitburg five years earlier.

Growing up on military installations in Germany and Italy, Stewart found himself different than most of the American kids around him: his first language was German; he grew up playing soccer instead of baseball, basketball or American football; the lunches he took to school almost never contained white bread; and many of the clothes he wore were hand-made by his mother who used patterns and fabric purchased at the Post Exchange.

"I had knock-offs before knock-offs were even cool," he said, explaining his mom often made and affixed labels to clothes to make them look like popular, name-brand items.

Beyond making clothes, Stewart said his mother possessed many talents.

"My mom, you know, she was a great woman, growing up with six sisters post-World War II," Stewart said, explaining that her formal education stopped at about the 12th grade when she started working in the factory along with her two older sisters to help their single mother support a household of seven girls. "She was very industrial, but that was her education as a kid."

When it came to simple things like excusal notes for school, Stewart had to write them for his mom to sign. At that time, she wasn't very good at writing in English.

Though lacking in formal education, his mom could pretty much do anything she set her mind to when it came to household chores, repairs, construction, etc. And she had to. After all, her husband was gone eight to nine months out of the year for most of the time her kids were growing up.

Stewart's dad had a three-decades-long career in Air Force Special Operations. The time he spent away from home resulted in him having a somewhat-distant relationship with his son. But the time was not without memories.

As a kid during the '70s and '80s, Stewart never really knew much about his dad's work, but he knew his dad was well respected and had a job that required him to always keep a "go bag" packed and ready. He knew his dad collected stamps and money from around the world as a way to help him keep track of where he had gone.

"During the late '80s when Special Operations was becoming really big, my dad was part of that," Stewart said. "When you look at some of the incidents that happened during the '80s—the TWA hijacking, Terri Waite, the Achille Lauro—all those things happened during my dad's time in Special Operations, and my dad was a part of (them) in some shape, form or fashion with what he did in the Air Force."

One of Stewart's dad's biggest accomplishments, never getting divorced, made him something of a rarity in the Special Ops community.

"In the last unit my dad was part of, the 7th SOS out of Rhein Mein, there weren't too many people in that unit that had any family," Stewart said, adding that so much time away from home—and living out of "go bags"—often led to divorce in Special Ops households.

While growing up in Germany, Stewart remembered nervous occasions—including one after the United States' airstrike on Libya in 1986—when terrorism fears prompted military officials to have security police escort school buses. He recalled that one service member at Rhein-Mein Air Base was killed by a bomb while he was there.

Incredibly, it was only after Stewart's dad took an assignment to Langley Air Force Base, Virginia, in the late 1980s that Stewart learned he was in the Air Force. His dad took the Langley assignment—his first desk job in decades—because he wanted to be able to spend more time with his family, and it required him, for the first time, to start wearing Air Force blue uniforms his now-teenage son had never seen him wear before. Uniforms plastered with lots of ribbons and medals on his chest. Gone were the all-purpose fatigues-style uniforms and Australian-style bush hats he had worn for so long.

Perhaps the result of watching his dad work so hard, both at home and away, Stewart longed to do something extraordinary with his life.

"Even back then, I thought it was really cool," Stewart said. "I had gone to so many air shows with my dad. As a young kid, I actually wanted to be a pilot or an astronaut. Those were my two big things that I always wanted to do."

Within a couple years of his family's move to Virginia, Stewart had begun a life he would later describe as one of a "knucklehead" living a dead-end lifestyle. He blamed it on having so much to see and do unlike his life in Germany.

Stewart dropped out of high school during his junior year in 1991, got his GED and began going to community college. At the same time, he was working and living with a girlfriend.

In 1994, Stewart was involved in a bad motorcycle.

Stewart recalled his dad visiting him in the hospital and telling him about how he expected him to do something bigger and better with his life.

"He told me he saw so much potential in me and I wasn't using it," Stewart said, "and that I was kind of being lazy."

Within a month or two of that accident, their roles were reversed after his now-retired dad suffered a heart attack and had to undergo bypass surgery.

"I remember sitting there, seeing him in the hospital in a very weird state, not the man that I'd seen before, very frail," Stewart said, "and I remember making a promise to him, telling him that

I'm not going to let him down, that 'you can't go yet, because there's a lot of things I have to do.'"

A short while later, Stewart began keeping that promise.

In 1995, he moved to Kearney, Nebraska, to live with his sister Sylvia and her family. It was an opportunity to get his education, to change his ways and refocus. And it worked out well.

Part of the arrangement with his sister required that he help babysit her infant son while she was working on her master's degree at the University of Nebraska-Kearney and her husband was at work as a teacher.

Up until that point, Stewart had been a very selfish person, concerned only with what he wanted to do in life. Taking care of and hanging out with the youngster taught him to love someone other than himself. At the same time, it helped prepare him to do that extraordinary something he had always longed to do.

## ‘Poster Boy’

Things continued to go well for Stewart in Nebraska. He was knocking out classes at community college and working two jobs—one at a restaurant, the other at a hotel—when he saw an Army recruiting poster while on a shopping trip at the local Walmart. With visions of doing extraordinary things, he called the local recruiter.

Though President Bill Clinton had the U.S. military in a drawdown phase following the end of the first Gulf War and people were being paid to accept early discharges, Stewart talked the recruiter into meeting with him.

During that meeting, Stewart told the recruiter about his days as a self-described “knucklehead” in Virginia and explained that several major moving violations on his driving record were the result of having a fast car and not wanting to listen to anybody.

The recruiter told Stewart that his driving history, combined with the fact that he dropped out of high school and opted to get a GED instead of a diploma, would keep him from getting into the Army right away. He would probably have to join the Army National Guard as a stepping stone toward going on active duty.

Stewart visited the Nebraska Army National Guard recruiter’s office next. There, he watched videos for several jobs he could train for in the Army. From among them, he chose medic and joined the Guard in November 1995.

In January 1996, Stewart began basic training at Fort Leonard Wood in south central Missouri. Eight weeks later, he graduated and moved on to Advanced Individualized Training at Fort Sam Houston in San Antonio, Texas. There, he realized he had found his niche in medicine.

"I noticed this was really the job for me," Stewart said. "To me, it came very easy, almost like working on cars. I understood the dynamics of it."

It marked the first time in Stewart's life that anything like that had ever come easy to him, where he understood it. Medicine was "the easiest job in the world."

After training in San Antonio, Stewart found he really liked the military life and asked his Guard recruiter to help him go on active duty. Several months later, he began a 180-day stint of active Guard status during which he accompanied a recruiter to high schools as something of a "poster boy" for the Army.

Then, with the help of a waiver, he landed a slot in the active-duty Army January 28, 1997.

"I took a bus to Omaha and, from Omaha, they put me on a plane, and I flew down to Killeen, Texas," Stewart explained.

At Fort Hood, he served as a medic in the 1st Cavalry Division's 3rd Battalion/8th Cavalry Regiment. After twelve months on station, he began trying to land an assignment in Germany, where he grew up. That didn't work out immediately, in part, because he was only a private. Instead of returning to the land of his childhood, he deployed with his unit to Kuwait for four months at about the time two U.S. embassies—one in Kenya, the other in Tanzania—were bombed by terrorists August 7, 1998.

While living in the field, Stewart took care of several patients who had been injured during training along the Iraq-Kuwait border and thought his job was the greatest thing in the world. Soon after, however, he received orders to Germany for an assignment with 40th Engineers Battalion, 1st Armored Division. He reported for duty there in December 1998.

A motivated young soldier, Stewart did everything he could to live up to the potential his dad had seen in him. He was laying down "markers" for his future.

In addition to serving as a member of the Color Guard and carrying the guidon during battalion runs each Friday, he did something that medics had never done before; he trained with the guys "down on the line."

"I wanted nothing more than to be the combat arms guy with a little bit of medicine," Stewart explained, saying such a stance was unusual. "In my experience, there are only two types of medics in the Army, those who love medicine and those who don't love medicine.

"You can tell, because some guys want to be these combat arms guys and don't know the first thing about medicine," he said. "Then there are guys who know everything about medicine but don't know the first thing about combat arms. I made it a point to get a balance on that."

While assigned to the 40th Engineers, Stewart was the only one in a training group of three dozen people trying to earn the Expert Field Medical Badge. On average, the course had an 11 percent pass rate. When the course had ended, he was the only person in his brigade to earn the badge. Another marker.

"I was doing the right things and being in the right places. I was getting promoted," he said.

That helped him earn a spot as the only medic out of a group of 15 in his unit selected for a deployment to Kosovo in 1999. There, Stewart got his feet "wet with war" and understood for the first time what war was really all about.

When Stewart returned to Germany as an E-4 after several months in Kosovo, he told his friend he would like to get to know Freija (sounds like "Frazier"), a woman to whom he had been introduced shortly before being deployed. His friend, recently divorced and not wanting to risk losing his buddy to a woman, tried to talk him out of pursuing her, but he persisted in courting this out-of-the-ordinary woman.

"If she was a dude," Stewart said, "she'd be a Green Beret. I know she would, because she's such a strong woman and she loves to do all those things."

Those things included ruck-marching—carrying heavily weighted packs on hikes and runs of 5 and 10 miles and longer—alongside Stewart as he trained for his newest career ambition, a shot in Special Forces.

The young soldier had made it his goal to become a member of the Army's elite fraternity after meeting a handful of SF soldiers and seeing firsthand the kind of people they were.

Even after Stewart learned that two really sharp, harder-than-nails members of his unit had been selected for SF training only to quit or wash out later, he kept his focus. And Freija helped.

"What woman wants to go with a guy ruck-marching when you're dating each other, you know?" he quipped. "She was all about me going to Special Forces, and she loved the military, and she liked to ruck, so she'd come out with me on Saturdays, and we'd go ruck-marching."

Stewart explained that Freija, a single mother at the time, sometimes carried her baby girl in a little backpack carrier while he was carrying his weight for the rucks.

"That's just how we did things," he said.

Apparently, it worked.

Freija married Stewart after only four months of dating.

"Up until this point in my military career, everything I tried I pretty much made with ease," Stewart said. So, when the opportunity presented itself, he asked an SF captain what he thought was a simple, straightforward question: "Do you think I have what it takes to become Special Forces?

"I remember him looking at me, staring me in the face and telling me, 'No. The fact that you have to ask me, that's not the kind of person we want in Special Forces.'"

The captain's words hurt Stewart's feelings and motivated him at the same time.

"Alright, you don't think I can do it," he recalled thinking to himself, "I'll show everybody that I can do it." He never even told his dad about this internal conversation.

With their time in Germany nearing an end, Stewart and his bride took advantage of the Army Married Couples Program and were able to land an assignment together at Fort Bragg, North Carolina, home of the Army's Special Forces in April 2001.

Now a junior E-5 with a stellar record, Stewart completed Airborne School at Fort Benning, Georgia, en route to an assignment with the 82nd Airborne Infantry Division. Freija, meanwhile, was assigned to the 44th Medical Brigade as a medic.

After arriving at Fort Bragg, Stewart continued to do everything he could to set himself apart as a soldier. That included competing in soldier-of-the-month competitions and doing everything possible to put himself on the "radar" for selection into the Sergeant Audie Murphy Club, an elite fraternity of soldiers to which he was exposed for the first time when his squad leader at Fort Hood was inducted and asked him to take part in the ceremony.

One way in which Stewart set himself apart was by fixing problems that his predecessor, an E-6, had left behind before being relieved of his duties. A measure of his leadership abilities can be found in the fact that two of the 10 soldiers under his supervision went on to become Army officers and that one became a Green Beret.

Stewart took time away from shaping up his unit to attend an SF briefing for people who thought they were interested in pursuing the opportunity.

"They had a slide show, showed some cool-guy videos and talked about all the incentives of money and everything else," Stewart said, "but that's not really what got me. What got me was, when I went in there, they had us sign a statement of non-disclosure."

Signing that document, of course, restricted him from talking about anything he learned there. He said he thought the secrecy aspect of Special Forces was "kind of cool."

After the briefers described the workout program and the paperwork he would need to complete before he could get into the program, Stewart decided it was doable.

"It wasn't like, 'Sign right here, and you're in,'" he said. "I had to put some work into it."

Stewart told himself, "I can do this," and he did.

He put in the necessary effort, completed all the paperwork required—including his Enlisted Record Brief, a summary of his Army career up to that point-- and, eventually, got orders to "Selection." The recruiter warned him, though, that he would probably meet some resistance from members of his unit when they learned he was trying to go into SF. And the recruiter was right.

"There's a big rivalry. People either like you and are supportive of you or they're not," Stewart said. "In my case, they were not supportive, because they were pretty much grooming me to be a senior noncommissioned officer at some point in the 82nd Airborne Division."

Fortunately, Stewart's sergeant major at the time did support him.

At Selection, everyone wore battle-dress uniforms minus name tags and rank insignias, because everyone—regardless of rank, officer and enlisted—had to pass the course the same way based on performance, not rank structure.

Everyday, there was at least one testable event and the rest were training events, but trainees never knew which one would count.

"The testable event today might be a run, but you don't know the length of the run," Stewart explained, adding later that, "You're never tested anywhere on anything in an area that you weren't trained on. If you can't retain what they're teaching you, then you will get failed."

"Special Forces just really takes what's great in a person and makes it better," he said. "They don't make great people. They train great, but if you don't have the raw talent somewhere within you.... "

Stewart used shooters as an example.

"Anybody can shoot, but true shooters have a natural ability that's already instinctively in there, and then they're trained to become better shooters," he said, adding, "Some people you can train to become good shooters, but they're just not going to be phenomenal shooters because they just don't have that in 'em."

Another good analogy highlighted the abilities of Pat Tillman, a linebacker for the National Football League's Arizona Cardinals who joined the Army after the attacks of September 11, 2001.

"He was a small guy and he did not meet the requirements that everybody thought he was gonna need as a football player, but he had a natural, raw talent that exceeded his size and ability," Stewart said. "He did things that guys twice his size were doing... because he had that natural ability."

After making it through Selection, Stewart went on to the "Q" Course—the Special Forces Qualifications Course. Perhaps tougher than the negative peer pressure he experienced before heading to Selection, however, was the fact that the so-called "War on Terror" had just kicked off and he realized he could have stayed with his platoon and went to Afghanistan and got into the fight.

A physician assistant friend offered Stewart some words of wisdom that offered some comfort.

"Selection and the Q Course is a marathon, not a quick event," he said, "and, whether you like it or not, war is still gonna be here."

"For me, that was a very difficult situation, because I left my platoon to go to the 'Q' Course and those guys went to war and some guys did die," Stewart said. "That always weighed on me that maybe they wouldn't have died had I not gone."

At the same time, those feelings of guilt boosted his desire to finish the course.

While Stewart was busy with the Q Course, Freija was coming up for reenlistment and both of them knew she was going to be deployed soon. To boost the chances of them being able to be stationed together in the future, she cross-trained to become a flight medic and graduated at the top of her class. Soon after graduation, she deployed to Iraq.

Freija's deployment to Iraq meant Stewart would have to complete the Q Course—one of the toughest courses known to man—as something of a "Mr. Mom."

While that role made him the target of much good-natured ribbing from his peers, it also gave him what he described as his "first experience of really handling what life in Special Forces was gonna be like, the amount of stress and being able to manage that."

Stewart admits that his marriage suffered a bit during that time, but said the couple began marriage counseling soon after his wife returned from Iraq and that marriage problems would never stand as an excuse for anything that happened in his life.

After more than two years of hard work, the vast majority of which was done as a single father while his wife was deployed, Stewart graduated from the Q Course in 2004. In addition to the standard SF training, the view in the rearview mirror of his mind was full of images from 14 months of medic-specific training and completion of the High-Risk Survive, Evade, Resist and Escape (SERE) Course.

Out of 420 guys who started the original 18-D (Special Operations Medical Sergeant) course, only Stewart and 12 others graduated as "first-time goes." Another 15 graduated after being "recycled"—the word for having to repeat the course—for one reason or another.

In addition to a graduation certificate, new status in the Army and a plethora of new knowledge and skills, Stewart walked away with his very own General Yarborough knife, serial number 2754.

"When you graduate from Special Forces, you get an engraved knife," Stewart explained, noting that it was something for which he had to sign his name in a book containing the names of SF warriors who had completed the course before him.

Immediately after graduation, Stewart gave the knife to his dad, along with his first Green Beret, and a note, saying, "From One Warrior to Another."

Pre-deployment training at Fort Carson, Colorado, followed, then Stewart went "downrange" to war with his SF unit. To Iraq.

In Iraq on his first SF deployment, Stewart got what he called his "baptism of fire" in war and became the senior medic on his team within a week of his arrival in country.

"I went there thinking that every life could be saved and every life should be saved," he explained. "You go there thinking that you're the most-trained person in the world and you're so confident... and find that not everybody can be saved."

## A New Assignment in Germany

By Spring 2008, Stewart was at the top of his career, having proven himself in combat as both a medic and a warfighter. At the same time, the buzz circulating through the SF community was about the creation of a new battalion, the 4th Battalion.

Due for a new assignment soon, Stewart fully expected to be assigned to the new battalion. As things turned out, however, his counterparts in another SF group got that assignment instead and guys in his group were given instructor assignments.

Stewart landed a slot at the Survival Division at the International Special Training Center, a half-century-old facility in Pfullendorf, Germany, once dedicated to Cold War purposes and now organized into four divisions: Medical, Patrol, Recognition and Survival.

A Level 1 sniper and combat-tested medic, Stewart drew upon experience gained during several SF assignments in Iraq and elsewhere as he instructed troops—most from other North Atlantic Treaty Organization countries and a few U.S. Army soldiers—in the fine art and science of the sniper. And he had a lot of experience from which to draw.

For instance, during one deployment to Iraq, his team conducted an all-intelligence-based mission set. That meant maintaining low-visibility and, basically, riding around dressed up like Iraqis and gathering intelligence during the day about the target sites that we were going to hit at some future moment in time.

At one point, his team generated 75 percent of national intelligence in Iraq proper. Not surprisingly, he was very compartmentalized about what he could talk about with anyone—including his wife and family—during that time.

"It's very stressful, because you're basically gathering intelligence on known insurgents and, sometimes, that intelligence doesn't make it to where it needs to be in a timely manner and people die," he explained.

"If I found out that there was an IED laying in this road over here, I had to send this report up and try to convince a regular Army unit that I knew what I was talking about—that there's this IED in the road," Stewart said, noting the fact that, if leaders of that unit decided to ignore the intel he provided, "then they have a patrol that goes out there and a person dies."

Another example Stewart pointed to involved having a source who couldn't share information over the phone and would only share it in person.

"By the time he makes it through all the checkpoints and I make it," Stewart said, "that intelligence is already old, because the action has already happened. It's very stressful."

As an instructor, Stewart had no more life-and-death scenarios, so he had to find other ways to measure failure and success. He found that, in part, by looking at his students.

One of Stewart's first ISTC course graduates—an E-4 at the time—went on to earn a Bronze Star with "V" device (for valor) for his work as a sniper only one week after his arrival in Afghanistan.

"He's an AFN commercial now," Stewart said, referring to American Forces Network, the military's broadcasting unit, which likes to share good-news stories about soldiers, sailors, airmen and Marines.

Finding satisfaction in the accomplishments of his students, however, only went so far.

"Every team guy will tell you this: Once they become a FAG, or a Former Action Guy, meaning they have to go be an instructor somewhere, not actually on a team, 99 percent of the team guys hate that," he said, "because what they came to Special Forces for was to be on a team and do team stuff. When they have to do admin stuff or be on the schoolhouse team, it's difficult.

"For me, I didn't realize how difficult that was gonna be," Stewart said, "because I was use to being on the team and the camaraderie and everything, and now I'm having to be an instructor."

In November 2008, members of Stewart's team stopped off in Germany en route to the Republic of Georgia where a conflict with Russia had surfaced. He wished he could go with them.

"Now, I'm seeing my team. They're getting ready to go into the fight and going to do really cool stuff behind enemy lines, and I don't get to be there," he said, "and I've been there with this group of guys for five, six years, and now I'm not. I'm a FAG—a Former Action Guy. I don't get to be part of it."

The stress of war, Stewart said, was "not a tangible thing that you can just put your hand on, like a gas pedal—stop and go, stop and go. It's a lot of sitting and waiting at the mercy of other people."

Stewart's difficulty with being out of the fight would pale in comparison to the difficulties he would soon experience. Still, he would find himself sitting and waiting at the mercy of other people.

## The Night That Changed A Soldier's Life

A few days after he reported for duty as an instructor at the International Special Training Center, part of the 7th Army Joint Multinational Training Command, Stewart headed out for what he thought would be a relaxing night of dancing and hanging out with friends at a local night club. With his eight-months-pregnant wife and young daughter not due to arrive in country for another month, he wanted to get out of his room at the Stuttgart-Marriott Hotel and decided to go dancing at a local night club, See-Studio. It would change his life forever.

The wheels of change in Stewart's life began rolling at approximately 2:30 a.m. August 23, when a twenty-eight-year-old German woman, Greta J. Heinrich, came over to talk to him.

Approximately 5-feet 10-inches tall while wearing black military-style boots, the well-endowed Heinrich had fair skin and a medium build, according to Stewart. Wearing a short skirt and a black halter top that exposed her midsection, she sported shoulder-length black hair that was something akin to the hairstyle worn by rock and roll singer Stevie Nicks during the '80s.

Heinrich's look was perfect for the venue, an '80s-oriented bar where one could go to hear American rock and metal music and see people dressing like they did back in the '80s—something, Stewart said, Americans like him found humorous.

Conversation led to dancing.

"She's dancing with me, and I'm not telling her I'm this Green Beret or anything like that, because I've been trained not to do that," Stewart recalled, "so, I'm telling her kind of like half-truths, if you will. I'm telling her I'm German (and) I'm from Trier, because, at this point, I really had no expectations of anything.

"I just figured it's small talk," he continued. "She's asking me how I know German, and I'm telling her I'm from here, and my mother's name is this, because in Germany, you can tell where people are from based off their last names—something the Germans ask all the time."

At one point during the evening, Stewart said she asked him what he did for a living and he told her about his work in medicine, avoiding the subject of being a Green Beret. In turn, she said she worked in the health industry, too. Things were working out. He found her attractive and asked her a question to which he thought he already knew her answer.

"Hey, do you want to come back to my hotel with me?"

She said, "Yes."

"Sure enough, we go outside, and there was a taxi cab out there," Stewart said, noting that, after Heinrich told a couple of her friends goodbye, they headed to the Stuttgart-Marriott Hotel in Sindelfingen, his temporary quarters until permanent housing became available.

En route to the hotel, Stewart said he asked the driver to stop at a petrol station to pick up condoms, noting that he had not planned to sleep with a woman prior to meeting Heinrich at See-Studio. When they found the station closed, Stewart said he asked the driver to go ahead and let them out there so he wouldn't have to do a U-turn and charge them additional meter time.

"So he lets us out, we crossed the four lanes of highway and we go up to the hotel room," Stewart continued. "We get through the door, we're kissing and everything else, and we kind of just have sex right there on the edge of the bed."

"We have sex—consensual," said Stewart, noting that it "wasn't fabulous. It wasn't something that was eccentric, off the wall or some kind of fetish.

"She takes a shower. I take a shower. The next morning, you know, she gets up to leave, and I'm like, 'Hey, I'll give you a ride to where you have to go.'"

When Stewart explained to her that he would go for a run to the spot where his rental car was parked two miles down the road, drive it back and give her a ride to her place, she turned down his offer.

"She's like, 'No, I have to be somewhere, so I need to get out of here,'" Stewart recalled, adding later that her destination that day—two hours after she left his hotel—was a wedding.

"So I said, 'Can—you give me your phone number?' and she said, 'Sure.'"

Stewart explained that the Vodafone he had was a very basic, pay-as-you-go cell phone he purchased at the post exchange, the military version of a department store. One could not even change the ringtone on it.

If, while trying to "unlock" the phone, you enter the password-PIN combination incorrectly three times, the phone locks up, and you're required to call the phone company and provide the company with your phone's sim card number, known in Germany as a "PUK" number, Stewart said. Given the correct number, they'll unlock the phone.

"The problem is, when you buy a phone at the PX, it's not registered to you," Stewart said, noting that a loophole in German law allows phones sold at the PX to stay unregistered.

Describing himself as "stupid and naive," Stewart said he threw the phone's box away and no longer had the PUK number for his phone. As a result, he and Heinrich couldn't unlock the phone and Heinrich couldn't put her phone number into his phone as she had wanted to. Alternatively, she wrote her phone number on a piece of hotel stationery.

With the phone issue now behind them, Stewart said he gave Heinrich 50 Euros for a taxi cab ride home, and she left.

He, on the other hand, hung around the room for a few minutes before changing into his running clothes, jogging to retrieve his rental car and then going to the PX. Later in the day, he said, he and one of his buddies drove to Trier to see some of his relatives on his mother's side. They returned two days later.

Stewart said he tried calling Heinrich on Monday with a new phone he had bought for $22 at the PX two days earlier. When she didn't answer, he left a message on her voicemail. Days and weeks passed, but he never heard from her directly again.

## 'Snowball Building'

It wasn't long after the one-night stand with Heinrich that Stewart's very-pregnant wife, Freija—who would be assigned 110 miles away at another Army post—arrived in Germany with their young daughter.

Stewart wanted to tell his wife about his infidelity, but was afraid to lose her the same way many of his SF brothers had lost their wives. So he waited until a day when he thought he might lose her for another reason.

On November 25, 2008, Stewart got a call from his wife that there was some kind of complication with her pregnancy. Doctors detected an abnormality in their unborn child's heartbeat. An emergency C-section followed. Not only was it "touch and go" for the child, but Freija was not doing well either and Stewart was crying like a baby the whole time.

"I basically prayed to God," Stewart said. "I said, 'Listen God, I will never cheat on my wife, and I will never hold anything over her head again,' because I had so much guilt for what I did.

"I said, 'I will never be that person again. I promise to be a better person if you save my wife and my child's life. I'm gonna change the way I've been.'

"I kept praying and kept praying and kept praying," he said.

Freija started to pull through and Stewart went to the next room to find his newborn daughter on oxygen, but alive and awake with her skin tone becoming more normal.

Amidst all of the turmoil of a difficult birth, Stewart wanted to tell Freija about his infidelity soon after the baby was born, but didn't want to ruin the day of his second daughter's birth. So he waited until the following day.

About that moment, Stewart said, "I'll tell ya, it wasn't a good moment in the history of Kelly Stewart, but it really made me feel better to get that off my chest.

"My wife, being the strong and great person that she is, wasn't happy," he recalled. "Her response was, 'We're not going to allow this to ruin the birth of our child, and it's something we're gonna have to work on.'"

The new year arrived, and Stewart's unit had just wrapped up some cold weather training when he decided to stop by the finance office on post to check on a pay issue about which he had a concern.

"When I went in there, I had a weird feeling about it, but I didn't know what it was," he explained.

Stewart was there to ask for a copy of his Enlisted Record Brief, a document that serves as a one-page record of his career in the Army, because he knew he was being looked at for promotion to E-8 for the first time. Strangely, he said, the female clerk assisting him appeared hesitant to provide him the requested document—and for good reason.

"When I got a copy of it, it had a 'flag,'" Stewart said, indicating that some sort of adverse action had taken place or that he was under investigation for some reason or another.

Stewart asked her to explain why his records were flagged and she began "tap dancing" around, advising him to speak with First Sergeant Richard Knapp, an E-8 and the senior enlisted man in the unit with which Stewart had just spent a week in winter training.

When Stewart made the call to find out why he had been flagged, Sergeant Knapp told him he had been instructed by the folks at the Army's Criminal Investigation Division not to talk with him about it. Still deeply curious, the 11-year veteran headed to the Judge Advocate General's office.

Stewart thought to himself that the flag must be related to something that happened downrange—perhaps, it had to do with the way he arrested a prisoner of war or how he had killed someone. He would find out soon.

At the JAG's office, Stewart explained his concern to a young military lawyer, Captain James Hill. In turn, Captain Hill called the prosecutor's office on the other side of the post and asked what was going on. When the folks at the prosecutor's office wouldn't tell him anything, the military lawyer told Stewart to tell anyone who wants to question him that he has legal representation.

"Now, I'm in a serious panic," Stewart said, "because I've got a captain in the Army telling me things don't normally happen this way, and all I see is a snowball building and I don't even know what it's about."

Two days later, Stewart checked in with Captain Oren Gleich, a military lawyer assigned to his case in place of Captain Hill, who was about to transfer out. When he asked if he had heard anything yet, the captain told him he was under investigation for rape but could not yet offer any particulars about the charges.

Captain Hill went on to describe the sequence of events (i.e., arrest, fingerprinting, questioning, etc.) that would soon take place in Stewart's life. He also reminded the soldier again that he should not answer any questions without his attorney present.

"At that point, it was pretty easy for me to figure out, because I had only slept with that one girl," Stewart explained. Then the lawyer told him he couldn't even say anything about the case to Freija, because (1) they could use his wife against him as a witness and (2) anything he said to his wife could be turned around and used against him by the government.

Captain Hill also advised Stewart that he had to tell his wife to call her unit's JAG office and get a lawyer so that she's protected in case the government comes after her with questions.

Now, Stewart is panicking more, because he's never seen anything like this happen.

Though his military lawyer couldn't recommend a particular civilian attorney who specialized in military law, he did give Stewart a list of lawyers in the area who practiced military law. He ended up hiring David Court, an American with 35 years' experience in the military justice field, as his civilian defense attorney.

During his initial visit with Court at his office in Frankfort, Stewart explained the situation and what he thought was the only possible circumstance behind the charges. Court asked why Heinrich would make such a charge.

"Dude, I have no clue," Stewart answered, adding, "The one thing is I have my wife's name tattooed between my shoulder blades," adding that Heinrich asked him about the tattoo shortly before she left after seeing it on his back at one point when he had turned away from her.

Court told Stewart he would see what he could find out, and their meeting ended.

A few days later, Stewart had surgery to remove a cyst from his chest and was placed on quarters (a.k.a., "recuperation") for two days at his home in Stuttgart. On the first day following the surgery, he received a call from Sergeant Knapp, telling him to come in the next day to talk about something. Suspecting Sergeant Knapp wanted to talk with him about the investigation, Stewart drove 110 miles to meet him the next day.

At the meeting, Sergeant Knapp handed Stewart a counseling form and told him he needed to go, accompanied by another sergeant in the unit, back to Stuttgart. Instructed to wear civilian clothes and travel in a low-visibility (i.e., unmarked) military vehicle, he was to talk with Detective Daniel Lorch at the German police station in Böblingen.

Upon hearing the E-8's instructions, Stewart called Court to let him know what was going on, and the attorney told him to make sure he didn't say anything to them except that he has a lawyer. Court also told Stewart to expect to be fingerprinted and photographed.

When Stewart arrived 30 minutes early in military fashion, he caught the Germans off guard, prompting one detective to say, "Oh, you're a little early" and ask for a few minutes to get ready.

Stewart said the detective began talking to him in German and asked him the question, "You understand German, don't you?" to which he replied, "Whether I understand German or not, that's not the question, but if we're going to have this meeting, it's going to be done in English."

After a little back and forth that included discussion about the language in which the session would be conducted and Stewart's declaration that, on the advice of his attorney, he would not be answering any questions, the detective probed a little more before finally excusing himself, saying, "Give me a few minutes, and then I'll bring you upstairs."

About ten minutes passed before Stewart was taken upstairs to an office where the male detective was on one side of his desk and a female, who Stewart thought was also a detective, was sitting right next to the soldier.

"My name is Detective Lorch," the male detective told Stewart before making a point to describe himself as the chief of the section/agency and not one of the investigators, "and I'm telling you this because it's important."

At that point, Stewart said, he interrupted the detective.

"Listen, I'm not being disrespectful to you, but, really, I have nothing to say to you nor do I care to hear anything you have to say. I'm basically up here because I've been instructed by my unit that I needed to come up here and have some fingerprints taken and some pictures taken. That's what I'm here to do. Anything above that, I'm not going to say anything. I'm not going to make any statements nor do I want to hear any."

When Detective Lorch began speaking again about how very serious the matter was, Stewart interrupted him again, showed him a form Court had given him and advised the detective to call the attorney.

Ignoring Stewart's words, the detective continued, prompting the accused sergeant to reiterate that he would not discuss anything and did not appreciate being badgered. That's when the female sitting next to him—an older woman who spoke good German and had blonde hair and features similar to Stewart's German mother—interjected.

"Well, normally, CID wouldn't give you all of this information that we're trying to give you here," she said.

"Well, that's neither here nor there," Stewart responded, cognizant of the fact she was playing the role of the "good" cop in a poorly-choreographed good cop/bad cop routine.

After Stewart remained steadfast in following his attorney's advice, he was taken to another room to have fingerprints and photos made.

"Of course, they're trying to do their police officer thing, and I get that," Stewart said before explaining that his training equipped him to be able to identify events such as one where police officers "mistakenly" brought two German men in handcuffs into the room where Stewart was about to be fingerprinted.

"You could tell it was a very staged event," he said.

Stewart went on to explain that they took four sets of digital—not ink—fingerprints but messed up three times along the way in an apparent attempt to annoy their suspect.

Because he had training in taking fingerprints, Stewart said, "Now, it was really pissing me off, because they were playing me like I was stupid."

Though she never showed her badge or other identification, the real identity of the female in the room came to light when, after the German's finished getting Stewart's fingerprints, she said she needed to get three sets of ink fingerprints for her office at Patch Barracks—she was an Army CID agent and, aside from the accused soldier, the sole U.S. representative at the meeting. Stewart never knew her name.

Stewart noted that, throughout the course of the meeting, other German police officers would enter the room on occasion to ask questions and make jokes in German to see how well he understood the language. Of course, he understood everything, because he is fluent in German.

They also caused him pain.

"I had just had this surgery done on my chest, so they were having me lift my arm up to roll my arm" for the fingerprints, he said, adding that he told them it was painful and asked them if they could lower the table. They would not.

When discussion about the surgical wound on his chest led to the discovery of tattoos on Stewart's chest, the Germans demanded he undress so they could photograph the tattoos.

Stewart objected to the prospect of undressing before them and called Court.

On a speakerphone, Stewart's attorney told the people in the room that his client would not undress. Eventually, however, Stewart agreed to taking off his shirt only so they could photograph his upper body.

After the fingerprinting and photo sessions ended, the German police officers again started asking Stewart questions and he again refused to answer, citing the fact that he's an American citizen, not a German. Then he told them that, unless they were going to arrest him, he was done with the session and was going to leave. They let him go.

A few weeks passed and, with the arrival of spring, the families of personnel assigned to the International Special Training Center gathered for a family day to enjoy food, fellowship and recognition for their work. Enjoying his first Family Day at the ISTC was Command Sergeant Major Richard "Spike" Klein, the unit's new enlisted leader who had arrived February 10, 2009, to replace First Sergeant Knapp.

Command Sergeant Major Klein knew Stewart well and, within the first 20 days of his arrival, sent him back to the Survival Division in a move that caused much consternation between the new sergeant major and Lieutenant Colonel

David L. Grosso, his soon-to-depart ISTC commander who had proffered the charges against Stewart. One of Command Sergeant Major Klein's toughest duties, however, was to inform Stewart at the Family Day event that he needed to report to Colonel Grosso at 6:30 that night.

When Stewart arrived at his commander's office at the designated hour, he found Captain Greg O'Malley from the prosecutor's office there and learned that charges had been filed against him.

"I'm like totally blown away as he reads off these four charges I'm charged with—sodomy, kidnapping, blah-blah-blah—and I'm like, 'Holy Cow!' What is going on here?'"

Stewart signed the paperwork and did not say anything before calling his lawyer, who told him, "It's no big deal. It's just the process," before informing him that an Article 32 investigation would come next.

By mid-May, an Article 32 investigation was fully underway to determine whether the charges warranted any legal action and should go forward. For the accused soldier, it was the first time he learned with certainty that Heinrich was alleging he had raped and kidnapped her more than nine months earlier inside his room at the Stuttgart-Marriott Hotel.

Embarrassed that it was taking place, Stewart attended the hearing accompanied only by his lawyers, Captain Gleich and Court. On the other side of the room, his accuser was accompanied only by her mother and the German state prosecutor.

Though he knew the charges alone had the potential to ruin his career, Stewart didn't think he would be going to prison. After all, he had done none of the things she alleged him to have done.

"Not really enlisting any help from any of my comrades or anybody else, I'm going in there like a man," Stewart said, "because I put myself in that situation, and I'm gonna handle this stuff."

The Germans had already told Court that, if the U.S. Army didn't take the case, they would try Stewart in a German court. The civilian defense attorney passed that thinly-veiled threat along to Stewart. With it, he told his client that his chances were better in a military court due to the type of evidence involved and because certain peculiarities of the German court system—including one that prevents alleged victims of assault, sexual or other, from being cross-examined in German court cases—would not work in his favor.

Amidst Court's reassurances that he didn't think anything would come of the allegations, Stewart opted for the military-court route as his best option.

After the Article 32 hearing, Stewart was removed from his instructor position in the Survival Division by Colonel Grosso and assigned to a desk job in the Training and Operations (S-3) shop. Everyone in his unit knew something big was going on.

On June 23, 2009, only 10 days before Lieutenant Colonel Donald P. Schurr took over from Colonel Grosso as ISTC commander, charges were served on Stewart.

Soon after his arrival, Colonel Schurr told Stewart he would not be able to attend his trial because he had leave scheduled to go to Italy and spend time with his wife and kids for the first time in five years. Additionally, the colonel told him that, while he had his support, he had no control over the process leading up to his trial.

Stewart learned from a high-ranking source within his chain of command that one general officer, referring the Stewart case, had told Colonel Schurr "to stay out of this and let this matter happen."

"That really added in some fear," Stewart said. "How can a general tell a battalion commander he doesn't have any influence or say on what's going on with one of the men in his command?"

# The Arraignment

Shortly after 1 p.m. on the afternoon of July 28, 2009, the arraignment of the accused in the case, United States versus Sergeant First Class Kelly A. Stewart, took place inside a courtroom at Rose Barracks in Vilseck, Germany.

The building, according to Stewart, was spartan in decor and small in size, resembling something akin to the one-room schoolhouse on the 1970s television show, "Little House on the Prairie." What would take place inside that building during the next few days, however, would look nothing like the family television series.

Three Army lawyers were detailed to the case by Lieutenant Colonel Francisco Villa, staff judge advocate for the 7th Army Joint Military Training Command. Major Charles Kuhfahl would serve as military judge (MJ), while Captain Jacob Bashore would serve as trial counsel (TC) with Captain O'Malley as assistant trial counsel (ATC).

Representing Stewart would be Captain Gleich as military defense counsel (MDC) and Court as civilian defense counsel (CDC).

The general nature of the charges was as follows:

- Violation of Article 120, UCMJ, two specifications of rape;
- Violation of Article 120, UCMJ, two specifications of abusive sexual contact;
- Violation of Article 125, UCMJ, two specifications of forcible sodomy;
- Violation of Article 128, UCMJ, one specification of assault consummated by a battery;

- Violation of Article 134, UCMJ, one specification of kidnapping; and
- Violation of Article 134, UCMJ, one specification of communicating a threat.

Judge Kuhfahl advised Stewart that he had the opportunity to choose the type of trial during which his guilt or innocence would be decided. Opting against a judge-only trial, Stewart said he wanted to be judged by a panel consisting of at least one-third enlisted soldiers.

In choosing that option, Stewart would be judged by a panel of ten soldiers who would vote by secret, written ballot. Two-thirds of them would have to agree in order for him to be found guilty of any offense. If found guilty, two-thirds would have to agree in voting on a sentence. If the sentence included confinement for more than 10 years, three-fourths would have to agree.

After Stewart pleaded not guilty to all specifications and charges, Judge Kuhfahl advised him of his right to be present at every stage of his trial and that, if he was voluntarily absent on the date of his trial, he could forfeit the right to be present and the trial could go forward without him.

"Now, I don't necessarily believe that you will be absent yourself," the military judge said. "This is simply a cautionary instruction that is given to all soldiers when there's a break between the arraignment date and the date of the trial."

When asked if he understood the instructions thusfar, Stewart said he did, and Judge Kuhfahl continued.

"It is important that you keep your defense counsel, both Mr. Court and Captain Gleich, and your chain of command apprised of your whereabouts at all times between now and the trial date. Do you have any questions about what I have just told you?"

"No, sir," Stewart replied.

The Article 39(a) session ended and, despite the extremely serious nature of the charges, Stewart was not ordered to be kept in confinement during the three weeks before the trial date.

Was that an indication that Army officials did not believe Stewart had committed any horrible crimes against the woman? Some think it was.

# DAY ONE

# Day One: Biased From the Start

One could argue that the legal proceedings involving defendant Stewart were biased in at least two major areas as the court-martial (a.k.a., "trial") began the morning of August 18, 2009.

Prior to the start of the trial, attorneys for both sides met with Judge Kuhfahl in conference to discuss whether or not the subject of accuser Heinrich's medical records from a lengthy stay at a mental institution in 2004 could be raised during the trial.

"We do not want them talking about this mental institution, that Helga was there, or that the victim stayed in that mental institution," said Captain O'Malley, trying to convince Judge Kuhfahl to side with the government. "We do not believe that's relevant to any of the charges about where they met or that they stayed in an institution in 2004 or 2005, under the facts of this case."

Who is Helga? Helga Gowar is a woman Heinrich met during her four-month stay in a mental institution where both were patients in 2004.

"We have no knowledge beyond what we were told by the victim as to the reason for that stay," Court countered on Stewart's behalf. "We believe that her mental state is always in issue. We believe that her response to stress, which is apparently her stated reason for going to that institution, is in issue here."

Unfortunately for Stewart, Heinrich invoked her rights under German law to not disclose her medical records. Likewise, the German government refused to release copies of Heinrich's medical records and spelled out the reasons for their decision in a letter:

Due to other obligations we are unable to exercise the right to observe the court-martial on 18 and 19 August 2009 in Vilseck.

Your request to obtain the treatment records of Klinik Christophsbad, Faurndauer Strasse 6-28, 73035 Goeppingen for the victim Greta J. Heinrich in the years 2004 and 2005 by court-order cannot be granted.

Even if you assume, with the dominant opinion, that there is no prohibition of seizure, in accordance with section 97, paragraph 1 German Trial Procedural Code (StPO), then, under the given circumstances, forcible access of Health Records by procedural methods against the will of the victim, would have to be considered, under general maxims, in violation of the principle of proportionality in a special sensitive area of the private sphere.

In the absence of a (currently missing) concrete claim of evidence and basis in fact, such an action would only serve the non-permissible purpose of baseless inquiry of the victim and the hoped for discovery of relevant circumstances (see Federal Supreme Court Decision NStZ 1997, 562).

**The fact that the trial was taking place in a U.S. military court based upon U.S. law (i.e., the Uniform Code of Military Justice) seemed not to matter to Judge Kuhfahl.**

**Asked by Judge Kuhfahl why they objected to the prospect of him allowing the defense to ask Heinrich why she was refusing to turn over her medical records, Captain O'Malley said, "There's no relevance shown by that at all, Your Honor."**

**Conversely, Court argued that the question "goes to candor with the tribunal" and said, "She has obviously got something that she wishes to withhold, and without that question, the panel will not have that impression of her; will think that she has been candid and told us everything, and that is not true."**

Judge Kuhfahl ruled as follows, saying, "The court does not find that there's any matter of consequence that that question would address, indicating anything is more or less probable in this case; therefore, the government objection is sustained, and I'm not going to allow that question."

Stewart and his attorneys were stumped by the military judge's ruling.

"It's my Constitutional right to have all evidence looked at, or all items looked at, by a judge," Stewart said. "Nothing becomes evidence until the judge deems it as evidence, but a judge still has to review it to determine whether it's evidence or not.

"If the judge chooses not to look at a particular item to determine whether it's evidence or not, then he's violated my Constitutional rights," Stewart explained, reiterating that Judge Kuhfahl had failed him by not petitioning or subpoenaing Heinrich's medical records.

"He would still determine whether those records were relevant or not, whether they would be admissible or not—that's still up to him," Stewart explained. "If I'm saying there was possible evidence there, he has to protect my rights as the accused to look at that to determine whether it is or isn't.

"He didn't do that," Stewart said. "That's where he violated my rights."

Panel members never got to hear about Heinrich's stay in a mental institution. They only got to hear from Heinrich that she was there as a victim of burnout. A major victory for the government.

"There was never a discussion about what Greta was in (the mental institution) for," Stewart said. "She testified that she was only in for simple 'burnout,' but she would never provide her medical records (and) the jurors never got to know that.

"If I was a juror," Stewart said, "and I found out that this chick was saying that someone had raped her, that she had spent time in a mental institution... and now she's saying that this American service member...is being accused of rape, it would add a shadow of doubt in my mind and any normal person's mind."

Another example of judiciary bias surfaced during the jury selection process.

"When we started this off, we asked the judge for a whole new venue of jurors," Stewart said, "because Major Bashore—then Captain Bashore—had just come from the unit that all 12 of my jurors came from. He was the legal officer for that unit, and they had just come off a 16-month deployment. If that's not bias, I don't know what is."

In addition to that, Lieutenant Colonel Bryan E. Denny, the president of the court-martial panel, had, in the not-too-distant-past, awarded the JAG officer a Bronze Service Medal, Stewart said.

From there, Stewart painted a scenario highlighting what might happen if he served as a prosecutor and had 10 fellow SF members serving on a court-martial panel.

"I'm gonna get up there as the prosecutor and say you raped this woman," Stewart said. "You don't think those 12 SF guys are gonna find you guilty when they know me? You don't think that whatever comes out of my mouth is not gonna be the gospel?"

What did Judge Kuhfahl, a very young judge without a lot of courtroom experience, do? Stewart found out well after the fact that he had asked the panel members a simple question—"Do you believe that Sergeant Stewart is innocent beyond a reasonable doubt until proven guilty and that you can perform your duties in a military manner?"—to which they responded unanimously, "Sure, we can."

Though Stewart's defense team was able to get rid of two potential panel members, including one "bird" colonel (i.e., O-6), they were left with the senior member of the group who, in addition to awarding Captain Bashore a Bronze Service Medal, was the rater and senior rater on the performance evaluations of five of the 10 panel members. In other words, their careers were in his hands.

Not surprisingly, Stewart had major problems with that kind of familiarity between members of the group that was supposed to be representative of his "peers."

"Now, think about that. You're my boss, and you're the one who does my evaluations, and you're a juror," Stewart explained.

"You don't think I'm gonna go with the way you want me to vote? Imagine yourself in this situation. That's how my court case started."

When the selection process ended, 10 men in Army uniforms—five officers and five enlisted men—were ready to serve as members of the court-martial panel.

The list of officers included: Lieutenant Colonel Denny (president), Lieutenant Colonel Douglas Sims II, Lieutenant Colonel (Chaplain Michael Yarman, Major Wallace Smith and Captain Joshua Buchanan. According to the Record of Trial, all of these men were married at the time of the trial.

The enlisted members were: Command Sergeant Major Mark Morris, Sergeant Major John Robinson III, First Sergeant George Spaulding, Sergeant First Class John Alam and Sergeant First Class Dontonio Roberts. According to the Record of Trial, three of these noncommissioned officers were married, one was not married and the remaining individual's marital status was not addressed.

During the trial, the panel members—the military equivalent of jurors—would hear testimony from a dozen witnesses during the trial.

In addition to the accuser and the accused, the list of witnesses included friends and acquaintances of both parties as well as a taxi driver and a German police investigator. A handful of military officers, including an Army medical doctor, and noncommissioned officers would testify as well.

Before the case reached its conclusion, one high-ranking official known as the General Courts-Martial Convening Authority (GCMCA) would play an important role without ever darkening the entrance to the courtroom.

For the case to reach the GCMCA, recommendations had to pass through two lower levels, the Summary Courts-Martial Convening Authority (SCMCA) and the Special Courts-Martial Convening Authority (SPCMCA), according to the Uniform Code of Military Justice (a.k.a., "military law").

As commander of Headquarters 7th Army Joint Military Training Command in Grafenwoher, Germany, Brigadier General

Steven L. Salazar was the highest-level officer involved in the case. He had taken over command of the JMTC, the parent unit of the International Special Training Center in Pfullendorf, from Brigadier General David R. Hogg July 9, 2009. By virtue of his new position, General Salazar became the GCMCA for Stewart's case.

Next in line below the general was Colonel Nils C. Sorenson, commander of the U.S. Army Garrison Grafcnwoehr, who served as SPCMCA.

Finally, Colonel David L. Grosso, the relatively new commander of the ISTC, served as SCMCA.

Before Stewart's trial would end, nearly two dozen people would play key roles inside the courtroom. And their roles would not be without controversy.

# Day One: Opening Statements

**"Ultimately, there's one Green Beret with two lawyers sitting on one side of the room and another Green Beret sitting behind them," said Stewart, describing the setting inside the courtroom. The government side of the room had "basically the whole legal department"—including five captains just taking notes and an official from the local German prosecutor's office."**

**The proceedings began with opening statements from attorneys on both sides of the legal battle.**

**Captain Bashore presented on behalf of the government shortly before noon August 18, 2009. Below is the transcript of his opening statement, as taken directly from the Record of Trial, which paints Stewart in a very bad light:**

> Mr. President, Members of the Panel:
>
> This case is about power, control, and deviant sexual violence. The reason that you're here today is because, on 23 August 2008, the accused forcibly sodomized, forcibly raped, had indecent sexual contact, kidnapped, threatened, and assaulted Ms. Greta Heinrich at the Marriott Hotel in Sindelfingen, Germany.
>
> The evidence will show that, in August 2008, the accused was PCSing into the Stuttgart, Germany, area; and during that time he was staying at the Marriott Hotel in Sindelfingen. Sindelfingen is nearby Stuttgart.

On the night of 22 August 2008, the accused went with some of his friends to a club called "Seestudio." The Seestudio was in Boeblingen, Germany, and Boeblingen is a sister town that butts up to Sindelfingen.

While there that night, the accused drank, danced, had a good time with his friends, and at approximately 2:30 in the morning, he introduced himself to Ms. Heinrich and asked her for a dance. Ms. Heinrich will come in and testify and tell you how the dancing went, and how the accused acted like a gentleman. When they were complete with that dance, he kissed her hand, and he told her, "Thank you"; then they went their separate ways off the dance floor.

Moments later, the accused comes back to Ms. Heinrich and offers to dance with her again; and again they dance. While dancing, the accused told her a little bit about himself. He told her that his name was Antonio; he told her he was a soldier; he said he'd recently been in combat; and he did all this in German. He also told her that his mother was German.

After about an hour, at approximately 3:30 in the morning, the accused tells Ms. Heinrich that he wants to be alone with her. Now, Ms. Heinrich will come in and tell you that she understood that to mean that he wanted a one-night stand, and she was okay with that— on one condition: that they go back to her place because she felt safe at her place. She had roommates.

The accused agreed, they gathered their coats, they told their friends goodbye, and they got into a taxicab. Immediately upon entering that taxicab, the accused took control of the situation, and he told the taxi driver he wanted a Red Bull; he wanted to go to a

Shell gas station to get that Red Bull. And as they got near that Shell gas station, the accused waived the driver on; he wanted to go to a different gas station, one up in Sindelfingen near the Marriott Hotel.

Ms. Heinrich will testify—she'll tell you that she was confused; she didn't understand why he wanted to go there; she objected; she was ignored. The accused continued to talk about himself, to talk about how beautiful Ms. Heinrich was, and how he'd been watching her all evening; that she knew she could get anybody in that club that night, and she had chosen him.

As the taxi passes the Marriott, the accused had the driver stop, and the driver actually had to turn around and come back. They both get out; Ms. Heinrich questions the accused why they are at this Marriott. See, at this time she did not know that the accused was staying there.

He explains to her why an American soldier would be staying in the Marriott; he reiterated the plan to go to her place. He said they just needed to pick something up; he wanted to get that Red Bull. So she follows him into the Marriott. They get to the fifth floor; they get up to Room 533. He goes inside; she stays at the door. He sees that she's apprehensive about coming in, and he coaxes her—he coaxes her in. "Do not be afraid. I'm not going to hurt you. I'm a man. I'm a real man." She comes in a little farther; he continues to coax her in.

He grabs that Red Bull, and he offers something for her to drink. She tells him she doesn't want something to drink because they're going to be leaving soon. When she tells him that, he changes, and he tells her, "No, we're staying here"; then he orders her to take off her clothes.

Ms. Heinrich tells the accused that that's not the way it's going to work. "You're not going to order me to take my clothes off"—you know, she wanted a little bit of romance.

When she told the accused that, he became violent, and he smacked her—he smacked her in the side of the face. She'll tell you how, at that point, she got very angry, started yelling at the accused. The accused became very calm, became tender, he became apologetic, and he again complimented her on how nice of a body she had; how beautiful she was, and he just wanted to watch her undress.

Ms. Heinrich will testify and tell you that she thought it was a game, and she continued to go along with it, and she took her clothes off. She'll say she took her own clothes off.

Once she took her clothes off, the accused became a different person; he became violent. She'll testify how he turned her around, and he threw her down on the front of the bed there in the hotel room, and she'll tell you how she tried to brace herself; that he threw her with such force that she really couldn't brace herself.

He grabs her hair; he pushed her down by the shoulder; and then he shoves his penis into her anus. And she'll tell you at this point there had been no conversation about anal sex. The accused had never asked Ms. Heinrich if he could have anal sex with her. And she'll tell you how she screamed out in pain; she doubles over on the bed.

When she recovers from that initial burst of pain, she goes into the bathroom. She thinks she's probably bleeding. And when she comes out, she tells the accused, "I'm not into that. What you did was wrong. I'm leaving." But while she was in the bathroom, the accused took her clothes. They had been by the foot of the bed; he puts them on the far side of the room, so, now, Ms. Heinrich has to go through the accused to get to the far side of the room to get her clothes, and then cross the room and exit.

She'll tell you, when she tried to go through the accused, the accused grabs her by the neck. He grabs her by the throat, and he chokes her. And then he proceeds to violate her, both physically and sexually, by placing his fingers in her anus, placing his fingers in her vagina, placing his penis in her vagina, grabbing her breast and biting it, all without consent, and he threatened her; he would not allow her to leave; and he assaulted her by hitting her on the face, the back of the head, the buttocks, and the thighs. And only when the accused was finished did he allow her to leave.

She leaves the hotel, gets in a taxicab, and goes home. She'll talk to you and tell you how she felt dirty; she just wanted to be clean.

She gets home, she tries to convince herself that it wasn't the way it was, she tries to convince herself that it was her fault—that she put herself in that situation with a strange man. She tries to convince herself it was just a wild night. Then, approximately two months later, when she was talking to a friend, that friend urged her to report this incident to the police, and she did shortly thereafter.

Now, you're going to hear from several other witnesses. You're going to hear from a Ms. Jasmin Dittmann and Mr. Rudolf Betting, and they were both with Ms. Heinrich at the Seestudio before they left, and they will describe to you the man that they saw Ms. Heinrich with, and they'll describe to you how they interacted before they left, and that they left together.

You'll also hear from Ms. Haug, and Ms. Haug is a very important witness because she was the taxi driver that picked Ms. Heinrich up that morning after she left the hotel room, and she will describe to you her appearance; how Ms. Heinrich was physically and mentally exhausted; how she looked like she was in pain; how she had trouble entering and exiting the taxicab; how she had trouble sitting down like a normal person.

You'll also hear from Detective Lorch, and Detective Lorch was the Polizei investigator who went through this case, and he'll talk to you about some of the investigation and the identification process.

And, lastly, you'll hear from Lieutenant Colonel Marshall Smith, a forensic psychiatrist, who interviewed Ms. Heinrich, and who will sit through the trial today, and he'll tell you about some of the common misconceptions panel members and society has, in general, about the way they believe the rape victim should act. He'll talk to you about some physical things from the evidence that he's seen; he'll talk to you about the late reporting and how that is very common; and how Ms. Heinrich's actions are consistent with the way other rape victims act.

And the government is confident, when you've heard all the evidence, when you go back into that deliberation room and you discuss these crimes and the evidence, that you'll return a verdict of guilty of all charges and their specifications.

Thank you.

**Directly after the government's opening statement, civilian defense counsel Court presented an opening statement on behalf of Stewart. Below is the transcript of that statement as taken from the Record of Trial:**

Mr. President, Members of the Court:

About a year ago—five days, six days shy of a year ago—a 28-year-old German girl, Greta Heinrich, goes to the Seestudio—that's spelled S-E-E, not like the letter "C", because it's near a little lake—in Boeblingen, Germany—Sindelfingen; she's been there before; she's there with friends, having herself a good time, dressed like you would expect a 28-year-old girl to dress when she's going out on the town.

And about 3:30 she tells her friends that she's leaving. Her friends had seen her dancing with and being with an individual that they can describe; they didn't really speak with him or talk with him; but she is more than happy when she's leaving that club because she knows what's going to be happening. That's what her friends see.

She will tell you, basically the way the prosecutor just told you, that she went to a hotel; that, although she originally wanted to go somewhere else, the cab driver stopped across the street from a hotel—four lanes of traffic; she had to follow the person across those four lanes to go into the hotel with him, past the reception desk, up in the elevator, and she stayed in that room for about four hours; slept in the bed; left the next morning; gave the guy her handi phone number—telephone—cell phone number—before she left; went downstairs; passed the reception office—didn't say anything; got into a cab; went home. The cab driver will testify; and then Ms. Heinrich will tell you that, a few days later, she went to her physician because she had some stomach cramps, stomach pains, and Ms. Heinrich will tell you that the slaps and blows that she said she received made her black and blue all over—on her face, on her thighs, on her shoulders.

The doctor she went to was a doctor she'd known for a long time; treated her as a kid. She's grown up in this area; a female doctor. She didn't tell the doctor anything about being brutally sexually assaulted, nor will there be any evidence that the doctor saw any injuries—bruises, black and blue—anything of that sort.

Ms. Heinrich also was treated for a bladder infection by this doctor in the ensuing weeks. No indication of violent forcible sex.

In November, Ms. Heinrich is speaking to a friend and, 10 weeks later, decides that she had been raped back in August. That led to a German investigation, and that led to us being here.

The defense believes that you will hear more than just what the government has related, and those that—most of you have sat before and understand what opening statements are and are not—but, when you've heard all of the evidence—not only the government's evidence, but the defense evidence—you will come to the conclusion that this is not a case of violent forcible sex; that this is a case of consent, that a young lady later decided, for reasons which may become apparent, that she wanted to say that she had been raped by an American—an American who was living in that hotel and had been living there for a while, and was known to be living in that hotel and that room, a fact which may or may not shed light on the likelihood that someone would commit that kind of a crime in his or her own four walls.

When you've heard all of the evidence, as stated, the defense believes you will come to the only conclusion, and that is that Sergeant First Class Kelly A. Stewart is not guilty of the charges and specifications.

Thank you.

**With the opening volleys finished, the outcome likely remained uncertain in the minds of courtroom observers without a stake in the outcome. During the trial's next 48 hours, however, witnesses would paint a more-complex picture of events about which 10 men in uniform, guided by a military judge, would have to pass judgment.**

## Day One: Five Witnesses

The government called four witnesses to testify on Day One of the trial pitting accuser Heinrich's version of events against those of defendant Stewart.

The government's first witness was Jasmin Dittmann, a practitioner of holistic sports and dance therapy who was repeatedly referred to by government attorneys as "Doctor Dittmann" during the trial. Though she testified as a friend of Heinrich, Dittmann admitted she had known Heinrich only since April 2008, approximately four months before the night of August 22, 2008, when the two had gone with friends to a coffee shop and then to the discotheque, See-Studio, in the town of Böblingen, near Stuttgart.

Dittmann's testimony during direct examination by the government produced the following items of significance:

- She said she had seen Heinrich with Stewart at See-Studio on the night in question;
- She said Heinrich had changed her appearance—cutting and coloring her once-long hair—during the three months following the night in question; and
- She said she had noticed "heavy changes" in Heinrich's personality during the same time period.

During cross-examination by the defense, however, Dittmann admitted she had seldom seen Heinrich between August 2008 and December 2008.

The second government witness was Rudolf Betting, a self-employed engineer from Denkingen and a one-time boyfriend of Dittmann.

Like Dittmann, Betting testified that he knew Heinrich as well and stated that his first contact with her was at See-Studio June 13, 2008, approximately two and a half months prior to the night in question.

Aside from being able to identify Stewart as the man with whom Heinrich danced and, later, left See-Studio, Betting told the court something during the defense's cross-examination that should have raised eyebrows about Heinrich.

When the defense asked Betting if he had told Heinrich that he remembered her leaving the club happily and of her own free will, he said he had—and then some.

"I saw that that way, and I stated it to her that I saw her, but she asked me not to say that in the testimony," Betting said, noting something that Stewart's civilian defense attorney had known about in advance of the trial.

During the defense's cross-examination, Betting was asked about Heinrich's behavior and responded by saying he had not noticed any changes in Heinrich's behavior. In addition, he described her as "very impulsive and emotional" and as a person who tends to speak her mind.

Following Betting's testimony, the government called Heinrich to testify.

Captain O'Malley asked Stewart's accuser to describe what had transpired during the evening in question.

Heinrich began her story by saying that she and her neighbor, Jule, met Dittmann and an acquaintance, Ralf, at Café Schilling in Böblingen at 9 p.m. Ninety minutes later, the foursome headed to See-Studio and, there, met another friend, Rudi. Interestingly, the last names of Jule, Ralf and Rudi appear nowhere in the Record of Trial—an indication, perhaps, of a less-than-thorough investigation by, among others, German police and U.S. Army investigators.

Asked to do so by the assistant trial counsel, Heinrich told the court how she had met Stewart.

"It was 2:30," she said. "The song that was playing was from Rammstein, 'You Smell So Good'; and, suddenly, he stood in front of me."

They danced for a while and, according to the Record of Trial, she said they spoke to each other in German.

At one point, however, she claimed Stewart pushed her away and walked away before later coming back and walking around her.

"I didn't understand it," she said when asked by Captain O'Malley how she had interpreted it.

Heinrich went on to answer several more questions about events leading up to her departure from the club with Stewart—shortly before 3:30 a.m.—for what she described as "a 'one-night stand' that, you know, it's a sexual meeting. It was clear to me that he wanted sex from me."

Heinrich told the court that, shortly before their departure from the club, she had suggested her place as their destination and that Stewart had agreed to that. She also told the court she would not have left the club with Stewart had he been wearing a wedding ring.

More questions from the assistant trial counsel followed about the cab ride that, Heinrich said, ended at Stewart's hotel instead of at her apartment as agreed. Then she painted a portrait of a man telling lies (i.e., that he was divorced and that he manipulated her into coming to his room on the 5th floor of the Stuttgart-Marriott Hotel).

"I was surprised when we stopped there, when we got out," she said. "I asked him, 'What are we doing here at the hotel?' and he said he lives here."

Asked if he told her why they were at the hotel, Heinrich said, "He said he would get something to drink."

Saying she thought they would leave after Stewart got something to drink, she offered her account of what happened after they entered the hotel and made it to the hallway outside his room.

"I didn't want to go in with him," she explained, adding, "I just had a bad feeling in my stomach. I mean I've never gone with a stranger."

Asked what Stewart said to her at that point, she said, "He must have noticed that. He looked at me and he said, 'You don't have to be afraid. I won't do anything to you; but I am a man—a real man.'"

She told the court she interpreted his statement as "just talking, you know, like blowing hot air. That didn't do anything to me."

The next thing she did, according to her testimony, was walk into the room when he opened the door, apparently willing to ignore the "bad feeling" in her stomach.

According to Heinrich, six hours of anguish followed inside the hotel room.

After a brief exchange about the layout of the hotel room, Captain O'Malley asked Heinrich to answer questions about what she said happened once she entered the hotel room.

"Please tell me, where did you go once the door to the room opened?" the government attorney asked, initiating a series of short questions and answers.

"I stopped very close to the door, about level with the bathroom," Heinrich replied.

"Why did you stop there?"

"I didn't want to go in. I mean, you know, we wanted to leave again. He was going to get something, and I was waiting."

"What did the accused do once you stopped?"

"He walked past me. Right away when the door opened, he walked past me over to the mini-bar and he got himself something to drink.

"What else did he say to you?"

"He asked me whether I wanted to have something to drink?"

"What did you say?"

"No, we're leaving right away."

"How did he respond to you saying that?"

"He said, 'No, we're staying here.'"

Heinrich went on to describe how she was not satisfied with that answer and "just stood there" before Stewart reacted to her.

"He grabbed my hand and he pulled me—he pulled me over to the bed; that's where he positioned me," she explained. "I mean he positioned me with—my back was toward the bed, and my view was toward the television. That's where he placed me."

"What did he say once he positioned you there?" Captain O'Malley asked.

"First he didn't say anything; then he walked around me, and then he was like behind me, on that side from the bed."

A brief explanation followed about where each person was positioned in the room, then she described what she said happened next.

"He said, 'Get undressed,'" Heinrich explained, characterizing the statement as an "order" he expected her to follow.

When she didn't comply, she said, he responded quickly.

"He, you know, extended his arm, and he hit me on the right cheek and the back of the head," she said. "He hit very hard. My entire head was shaking."

Describing herself as angry and wanting to leave, Heinrich told the court she wanted to walk to the door, but "then he came."

"He got in front of me, stopped me, and, you know, he was trying to calm me down," she said. "He kept saying, 'Sorry, sorry,' and he said he wanted that I get undressed alone because I'm so beautiful; I look so beautiful."

Asked what she was thinking at that time, she said, "I was very angry that he had hit me; but, since I was objecting, since, you know, I was fighting back, I thought he understood—he understood he couldn't do this to me."

Next, she said, "He said I should please get undressed." And she did.

"I was ashamed," she explained. "I was looking down onto the ground, but I did get undressed."

Her reasoning?

"I was angry because of the hit, but I was too proud—I was too proud to simply leave," she told the court.

Asked to described where she was standing at that point, she said, "In front of the bed where he had positioned me" with her clothes "on the floor beside me."

Asked what Stewart was doing during the time she was getting undressed, Heinrich said he was undressing himself and saying nothing except that he wanted her to leave her boots on because "they turn me on."

After saying that, she said he turned her around and threw her on the bed very fast as was pushing her around.

At that point, according to the Record of Trial, the assistant trial counsel noted, "The witness made another motion with her hands, both hands raised about head level, made a turning motion, like moving her right hand out, left had towards her body, like turning something; and then she put both hands forward, as if a push—to be pushed down."

"Once he had turned you around and pushed you down, what did he do?" Captain O'Malley asked his witness.

"He had his knee in my buttocks and, you know, pushed down; and with his right hand, he was pressing down my shoulder; and with his left hand he was reaching into my hair. I was screaming and I was struggling, but he just pushed me down."

"Once you were pushed down and he had pushed you and grabbed your hair, then what did he do?" the government attorney asked.

"I was struggling; I was screaming," she said. "I was—you know, I was fighting back, but I didn't have a chance; he just pushed me down."

Asked to describe how quickly that happened, Heinrich said, "Within seconds—from now to right away; that's when he pushed me onto the bed, and he rammed me.

Their exchange continued.

"What do you mean by 'rammed' you?"

"Anal intercourse."

"What did he place inside your anus?"

"His penis."

"How did you react?"

"I screamed and I tried to get free, but I didn't have a chance; he pushed me down."

"Had you, earlier in the evening, discussed having anal sex with the accused?"

"No, we didn't talk about sex at all."

"What were you thinking at this time?"

"I was in pain. I had such terrible pain I thought I was going to throw up. I mean I thought like I burst open and there's blood everywhere. I never had such bad pain before."

"What did you do then?"

"I rolled over to the side. I mean he just rammed it in once, and then he went away, and I just rolled over to the side. I was in sort of like a fetal position, scrunched up, and lay there."

"Why did you assume that position?"

"I was in so much pain. I was just, you know, hunched together."

"What did you do after you went in that position?"

"I got up, and I went to the bathroom."

"Why did you go to the bathroom?"

"Because I thought I was bleeding everywhere."

"What did you do once you got in the bathroom?"

"I checked, as I was on the toilet, whether I'm okay."

"Were you okay?"

"No. I wasn't bleeding, but I was in pain. I had a lot of pain."

"Did the accused have your permission to insert his penis into your anus?"

"No."

"How long were you in the bathroom?"

"One minute—very quickly."

"What were you thinking when you were in the bathroom?"

"I thought something went terribly wrong. I wanted to leave right away."

"What did you intend to do when you left the bathroom?"

"I went straight to the bed where my clothes had been lying, but they weren't lying there anymore."

"Where were your clothes at the time you exited the bathroom?"

"On the chair in the corner—right back there in the corner; that's where he put the clothes."

Heinrich was then asked to show the court the locations of a variety of things, including where she found her clothes and where Stewart was standing as she exited the bathroom.

Asked what she did when she left the bathroom, Heinrich explained.

"I wanted to go to my clothes, and I saw that they were lying there on the chair."

"Did you go over to your clothes?" Captain O'Malley followed.

"I wanted to," she replied. "I said to him, 'That was not okay. I'm leaving now,' but he blocked my path."

"What did he say to you as he blocked your path?"

"He grabbed me with his right hand by the throat, and he said, 'You blow me one, cunt, and you will swallow it.'"

At that point, the assistant trial counsel noted that Heinrich "grabbed her right hand and grabbed her throat, making a choking motion."

"How did the accused look at the moment when he grabbed your throat?" Captain O'Malley asked.

"Evil, like an animal," she replied. "Evil."

Heinrich explained that she looked into his eyes and was afraid.

"I thought he was going to kill me."

Prompted by more questions, she said Stewart was holding her throat very hard, making it so she could barely breathe, and he was holding her hair, pushing her down.

Asked what happened next, Heinrich said, "He pushed me down onto my knees, and he put his penis into my mouth."

"What did you do once he had forced his penis inside your mouth?"

"Nothing at all. He got an erection right away, and I swallowed it the way he wanted me to."

She said she performed oral sex on him for "very, very, very briefly" against her will and, afterward, she said, Stewart told her she should wait while he took a shower.

What happened during the time he was in the shower?

"I sat on the bed and I just looked," Heinrich said. "He went into the bathroom, but he didn't close the door, and I was just sitting there; I didn't move; I was in a lot of pain."

"What were you thinking at that time?" she was asked.

"I thought that nobody has ever humiliated me like that."

When asked why she didn't leave the hotel room during the shower that took Stewart two to three minutes to complete, she said, "I was afraid, and I was in pain. I have never before in my life had such awful pain. I could not move."

After Stewart came out of the bathroom, Heinrich told the court Stewart wanted to continue on.

"You know, he rolled me over on the side, and he lay down behind me, and he tried to push his penis into me from the side."

She said his penis entered her vagina only very briefly—and without her permission, she added later—because she was, "blocking it."

That's when, she said, "he went at it with his fingers" while holding the back of Heinrich's head by her hair.

Heinrich went on to say Stewart hit her in the face, on the breast, on the buttocks and on the hip—again without permission—while not saying a word to her until after he stopped.

Then, she said, he talked, saying, "You have it. I gave it to you the way you needed it, and you needed it hard."

Asked how she reacted to those comments, Heinrich said she didn't say anything, but Stewart kept on talking.

She said Stewart told her, "Normally, you have to control the sex."

Next, she said he told her, "You do what I want you to, and I won't do anything to you. Then I will be good to you, also. Otherwise, you know what's going to happen."

Asked what she thought he meant by those statements, Heinrich said, "I didn't think anything. I just was scared and in pain."

What happened next, she said, was that Stewart pushed into her right breast with his fingers and then bit into the nipple very hard, causing her to scream, all the while still holding her then-long hair with his left hand.

Next, she said, "He said I should lick his balls," and she did.

Why? Because, she said, "I would have done anything so he would stop."

Next, she said he told her, "I should kiss his butt hole and I should lick it out."

In response, she said, she told him, "You can lick your own asshole. I won't do anything like that."

In turn, she said, Stewart responded violently, trying to push her head down there, but she was able to avoid performing that task.

She said Stewart got angry and hit her hard before issuing another demand.

"He said, 'Well, then you blow me another one, you cunt, and you will swallow it,'" she said. And, much like the first time, she did it.

After Stewart ejaculated, she said, "He stood next to the bed, and he was pounding his chest, and he said, 'That was really good.'"

The assistant trial counsel asked Heinrich what she was thinking as he did that, and she offered a dramatic answer.

"That I will not survive this; that it won't stop—never," she said. "I was afraid he would kill me.

After beating his chest, Heinrich said, Stewart told her it was time to go to sleep and uncovered the left side of the bed, pushed her down and then covered her before going to the other side of the bed and laying down with his back to her.

"What were you thinking once he laid you down in bed?" Captain O'Malley asked.

"I thought, 'What a sick situation,'" she said. "I mean the situation just wasn't fitting—first all this violence, and now we're lying there like a lovers couple; and, you know, we were just lying there, and he's even turning his back to me."

Asked by the attorney to interpret the meaning of Stewart turning his back to her, she spoke of being humiliated.

"I mean it was like a double humiliation," Heinrich told the court. "After everything he did to me, then he turned his back to me."

After both of them were in bed, Heinrich said, "I was listening to his breathing, to his breath; and then, when I thought he was sleeping, I tried to get up."

Where was she trying to go? The assistant trial counsel wanted to know.

"Outside-just outside of the room," she answered.

When she stood up, she said, Stewart turned around really fast, grabbed her by the arm with his left hand and said, "Where are you going?"

"I have to go to the bathroom," was her response, she said, adding that she remained on the bed. Scared.

Asked what she did next, she said she waited.

But for how long?

"I couldn't tell you. I have no idea," Heinrich told the court. "I mean at first I thought it was between 3:30 to 8:30; it's—I mean I was just waiting.

"At one point I saw the daylight—daylight through the curtains, and then I thought I'll try it again."

Asked to tell the court what happened when she got up the next time, she explained.

"I had to walk around the bed. I walked around the bed, but the whole time I kept looking at him. I mean I had to go—my clothes were directly on the chair behind him, so I had to walk around him."

"What direction was he facing?" the assistant trial counsel asked. "Was he facing towards your clothes or away from your clothes?"

"In the direction of my clothes, to the window side," Heinrich answered, adding that she kept her eyes on him the whole time because she was afraid he would wake up.

Once able to get her clothes and dress, Heinrich said, "I wanted to walk to the door, and that's when he opened his eyes.

"He got up and he said, 'Where are you going?'"

Heinrich said she responded by saying, "I'm leaving."

In turn, she said, "He grabbed me, and he led me over to the table—that's where a pen and stationery from the Marriott Hotel was—and he said, 'You will write down your cell phone number, and the right one; otherwise, you're not leaving.'"

She said she did what he asked and wrote down the right number, saying, "I would have done anything to get out of the room. That was my last chance."

After writing down the number, she told the court, Stewart told her to go, then went back to the bed, laid down and closed his eyes.

At that point, she said, she "went very slowly to the door and opened it; and then, outside in the hallway, I ran to the elevator and took the elevator downstairs."

The assistant trial counsel asked Heinrich why she ran to the elevator.

"I was afraid he would follow me," she said.

Once she reached the ground floor, she said she went to the reception area by the exit, got into a cab and told the female driver to take her to the Café Schall in Böblingen because it was near her home.

Asked to describe the taxi driver, Heinrich told the court she had dark hair, was heavily built and in her middle 50s.

Asked if she knew the driver's name, she said, "Now I know it, but before then I didn't."

When the assistant trial counsel asked Heinrich why she told the taxi driver to take her to Café Schall in Böblingen, the witness said, "Because that's where I live."

Pressed to tell the court why she wanted to go home, Heinrich said she wanted to go home and have a shower "Because I was dirty. The man made me dirty everywhere."

Asked why she didn't tell the taxi driver to take her to the police station, she said, "I wanted to go home. I only wanted to go home."

Prompted by the assistant trial counsel to continue, Heinrich said she felt safe in the taxi but was in pain: "Everything hurt."

The attorney's questioning then turned back to the hotel room and what she noticed about Stewart's body while he was undressed.

"He had two piercings through his nipples," Heinrich told the court. "On each nipple, he had a piercing; and he had a lot of tattoos."

After she described the tattoos and their locations, the questioning turned to why Heinrich didn't go to the Polizei soon after the alleged incident and report it.

"I blamed myself," she said, because she went with a stranger to a hotel room. "I was very ashamed."

Asked when she finally went to the police, Heinrich said it was November 7, 2008.

Did she think, the assistant trial counsel asked, while lying in bed in the hotel room almost 11 weeks earlier, that she had been raped?

"I thought he raped me," she told the court. "I felt it."

Asked why she waited until November to report the alleged incident, Heinrich said a friend, Helga Gowar, had convinced her during a phone call November 5, 2008, that she should.

"You know, I was telling Helga about it, and she said to me, 'Wake up, girl; wake up.'"

At this point, Heinrich's testimony turned toward the subject of her making the police report and the investigation—including a visit to the scene of the alleged crime and her identification of a photo of Stewart as the alleged perpetrator—that followed.

When Captain O'Malley asked Heinrich how she reacted when she was shown a photo of Stewart by the Polizei, Stewart's civilian defense attorney objected, quickly realizing that Heinrich could feign a reaction that would likely influence panel members. The objection was sustained by the military judge.

After some administrative matters were discussed, the assistant trial counsel continued the cross-examination of Heinrich by asking if she had sought medical attention for her alleged injuries.

She responded, saying she had had a urinary tract infection and went to a doctor the week right after the alleged incident.

Strangely, she said in response to the attorney's question, she did not tell the doctor she had been attacked and didn't show him signs of the attack, despite telling the court her "entire body was covered in bruises, my right breast was so sore, infected, and swelled up."

The assistant trial counsel asked her why she didn't tell the doctor about the attack.

"Because I was ashamed," Heinrich said.

And why didn't the doctor notice the bruises during a physical examination? That question would go unasked for the time being.

Asked if she had sought professional mental health counseling to deal with this alleged attack, she said she had and provided some details.

"In November, I went to THAMAR. THAMAR—that's an agency that helps victims of sexual violence; and, then, in the beginning of December, I went to Mrs. Mornhinweg," Heinrich said.

When asked if she was still seeing Mrs. Mornhinweg, Heinrich said she had not seen the counselor since the end of June 2009.

Though the defense objected on grounds that panel members might see her answer as providing "proof that she's a victim," Judge Kuhfahl overruled the objection and allowed Heinrich to tell the court how her lifestyle had changed after the alleged attack.

"I'm afraid a lot," Heinrich told the court. "I'm afraid to go—be with people."

She added that she doesn't sleep a lot, doesn't go dancing and doesn't go out with people a lot anymore.

Asked if her appearance had changed since the alleged attack, she told the court she had cut her hair "really short" and "I don't want anybody ever to grab and pull on my hair again."

In testimony later during the trial, Heinrich said she didn't cut her hair until "it all came back to me" after going to the police in November 2008.

Regarding other actions she took after the alleged attack, she said she had gone to THAMAR, "the counseling place," three to four times.

When she was asked if she still had the cell phone number she had given to Stewart before leaving his hotel room, she said she had had it changed "so that nobody can reach me."

Again, timing was an issue.

In testimony later in the trial, she said she thought she had changed the number "shortly after" she had gone to the police. In the next breath, however, she said, "I think it was like the 6th of November," one day before she went to the police.

In summary, her testimony during direct examination by the assistant trial counsel on the first day of the trial revealed the following:

• Heinrich said that, when she left the club with Stewart, "It was clear to me that he wanted sex from me";

• Heinrich said that she entered his hotel room despite having a "bad feeling" in her stomach;

• Heinrich claimed she had been "too proud to leave" the hotel room in which she said she had feared for her life;

• Heinrich said that, because she was afraid and in pain, she did not leave the hotel room during a shower that took Stewart two to three minutes to complete;

• Heinrich admitted that, while visiting her doctor about a urinary tract infection a week after the night with Stewart, she did not tell that doctor about the alleged attack that she said had left her "covered in bruises" and the doctor did not notice any evidence of such an attack when he examined her;

• Heinrich responded to questions about how her lifestyle and social habits had changed since the night of the alleged attack by saying, "I'm afraid a lot. I'm afraid to go--be with people," and "I don't go dancing a lot anymore, and I don't go out with people a lot anymore"; and

• Heinrich admitted that she waited almost 11 weeks before reporting the crime, cutting her hair and changing the cell phone number she said she had been forced to give the man whom she later claimed had raped her.

**Next, Stewart's civilian defense counsel cross-examined Heinrich.**

**After establishing that her age at the time of the alleged incident was 28 and that she had met Stewart for the first time at 2:30 in the morning, the civilian defense attorney fired a zinger at Heinrich.**

"And, an hour later, you were prepared to have a one-night stand with him?"

"Yes," Heinrich replied.

The questions then turned to her departure from the hotel and why she didn't stop to tell the clerk at the reception desk or the female taxi driver what she said had happened to her in Stewart's room.

"I told (the taxi driver) that I had met an American—I mean that came out in the conversation; but, you know, I didn't tell her that I was raped," Heinrich said.

When questioned further by the defense attorney, she admitted she had not said anything about the incident to anyone until November 5.

Asked about her visit a few days after the alleged incident to the office of a doctor she had known since she was a child, she said she was not physically examined and she did not tell anyone at the doctor's office about the bruises all over her body. She said she was there for the treatment of a stomach pains.

"When a bladder infection was diagnosed, did you tell them that you had had forcible sexual activity?" the attorney asked.

"No, only in December; that's when I told them," Heinrich replied.

Asked to elaborate about her visits to Mrs. Mornhinweg for what she called "trauma therapy," Heinrich revealed she had had her first session with the "psychotherapist and dance therapist" early in December and went weekly except for three weeks due to vacation. She also said Mornhinweg was not a trauma therapy specialist.

Asked about her visit to Frau Mornhinweg in December 2008 not being her first visit to a psychotherapist, Heinrich explained that she was treated at a clinic for four months in 2004 for inpatient treatment of what she called "burnout."

That discussion prompted a brief meeting between attorneys for both sides and Judge Kuhfahl.

Stewart's attorney requested permission to ask questions about Heinrich's refusal to release records about her psychotherapy treatment in 2004, telling the military judge the fundamental question to Heinrich would be, "Why have you refused to let the defense and the government have copies of your records from that time?"

When asked by Judge Kuhfahl what matter of consequence the records would prove or disprove and why the records were relevant, Stewart's attorney asked first for the judge to ask the witness to leave the courtroom during their discussion. After her departure, the civilian defense attorney continued.

"Your honor, just like the government's argument that her post-incident action gives the panel some suggestion of her credibility, and how she acted, and whether it's believable what she is saying, her unwillingness to cooperate with the government or the defense as to her prior mental condition also should give the panel something to consider in determining her credibility.

"The defense does not dispute we have no records; we do not know what is in the records; but that, in and of itself, is of concern. We believe that is a clear inference that she is not as candid with the tribunal, and the government, and the process, as she is implying by her testimony and the way she presented herself under direct.

"We believe that the government is, as they are entitled to do, trying to have it both ways. They want to bring in post activity to show she's credible; but they don't want us to ask her questions about why she's not willing to work with the system to determine her credibility. All we want to do is ask her the question of why she has not let us have copies of those records."

The assistant trial counsel countered the defense's argument.

"Your honor, the victim has invoked her rights under German law to not disclose her records. The government has then gone to the Stuttgart prosecutor to request those under German law. The prosecutor has refused to give those up.

"The country of Germany is basically refusing to give us the records. Ms. Heinrich should not be held accountable for her country not giving us these records, as the defense is trying to blame her completely for this."

Judge Kuhfahl interjected.

"All I want to know right now is, one, do you object to the defense asking the question, "Why have you refused to turn over your medical records?"

"Yes, your honor," the assistant trial counsel responded, adding, "There's no relevance shown by that at all, your honor."

Acknowledging the response, Judge Kuhfahl said, "Okay," and asked the defense counsel if his argument for relevance centered on credibility.

"It goes to candor with the tribunal, your honor, which is a subset of credibility," said the defense attorney. "That is what the government was bringing out with all of the actions, post-event—cutting her hair, reportedly not going out with friends, and so on.

"It is the counterweight to that in terms of her willingness to be candid, be open with the tribunal," he continued. "She has obviously got something that she wishes to withhold, and without that question, the panel will not have that impression of her; will think that she has been candid and told us everything, and that is not true."

Judge Kuhfahl responded by telling the attorneys he didn't know why Heinrich had not agreed to turn over her records and that he wasn't going to assume anything.

"The Court does not find that there's any matter of consequence that that question would address, indicating anything is more or less probable in this case," the military judge said. "Therefore, the government objection is sustained, and I'm not going to allow that question."

Judge Kuhfahl did, however, allow the defense attorney to question Heinrich about the definition of "burnout," the reason she sought psychotherapy treatment in 2004, but that opportunity paled in comparison to what Heinrich's actual medical records might have provided the court.

Heinrich was called back into the courtroom and the defense attorney asked her if, indeed, she had received treatment related to her story of what happened in the hotel and if part of that treatment involved talking through what she said happened.

To both questions, she said, "That is correct."

After a brief exchange about Heinrich's employment history, the defense attorney asked her about what she told Rudolf Betting before he testified earlier in the day.

"Did you ask him not to testify about part of his knowledge of the night of 22/23 August?" the defense attorney asked.

"That is not correct," she replied.

"Did Rudolf Betting tell you, in preparation for this trial, that he would testify you looked pleased, happy, and voluntary when you left the club?"

"He did not tell me that," she said. "He only said he could describe him very well."

The civilian defense attorney then turned his questioning to Heinrich's report about the evening with Stewart, including her story about the taxi ride from See-Studio to the Stuttgart-Marriott Hotel and her changing stories about who kissed who that night (i.e., she told the German police that she kissed Stewart, but told the court he had kissed her).

Other questions followed.

"You told us, up until this point all along, you never wanted to go with a stranger to his hotel, correct?" the defense attorney asked.

"That is correct," she replied.

"But, on this evening, you did."

"Yes, for the first time; that's right."

"And you told us you didn't want to go in the room; then he made macho talk; and, since it didn't impress you, you did go in the room, correct?"

"It's not right that way," Heinrich answered, explaining later that, "I had a bad feeling. I had a bad feeling because I went with a stranger, and I didn't want to go in; but he wanted to get something to drink, so we did, because it was clear to me that we would leave again."

An exchange of questions and answers about the room's layout and Stewart's movements within it followed; then Heinrich described how she didn't fight when Stewart grabbed her by the hands and pulled her toward the bed.

The defense attorney asked Heinrich if Stewart was "standing there admiring you?"

"No, that I didn't see," she said. "I mean he walked around me—that much I saw; and then he was standing behind me—I didn't see that."

Seconds after Stewart walked around her and told her to undress, the German woman said, he hit her on her right ear and back of her head.

After that, she said, she turned toward Stewart and said, "No, my friend, not in that tone of voice."

Asked if, at that point, she started to leave, she said she had not.

"I mean I started to scream; I started the struggle," Heinrich said. "I yelled at him and I said, 'No, not with me. If you like shit like that, that's okay, but I don't," and then I wanted to leave."

That's when, she said, Stewart changed his approach.

"So he gets around in front of you and then starts calming you down, saying, 'You're so beautiful,' and, 'You don't have to worry; it's okay.' He uses the calming words at this point, correct?"

"That is correct," Heinrich said, 'and he said, 'Sorry, sorry,' and he calmed me down."

"And, after that, you voluntarily got undressed?" the defense asked.

"Not at first," she explained. "I was angry; but then, yes, yes, I got undressed, that is right."

Asked if she had talked with Stewart about the type of sex in which they would engage, she said she had not.

"We didn't talk about sex at all," Heinrich explained before confirming that it was understood by both parties that their one-night stand would involve sex.

Questions followed about how many times she screamed during the night and why she didn't leave the hotel room while Stewart was in the shower.

Though she explained that the loud music likely concealed her very loud screams, she gave no reason—other than that she was "lying there, because I was in pain"—for not trying to leave the hotel room during Stewart's two-minute shower.

The defense's questioning of Heinrich continued, moving to a discussion of how, she said, Stewart tried to force her head toward his rectum.

"Did he use one hand or two hands to do that?" the defense attorney asked.

"One hand—with one hand," Heinrich replied. "One hand was in my hair—he grabbed my hair—and with the other hand he was pushing down my shoulder."

"So, he's pushing on your shoulder with one of his hands, has his hand in your hair with the other; and, with that, he's moving your head toward his rectum?"

"He was pushing me down with the hand on the shoulder," she said. "That's the hand he used to push me down. The other hand was holding my hair.

"That's where he held my head up and he tried to position it. He was lying spread eagle on the bed, and he tried to push my head there."

"So, after the last sexual activity, he stood next to the bed, pounded his chest, and said, 'That was really good.' Is that your testimony?" the defense continued.

"That is right," Heinrich answered.

"And then he said, 'Okay, we'll go to sleep.'"

"That is right," she repeated.

"And it bothered you quite a lot that, when the two of you lay down on the bed, he rolled so his back was to you?" the defense asked.

"That is not correct," Heinrich said, correcting the defense attorney. "It didn't bother me, but he humiliated me."

After pointing out to Heinrich that she had used those words more than once when telling her story, the defense attorney asked her what she meant by saying, "After everything that happened, he then turned his back to me."

"Yes, because it only emphasized how he was humiliating; how this was humiliation," Heinrich said, "because he treated me like I'm the last dirt on this world, after everything he did."

After denying that she had ever used the words, "after we made love," during her testimony, Heinrich explained what it was she had said that sounded similar.

"I said that the situation was totally twisted, and screwed up, and upside down," she explained. "I said that he lay me down and covered me as if we were a couple in love—as if we were a lovers couple—but that's not what we were. He forced me to do those things."

The defense attorney asked Heinrich to confirm that she left the hotel room around 8:30 a.m. August 23, 2008, and that she gave her phone number to Stewart.

"And, when you got ready to leave," the defense attorney asked if Stewart had said, "You have to give me your right telephone number or you can't leave."

According to Heinrich, Stewart said, "You will write your number down—and the right one; otherwise, you're not leaving," so she wrote down the correct number.

"How would he have known if you didn't?" the attorney asked.

"I never even had the idea to give him the wrong number," Heinrich said. "I would have done anything to get out of this room."

"Once you gave him your telephone number, he said, 'Then go'?"

"That is right," she said, "and he lay down in bed again and turned away again."

In a brief diversion from events in the hotel room, the defense attorney asked Heinrich if she recalled anything in the way of tattoos on Stewart's back.

"I think it was a female name, like Frieda, Freya, Freda," Heinrich said. "It was written in cursive writing."

The next question was unrelated to the previous two.

After saying he was "a little unclear" as to part of Heinrich's testimony with the government toward the end, the defense attorney asked Heinrich if, while she was still in the hotel room August 23, 2008, she believed she was raped?

"I did not believe it," she answered. "I felt it."

"But you did not tell anyone that you had been raped until November of 2008?" the attorney shot back.

"That is correct," Heinrich said.

At that point, the defense ended its cross-examination of Heinrich, and the court adjourned for five minutes. When the court reconvened, Judge Kuhfahl asked if any of the panel members had questions, and they did.

***[Editor's Note:*** *Questions submitted by the panel members during the trial were read by the military judge.]*

Major Wallace Smith asked Heinrich if she ever yelled or said, "No" or "Nein" in an attempt to get Stewart to stop what she said he was doing to her in the hotel room.

She said she had and elaborated.

"The first time, when he threw me on the bed and anally raped me," she said.

Asked if that was the only time she said, "No," she explained that she "said it again when I came out of the bathroom—that this wasn't right and that I will leave now."

A question from Colonel (Chaplain) Yarman had to do with Heinrich's cell phone.

"Do you remember the date that you changed your cell phone number?"

Heinrich responded by saying, "I think it was shortly after I had been to the police. I think it was like the 6th of November."

Captain Joshua Buchanan wanted to know if Heinrich ever attempted to tell the taxi driver who drove her and Stewart to the Marriott she didn't wish to go to the hotel.

Heinrich responded, saying she did not and that she "felt safe in the cab."

Asked if she told the taxi driver he was not going in the right direction, she said she had.

"I told him that this is the wrong direction," Heinrich said, "that we're going very far away from my apartment, yes."

Upon further questioning, she said the driver did not respond to her.

"He was talking to the soldier and laughing with him; they were making jokes; they were talking about me."

"Do you know whether the cab driver understood you when you said you were not going in the direction that you wanted to go?"

"I do believe he understood me, yes," she explained, "but the soldier said to him that we have to go to the gas station at the Marriott Hotel, and he listened to him, yes."

Another question from Captain Buchanan had to do with when Heinrich told Betting about the alleged incident for the first time.

At one point, she said she had told Dittmann about it November 1, 2008. Next, she said the first person she told about it was her friend, Helga, by phone the evening of November 5, 2008. Finally, she concluded that she must have told Dittmann about it one or two days after telling Gowar. In turn, she said Betting heard about it from Dittmann a few days later.

Upon being asked, Heinrich confirmed that she had had a chance to speak with Betting about the alleged incident about two months later—"either the end of December 2008 or January 2009"—while dancing and again in May 2009.

When questioning ended, the assistant trial counsel began his brief redirect examination of Heinrich by asking her to describe her relationship with Betting.

"We don't have a relationship," she said. "He didn't get over the breakup with Jasmin, and he keeps calling us in the middle of the night, and he keeps hassling us with emails."

Asked by the civilian defense counsel during recross examination how recently she had had e-mail contact with Betting, Heinrich said he had sent her an e-mail Friday, August 14, 2008, but she did not reply to it.

When asked if she told Betting via e-mail that he "really, really had to testify because he knew what the person looked like," Heinrich confirmed she had.

"I told him that he is very important because he's the only person, besides me, that can describe him and that has seen him," she said, "so I told him he's very important; that is correct."

"Did you, in another email after that, tell him that it was a good thing he didn't have to come after all, and you and Jasmin were glad about that?" the defense added.

She said she had and the questioning ended.

Heinrich's testimony consumed a third of the twelve-hour day.

A cab driver since 1984, Monika Haug was called to testify by the government late in the afternoon on the trial's first day because, prosecutors claimed, she was the one who had driven Heinrich from the Marriott Hotel to her home the morning of August 23, 2008. Her testimony lasted well past 7 p.m.

Notable in Haug's testimony were her initial impressions about Heinrich as she walked out of the Marriott Hotel and toward her cab, which she said was a seven-seat Ford Galaxy van that is higher and larger than the average German taxi.

According to the Record of Trial, Haug said Heinrich was "not walking straight; you know, she was weaving from one side to the next."

"Normally, if you would walk, you would walk straight," Haug continued, "but I mean it could be that something else was wrong with her, I mean because I recalled my impression right away when she was in the cab that she had alcohol to drink.

"When she got into the cab," Haug continued, "that impression didn't verify itself, because she didn't smell like alcohol."

In describing aspects of Heinrich's physical appearance, Haug said, "She made a very unkempt impression" before going on to describe her messed up hair and clothing.

In addition, Haug explained that Heinrich appeared to be in some pain and wasn't very talkative during the cab ride back to her Böblingen home.

When the government asked Haug to describe Heinrich's mental state, the defense objected and the military judge agreed.

A short while later, the defense began its cross examination of Haug by confirming with her that she had given a verbal statement to German police December 22, 2008.

"When you first saw (Heinrich) approaching your cab, what was your impression of that woman?" the defense attorney asked.

Judging by her response that followed, Haug appears to have been fearful the statement she gave German police officials eight months earlier might come back to haunt her.

"If you then later will imply that this is what I said about the women, then, no, I don't want to say anything because I want to give it back the right way," Haug said. "When I said before my first impression I was—the first impression I had from her—wait, I have to—let me rephrase this.

"I had, since I'm driving a taxi, picked up many women from this hotel. The first—when she walked toward the cab, when she walked toward the cab, I had the impression, 'What happened to these women?' But, also, as she was walking toward me, toward the cab, that's when I realized then that she cannot be a woman free from the business, that she cannot be a prostitute, but there had to be something else."

Though the taxi driver believed Heinrich was not a prostitute, she apparently had more difficulty telling time. Translated to English, the German police report of Haug's interview begins with this paragraph: "Mrs. Haug, you are a taxi driver for the company Vollmers. Based on our information you had a tour from the Marriott-Hotel in Sindelfingen in the morning of 24 Aug 2008. At that time you were allegedly driving a woman. What can you tell me about it?"

Haug's reply, according to the same report, began this way: "That morning I was waiting for customers at the Marriott Hotel. It was Saturday morning; I was there already since about 0630 hrs. Saturday mornings some guests often want to the got he airport that is why I waited there. Then a woman came outside through the spinning doors, I believe it was about 1100 hrs, but I am not sure about it anymore."

When one realizes that Heinrich took a taxi from the Marriott to her Böblingen home a full 24 hours earlier on the morning of August 23, 2008, Haug's entire testimony begins to lose credibility. It loses even more when one recalls that she explained to German police officials months earlier that her recollection of the passenger in question from months earlier was not good.

"I'm sorry I don't see her in front of my eyes anymore right now," Haug told the German police officers. "I believe she had blonde dyed hair. I don't remember her clothing or age right now anymore."

On the night in question, Heinrich had shoulder-length black hair.

Stewart found it oddly coincidental how, one year after supposedly picking up Heinrich, the taxi cab driver was able to remember details (i.e., Heinrich was wearing knee-high boots, had long black hair, etc.) that she couldn't remember six months prior and add details (i.e., "Every time I drove over a bump, I could hear her moan like she was in pain, and I asked her if she was okay.").

"That's what I like to call 'coaching,'" he said, adding, "It's phenomenal to me. And the jurors don't know that, because that's not what was presented to them."

The first defense witness to testify was Major Patrick Grow, a colleague of Stewart at the International Special Training Center. Judge Kuhfahl allowed him to testify out of order to accommodate previously-scheduled travel plans.

Despite government attempts during cross-examination to get Major Grow to paint Stewart as a soldier who often lives in a gray area when it comes to behavior, the witness did not waver in his support of his colleague.

"Sir, of the non-commissioned officers that I have seen and worked with, I would say he's in the upper $90^{th}$ percentile," Major Grow said, "and I only say that because I personally have not served with him in combat, but I do know the guys in the same regiment and the same battalions that have, and it's a small community, and they have a very high opinion of him, as well."

Following Major Grow's testimony, the defense recalled Betting to the witness stand in what seemed an attempt to emphasize a point made earlier (i.e., that Heinrich wanted Betting to not mention that he saw her leave See-Studio "with a happy expression in her face").

Defense attorney Court asked Betting if he recalled when he first spoke with Heinrich personally about the events of 22/23 August 2008?

He said it was in November 2008 and went on to describe the occasion.

"It was a Saturday evening. I picked up Ms. Dittmann from—I took her from where I lived, Denkingen, to Tuebingen, and then I went to Boeblingen to pick up Ms. Heinrich, and I took both of them with me to Ludwigsburg to the Rock Factory--Fabrik" which, he explained "is the biggest rock disco"— "and then, at about one o'clock, Greta said to me, 'Rudi, do you have any memory of that evening in the Seestudio?'"

Asked by the defense attorney to share the answer he gave Heinrich, Betting complied.

"I said to her I could never forget this evening because that was the night when I could call Ms. Dittmann my girlfriend." Later, he confirmed that that evening was the last time he had spoken with Heinrich about the night in August at See-Studio.

"I told her I could explicitly describe that evening, and I did," he told the court. "I told her exactly—you know, I said I could identify the person, and I described the person to her, and I described the events that happened on that evening, just like I had done here in court."

Asked again by the defense attorney if it was on that evening that Heinrich asked him not to mention part of what he remembered about the night, he said "No" and explained.

"It was on the 22nd—the 22nd of last month, July—no, wait—the 22nd of July," Betting said, "that's when Ms. Dittmann broke up with me; and then, approximately one week later, in my desperation, I called Greta.

"She asked me, because I had said she left the Seestudio with a happy expression in her face, and she asked me that I please should not mention this," Betting continued, prompted by the defense attorney.

In closing, the defense attorney asked the witness if there had been any email traffic between Heinrich, Dittmann and himself.

He replied, saying that emails were exchanged only between Heinrich and himself and that conversations with Dittmann took place by phone.

Asked who had initiated the email exchanges, Betting said it was Heinrich.

Betting was the last witness to testify on the first day of the trial, a day on which no physical evidence was presented.

# DAY TWO

# Day Two: Six Witnesses

Six witnesses testified on Day Two of the trial. The first three to testify were called by the government. They were followed by two witnesses for the defense and one final witness for the government.

The first witness, Criminal Haupt Commissar Daniel Lorch, was the officer in charge of the eight-man investigation unit at the German criminal police office in Böblingen since 2000.

The nine-year veteran of the local police force answered a litany of questions from Captain Bashore about the basic police work that led to Stewart's apprehension following Heinrich's report of the alleged crime.

Asked what he knew about the suspect in the alleged crimes reported by Heinrich, he said, "Ms. Heinrich could give a very good description of him, you know" and went on to provide that description which he credited to Heinrich.

"She said that he's male; he's white; beginning to the middle of 30; approximately 1-meter 76 to 1-meter 78; he was muscular, strong; muscular but not fat; he had large tattoos on his upper arms and shoulders; and piercings through both nipples; and that he was probably from the military, at least that's how he introduced himself; even with the first name Antonio; and he was probably American or at least half-American."

In addition, Lorch said Heinrich was able to describe the layout of the room at the Marriott Hotel where the alleged crimes took place and identify Stewart in a photo.

Then the trial counsel asked Lorch about his efforts to locate a taxi driver.

"Did you attempt to fi--or did you find a taxi driver that drove from the See-Studio to the Marriot Hotel with the accused and Ms. Heinrich?"

"No," Lorch replied.

"Did you look?"

"No, I wrote to all 35 cab companies that are in that area, I personally called, I mean we tried everything but it wasn't--I wasn't able to personally iden--to identify the specific driver," Lorch said.

"But your office did identify Ms. Haug, is that correct?"

"Nein," Lorch answered.

Apparently confused by his answer, the trial counsel asked the question again.

"Haug? Did your office identify Ms. Haug as a taxi-driver?"

This time, Lorch gave the answer the trial counsel wanted to hear.

"Yes, that's correct, she was the driver who drove her home--."

Defense attorney Court voiced an objection, saying Lorch's statement amounted to hearsay, but it was overruled by the military judge and the trial counsel continued.

"And did your office have an opportunity to interview her?

"Yes."

"And are you aware of what day of the week is 23 August 2008?"

"Yes, it was a Saturday.

During cross-examination, the civilian defense attorney asked Lorch several soft questions about the layout of the hotel room and then asked him if he had found any witnesses who said could corroborate Heinrich's claim that she screamed loudly that night. He said he could not.

The second witness, Lieutenant Colonel (Dr.) Marshall Smith, was an Army physician and psychiatrist serving as chief of outpatient behavioral health at the Army's Landstuhl Regional Medical Center.

The government spent 10 minutes reviewing the doctor's background, education and professional experience—including his work with victims of sexual assault and related crimes—in an attempt to establish that the colonel was, indeed, a subject-matter expert. His answers dovetailed well with the government's line of reasoning—that is, that it's common for a rape victim to behave the way Heinrich did on the night of the alleged assault and during the months that followed until she reported the alleged crime.

Next, the trial counsel and the doctor conversed about how rape victims behave, about myths and public misconceptions surrounding that behavior and even about how it's possible for a person to not bleed after forcible anal intercourse. His answers continued to dovetail with the government's line.

During cross-examination, the civilian defense counsel asked Colonel Smith questions in several of the same areas covered by the trial counsel. One volley of questions and answers, however, produced replies that should have stunned panel members. Below is how they were recorded in the Record of Trial:

Q. Sir, were you aware that Ms. Heinrich was in psychotherapeutic treatment weekly for seven months, absent three weeks when she was on vacation, prior to her being interviewed by you?

A. No, I was not.

Q. Were you aware that she had talked about her reported experiences in each of those psychotherapeutic sessions before she spoke to you?

A. No, I was not.

Q. Would you agree, sir, from a psychological point of view, or psychiatric point of view, that the more a person tells a story the more ingrained it becomes in the person?

A. That's--I agree with that.

Q. And would you also agree that over time a person can convince him or herself of something as being true?

A. That's possible.

Q. The descriptions that Ms. Heinrich gave of her reasons for not doing what might be intuitive, were all her own personal subjective reports to you, correct?

A. That's correct.

Q. And those were all given after her seven months of psycho-therapeutic discussion of what happened, correct?
A. Correct.
Q. And one of the goals of psycho-therapy, in a situation like that, is to have the person talk through what the person says occurred, correct?
A. Correct.

The question that went unasked—at least directly—by the civilian defense counsel was this: "How did you make your evaluation on a patient about whom you didn't know her previous medical history?"

The trial counsel questioned Colonel Smith one more time during redirect, but did little more than rehash what they had covered in the earlier cross-examination. After that, Judge Kuhfahl asked the doctor when his initial interview with Heinrich took place, and he said it took place in June 2009, lasted for three hours and was his only session with the woman.

During re-cross examination, the civilian defense attorney asked Colonel Smith if he was certain his session with Heinrich took place in June. He was not.

"It may have been July, I know it was either June or July," he said.

"And would another reason for false report, for example, be a financial gain?" the civilian defense attorney asked.

"That is listed as a potential reason why someone would make a false report," he confirmed. That's especially important since, in Germany, victims of assault—sexual or other—receive financial compensation from their government.

After the doctor finished testifying, the government recalled Jasmin Dittmann in an apparent attempt to paint the previous-day testimony of Rudolf Betting, her now-ex-boyfriend, as that of a man biased against Stewart's accuser, Heinrich, because of his now-severed friendship with Dittmann. Little new ground was covered.

The next witness, called by the defense, was Sergeant First Class Gregory S. Settle, an 11-year Army veteran and SF colleague who had worked with Stewart on a daily basis for approximately one year as a survival/sniper instructor at the International Special Training Center in Pfullendorf, Germany.

As the only remaining defense witness other than Stewart, he spoke highly of the accused during cross-examination and re-cross by the civilian defense attorney and appeared not to bite on a handful of government attempts to paint Stewart as a rule-breaker.

After Sergeant Settle stepped down from the witness stand, the defense called Stewart to testify for the first time.

Stewart took the stand, he said, after having been told by his civilian defense attorney just before closing arguments were to begin the previous day that he rarely advises his clients to testify but would in this case. Why? Because his case was a proverbial he-said-she-said matter, the panel members knew he was at the hotel—Heinrich knew his mother's name and could identify his tattoos—and it would piss off the panel members if he didn't testify.

After asking Stewart basic questions about his name and where he was living on the dates of the alleged crimes, the civilian defense counsel began asking about the day he went to the See-Studio.

First, Stewart admitted to having met Heinrich at the club the evening of August 22, 2008. Next, he answered questions about the meeting:

Q. Please tell the panel how you recall meeting her?

A. Myself and some other people in the club were dancing, Ms. Heinrich was dancing there and she approached me and was dancing with me and, you know, I enjoyed the dance and I did dance with her.

Q. At some point in that evening did you talk to her about your name?

A. Yes, I did, sir.

Q. What do you remember saying about your name?

A. Well, she asked me what my name was and I told her it was Kelly and she asked for a full name and I told her it was "Kelly Anthony Stewart, but it's not really Anthony." And she said, "Why is that?" And I said because my mother is German and my father was in Vietnam at the time of my birth. And that past tense and pre-tense with Germans, when she filled out the American birth certificate she put Kelly Anthony. Originally I would have been Anthony, so as a nickname growing up around as a kid, or my dad joking on with me and my mom being German messing up my paperwork, they used to call me Antonio as a joke, and that was kind of the nickname that I had.

Q. And you told her this as you were introducing yourself?

A. Yes, sir.

Q. On that evening did you wear a wedding ring?

A. No, sir, I did not.

Q. Please, explain that?

A. There are several instances when I don't wear my wedding ring. All the times that I've been in Iraq I never personally wore my wedding ring, I wore it in my body armor with an American flag, but I personally never wore it on my hand, just because the nature of the business that I do so that people will not know I am.

That particular evening, when I left my car I was going out as kind of a single guy going out, not having a whole crew of people, I took off some of the important stuff, my wedding ring, I took off my watch, I only took a limited amount of cash and left the rest in my car, that's just how it is, because I don't want to get robbed.

Q. At some point in the evening did the two of you decide to leave the club?

A. Yes, sir.

Q. How did that develop?

A. Well when we were dancing on the dance floor I thought, you know, she was real nice lady--I mean, she was real--I mean, we connected, we talked about some stuff. We talked about my experiences here in Germany, that she had worked with handicapped people, and I explained that I've been doing medicine for about ten years. I don't tell anybody that I'm Special Forces, I talk about my capabilities as being a medic and my experience as a medic, that's, you know, if we--if anybody here in this court I meet you and I was in civilian clothes I wouldn't tell you that I was Special Forces. And so we had some like interests and she was a real nice girl, I mean, great conversation and she was interested in me and I was interested in her.

Q. Okay, did you tell her anything about military installations that you were either assigned at, or visiting, or working at at that point?

A. Yes, sir, I mean she asked my duty assignment and kind of what I do in the military. She knew that I was an American, and I'm not at liberty to discuss anything that I do, so I told her I was working at Patch, which is a true statement because I was in-processing. My whole point, even though my duty assignment is in Pfullendorf, Germany, which is 220 kilometers to the south, this is only American military installation and during the in-processing I still have to attend Head-Start, I still have to attend TMP license and all that, so my duty assignment was Patch, Panzer, and Kelly Barracks, all three installations, for various reasons, cause I have a TS security clearance, SOCEUR is in one place, EUCOM is in another one, and AFRICOM is another one. And because of those things those are my three duty stations for in-processing.

***[Editor's Note:** SOCEUR = Special Operations Command Europe; EUCOM = European Command; and AFRICOM = Africa Command]*

Q. About what time do you believe you left the club that evening, the two of you?

A. You know, looking back now we're talking almost a year, I'd have to put it between two and three o'clock in the morning, Mr. Court.

Q. How did you depart the club, that is, by what means of transport?

A. As you exit the See-Studio, there's basically like a lake that's there, but the taxi-cabs, the local taxi-cabs, are right--actually able to park right there and they pick up everybody that's going on and off and there's a taxi-cab there, we discussed it that we were leaving together and that we were going to take a taxi together.

Q. Was there a discussion ahead of time as to where the taxi would go?

A. Yes, sir. When we were in the--prior to us leaving, I did discuss "hey, you want to go to your place? Do you want to go to my place?" And the conversation came up that she lived in some type of common household where there was a lot of people, and I can't elicit or talk about what that means, but she's like, "I want it to be a little more private, can we go to your place?" And I explained that I was staying at the hotel and that we would have to take a taxi-cab because I wasn't going to drive my car, because my car from where See-Studio is, within 100 meters over a bridge is the parking garage where my car was and that's why we took the taxi-cab, because it was a little longer of a drive to my place.

Q. Okay, you said that you had been dancing that evening. Did you notice her footgear?

A. Yes, sir, I did.

Q. What was she wearing on her feet?

A. It's a rock and roll bar, so I am sure everyone can gather what that means, but she had knee-high boots on that were military-style boots laced up like Doc Martins and, you know, a dress and then a top.

Q. Okay, as far as at any time at the club, did she complain about her feet hurting?

A. Yeah, I mean, we were there for a while and during the dancing and stuff we would take breaks and then we were talking over to the side. And she--the reason why we were taking breaks between the songs was because she was like, "You know, these boots are killing me because they come all the way up to my knees and they're laced up."

Q. All right, after you got to the hotel, did you do anything that you're ashamed of now?

A. Yes, sir.

Q. What was that?

A. You know it's a--it's uncomfortable sitting here, because for a year I've not been able to talk about anything, you know, and, you know, I made a mistake because I cheated on my wife, you know, and--and I'm not proud of that, I'm ashamed of it, you know, not so much to tell you guys I'm ashamed to my wife, you know, I'm ashamed that I made that decision consciously and--and it was wrong.

Q. Did anything that happened in the room at the Marriot that night happen by way of force?

A. No, sir.

Q. You said you cheated on your wife?

A. Yes, sir.

Q. Did you ever tell your wife that?

A. Yes, sir, I did.

Q. When did you tell her?

A. Directly after the--following of the birth of my first kid.

Q. When was that, sir?

A. That was the 25th of November.

Q. About how long, to your recollection, did Ms. Heinrich stay in the hotel room with you?

A. She stayed there till the next morning, it--I say, with good memory that, I remember looking at my phone in the morning as she was leaving and it was around 9:00 or 9:30. And I can only say 9:00 or 9:30 because there was an issue with the phone when I was getting her phone number.

Q. Please explain about getting her phone number.

A. I mean, basically it was early in the morning and Ms. Heinrich wanted me to take her to the house and I reminded her that my car was over there at the place and I had to take a taxi-cab, and she was like, "Oh yeah." And I said, "Well, I mean, I can pay for the taxi-cab to take you to the house or you can go in the taxi-cab with me to the car." And she said, "Well it would be quicker from here for me just to take a taxi-cab to my house." And I paid for the taxi-cab for her to leave and I asked her--well, she had asked me that she didn't have to pay for it and I said, "No, I don't have a problem. I'd like to pay for it because, you know, you came here and I'll pay for you to get back." And I asked her for a phone number, she's like, "Yeah, let me give it to you." And I got my phone out, but it was this--if you guys have ever been to the PX and you get the cheap Vodafone that does nothing/has no options, I wasn't able to scroll through it to figure out how to save anything in there, but the time-stamp was on there because it was in a locked mode and I couldn't figure it out, nor could Ms. Heinrich figure out how to unlock this cheap Vodafone to be able to put in a phone number, so she wrote on the stationary that was right there on the desk where my laptop was.

Q. Did her attitude change at all during the course of the evening upon seeing anything on you?
A. Yes, sir.
Q. Please, explain that?
A. When we both woke up in the morning and she was getting ready to leave I was actually facing away from her and on the back of my neck, between my shoulder-blades is my wife's name and she asked me about it and I said "It's my wife's name," and--
Q. Was that the first time she had heard you were married?
A. Yes, sir.
Q. Had you ever consciously lied to her about being married or did it just not come up?
A. No, sir, it never came up in any conversation prior to that.

Asked, after the fact, to describe his feelings about taking the stand, Stewart said he didn't have any fears.

"Not because I was cocky, nothing like that," he said, "but because I knew what did and did not happen, and I figured, if I rationally told these people what actually happened, that they would be able to see the truth.

"I took the stand, I told my story about what happened," he continued. "I was upfront then, and I accepted my responsibility—that I made mistakes. And I told 'em that. I didn't have to tell 'em that.

"I didn't have to sit there and say, 'She's a crazy person.' I told them the mistakes that I made. I accepted responsibility for the situation that I put myself in, which is I committed adultery. I should have never put myself in that situation, and I was wrong for that. And I told 'em that. And I was sorry for that."

The government's cross-examination followed with the trial counsel asking Stewart questions about friendships he had established in Germany since his August 2008 arrival in the Stuttgart area. Before long, however, it turned into a somewhat-

**heated exchange—something Stewart later described as being similar to a courtroom scene from the movie, "A Few Good Men." In that scene, a Marine colonel (Jack Nicholson) on the witness stand was accused by a young Navy defense attorney (Tom Cruise) of ordering a "Code Red"—an illegal beating of a Marine by members of his platoon that resulted in his death and a subsequent cover-up. Several minutes of heated exchange between the officers resulted in the colonel finally losing his cool and admitting he ordered the attack.**

**"Every schooling and every assessment that the military has done on me to assess that I'm stable," Stewart said, "and that I'm trusted with national security issues and that I can be trusted to make the right, conscious decisions, now is being turned around (so that) every one of those (are) predatory skills that I used to go after Miss Heinrich."**

**Still, the trial counsel tried to paint Stewart, a man who had risen into the top three percent of the Army, as a master manipulator whose SF training helped him know how to control a person like Heinrich.**

**Below is the text of that exchange as it appears in the Record of Trial:**

Q. And you were brought to Germany to be an instructor in the survival division?
A. Yes, sir.
Q. And you would consider yourself a--this is somewhat subjective, but a highly trained soldier being a Special Forces soldier?
A. Can you repeat the question, sir?
Q. Being a Special Forces soldier, you would consider yourself highly trained? You have more training than the average soldier in combat-type stuff?
A. Sir, I can't talk about other soldiers, for instance, the panel is here, their experiences versus mine, I'm not qualified to talk about--
Q. I'm not asking--

A. --I can tell you that I have training in the United States Army.

Q. You don't consider yourself highly trained?

A. I consider myself trained by the Army, sir.

Q. Okay, you've gone through the "Q" Course?

A. Yes, sir, I have.

Q. You've gone to the Target Interdiction Course?

A. Yes, I have.

Q. And that trained you how to be a sniper?

A. Yes, sir.

Q. Have you gone through SERE* training?

A. Yes, I have, sir.

Q. And not just SERE training, but the high-risk SERE training?

A. Yes, sir, I have.

Q. And that course--those courses are all fairly intense, right?

A. Yes, sir,

Q. Much more intense than your basic training, AIT, your average BNCOC/ANCOC-type courses, is that correct?

A. Any discussions on the details of my training--

Q. Just asking if they're intense, Sergeant.

A. Sir, I'm trying to answer the question. Any details or my opinions about any of the training that I have attended in the United States Special Forces Qualification Course, I'm not authorized to discuss with you. Now, if in closed session, the judge would like to ask me those questions, I might be able to discuss it with him, but I myself have been instructed, and I have a PAO guy, any of my training I'm not at liberty to discuss with anybody.

Q. So you can't say that those courses are mentally challenging?

A. I think any courses in the United States Army are mentally challenging, sir.

Q. You can't say that they're psychologically tough?

A. I think Basic Training was psychologically tough on me, sir.

Q. Now I pulled this off of the internet, this is open-source information I'm going to ask you about.

A. Okay, sir.

***[*Editor's Note:** SERE is an acronym for Survive, Evade, Resist and Escape training.]*

CDC: Objection, Your Honor, to that testimony by the government.

TC: I'm not getting answers to my questions, Your Honor, I've got to preface--if he's going to refuse to answer my questions, I've got to tell him where I'm getting this stuff if he's going to invoke his Special Forces training to prevent him from answering questions or policy, I'm sorry.

MJ: Objection overruled. Ask the question.

Q. At the SERE course you're taught how to resist violent captors, is that correct?

A. Again, sir, unless I'm authorized by the SOCEUR Public Affairs Officer, I can't discuss the training that I received at the SERE-level C School.

Q. You're taught how to resist torture?

A. Again, sir--

Q. We're going to go through this, so, that's fine--

A. No, again, sir, I don't know what I'm authorized to discuss with you because I'm not the releasing authority of my training.

Q. I got this off of Wikipedia.com.

CDC: Objection, Your Honor, that is not evidence before the court, that is merely an assertion by counsel.

TC: And the accused will not answer my questions.

MJ: Objection sustained. Ask the question, if the accused answers he answers.

Q. You were taught how to resist torture?

A. I was taught to resist and to return with honor.

Q. You were taught how to resist interrogation techniques?

A. Again, I was taught to resist and to return with honor.

Q. You were taught to resist exploitation, isn't that correct?

A. I was taught to return with honor, sir.

Q. And you were taught how to combat psychological ploys of your captors, isn't that correct?

A. Could you rephrase the question, sir?

Q. You were taught how to combat psychological ploys of your captor?

A. Again, any teachings, techniques, plans, or policies that that school has I'm not authorized to discuss with anybody in here, because this is an open forum.

WIT: And if the questions are going to continue down that road, Your Honor, I'd ask that it be at a closed session because currently we are in an open session with an open court and I am not the approving authority or the releasing authority of the information or training that I received there.

**"They just wanted me to admit that I spoke German, that I am trained in all this 'secret squirrel' stuff to beat and interrogate people and everything else," Stewart said, noting that it's a facade and that Green Beret professionals like himself are trusted to do national-level stuff for the president of our country on a daily basis.**

**"The one thing I wouldn't say in there was... a lie. I told the truth (in response) to the questions that were asked of me. I asked**

the questions the best that I could answer without telling a lie and without compromising myself in a situation that I would get treason for, basically, letting out how we train.

"And the reason why I say that is because it's an open court, and this is a 'what if.'

"If I had went up there and said, in a statement, that we do some type of training like, 'We do free fall blindfolded, you know, to work on the psychological aspects of the mind...' that reporter that I knew was in the courtroom... what would that person have written in the *Stars & Stripes?*"

Following the heated exchange between Stewart and the trial counsel, the questioning continued into other areas, including Stewart's German language skills, his mother's German heritage, his tattoos and body piercings and his wife, Freija. Before too much time passed, however, talk returned to the time the soldier spent at See-Studio the night of August 22-23, 2008.

Contrary to Heinrich's testimony that she had not had any alcohol the previous day, Stewart said she had had a vodka and Red Bull which she drank during breaks from the dance floor.

An exchange between the trial counsel and Stewart about who approached who on the dance floor followed, though it produced no firm conclusions other than that Stewart and Heinrich had began dancing in proximity with one another around 2:30 a.m.

Stewart said he treated Heinrich with "gentleman-like behavior" and thanked her for the initial dance before rejoining the soldiers he was with at the club that night.

The trial counsel next turned to questions about Stewart's second interaction with Heinrich, which he said he initiated and involved more dancing and flirting with him speaking to her in her native language.

Stewart denied trying to conceal his true identity and said he did not tell her early on that his name was Antonio.

"As I explained earlier, I told her my full name and she asked me my mom's family name, and I went into the story about how my name as a kid, joking around the house, was Antonio," Stewart explained. "It was a nickname."

A short while later, Stewart confirmed that he had not told Heinrich he was married until after he had sex with her and that he had indeed asked if he could be alone with her around 3:30 a.m., approximately 60 minutes after they had met at See-Studio.

Countering Heinrich's testimony, Stewart told the court that he had never agreed to go to her apartment and that he understood that they were leaving the club with the purpose of having sex—or, in Heinrich's words, "a one-night stand."

Next, the defense objected when the trial counsel asked Stewart whether or not he had made other advances toward women other than his wife since arriving in Germany, the objection was sustained by the military judge and the trial counsel moved on to new territory.

The government's next line of questioning centered on events surrounding Stewart's departure from the club with Heinrich and the taxi ride to his hotel room that followed. It was on the latter that Stewart's testimony differed greatly from that Heinrich had given the previous day.

Stewart said he told the taxi cab driver they were going to the Marriott Hotel in Sindelfingen and asked if he could stop by the Esso Station near the hotel to pick up some Red Bull, because there wasn't any in the mini-fridge in his hotel room.

When they got to the station, however, they found it was closed and, because it was barely 50 meters from their final destination, the hotel, they got out and walked.

When asked about topics of conversation he discussed with the taxi driver en route, Stewart denied having talked with the driver about being divorced, about his family or about him being the "black sheep" of his family.

Instead, he told the court, he had spent most of his time in the van kissing Heinrich.

During the next few minutes, Stewart was asked a series of questions framed so as to draw stark contrasts between Heinrich's version of events and his own.

Stewart denied the trial counsel's contention that, when they got out of the taxi cab at the hotel, Heinrich told him she didn't understand why she was there, that she didn't know he was living there, and that he had told her he was only going to go upstairs to pick up some Red Bull from his room.

The next set of questions took Stewart in another direction.

While he admitted taking Heinrich to his hotel room, Room 533 on the fifth floor, he denied that she was apprehensive about going to his room, that he had to coax her into his room and that he demanded that they stay in his room.

Stewart denied ushering or leading her to a position in front of the bed but admitted complimenting her and telling her she was beautiful and had a nice body.

He denied telling her to get undressed and denied slapping her in the face, head, breasts or buttocks, saying things did not proceed that way.

He denied ever grabbing her hair or grabbing her breasts forcefully or biting her breasts.

And he denied becoming angry with Heinrich.

"I mean--we got in there; we were kissing; the bed is, as you come in there in the room, Ms. Heinrich started undressing me, I had a t-shirt on; she was undressing my shirt, I undid her top; things were kind of passionate between the two of us, she was getting my shirt off and I was getting her shirt off; and then Ms. Heinrich lay down onto the bed; I climbed on top of her; Ms. Heinrich helped, you know, get my pants down and we had sex."

Questioned further, Stewart said Heinrich got undressed, but left her black Army boots on and, with his pants around his ankles and shoes still on, they had sex for the first time.

In addition to having sex twice, he said, they gave each other oral sex, but nothing more. No anal sex. Nothing even close to it.

"After the first time, when we finished, I got up, finished taking off my pants, I went into the shower, Ms. Heinrich finished taking off her boots and her skirt that was pulled down, it was only on one leg, and she ended up putting those on the chair while I was in the shower," he told the court. "I took a shower; I came back out; we watched a little of the TV; we had some more conversation; we started kissing some more and we had sex again."

Next, the trial counsel asked Stewart if normal sexual intercourse includes anal sex. Stewart replied by saying the question was confusing, because different people have different views of what normal is. That prompted the trial counsel to ask him if he thinks it's normal to have a one-night stand and, without asking any other questions, to proceed to anal sex?

Not only did Stewart tell the prosecutor he doesn't think it's okay to have a one-night stand, but he said he doesn't think it's okay to have anal sex period and that he thinks anal sex—including anal penetration by a finger—is wrong.

That portion of Stewart's testimony ended with the accused soldier, according to the trial transcript, pointing to his chest and telling the court, "I'm not judging anyone that does that, but as far as Sergeant First Class Stewart, I would never do something like that to a woman."

The trial counsel moved forward from that point, asking Stewart if he had ever engaged in or asked his wife to engage in anal sex with him. After the soldier said he had not, the attorney asked two more questions about Heinrich's claims that she had been anally penetrated front, apparently trying to keep the issue front and center for as long as possible in the minds of panel members. Stewart, however, remained steadfast in his denials and the attorney moved on to other questions about the events that took place in the hotel room during the early morning hours of August 23, 2008.

One of the topics covered was the two- to three-minute shower taken by Stewart:

Q. You came out of the--you took a shower alone?

A. Yes, I did, sir.

Q. When you came out, was Ms. Heinrich still naked?

A. At that time she became naked. As I said, when I went into the shower I had to finish taking my clothes off. Ms. Heinrich still had her boots and her dress was--her skirt was still around one leg. As I came out of the shower she was already naked on the bed with the white--there's a bed-decking on there and there's a sheet, because the air conditioner was on she was underneath the sheet because the room was cold.

Q. So before you went to take the shower, her clothing consisted of a skirt being around one leg and her boots?

A. Yes, sir.

Q. When you came back out of the bathroom, isn't it true that you had her lay on her side?

A. No, she moved over onto her side of the bed that we were laying on and she was on her side because we had just got done and she was kind of just laying there--

Q. So she was laying on her side?

A. Yes, sir.

Q. And you came up behind her?

A. Yes, sir.

Q. And you penetrated her vagina from the rear?

A. No, I did not, sir.

Q. You penetrated her vagina with your fingers?

A. No, sir, I did not.

Q. Did you fondle her?

A. No, sir, at that time we were just kind of--I was holding her arms and she was leaning back and was kissing me and then I ended up rolling onto my back and then Ms. Heinrich got on top of me, she was kissing me and then we ended up having--that's when we started the second time of sex to where she was on top.

**After those questions, the trial counsel reverted to asking Stewart more accusatory questions stemming from Heinrich's claims that he had grabbed her hair during their second round of sex, slapped her and forced her to do unspeakable acts with him. Before he was done, the trial counsel ended with a doozy: "And when you were done, you thumped your chest [the trial counsel pounded his chest with closed fists] and said, 'this was very good'?"**

**"No!" Stewart replied before denying all of the allegations that preceded it and others—including her claim that he grabbed her by the arm—that followed.**

**The trial counsel followed with questions about the time leading up to Heinrich getting dressed and leaving Stewart's room.**

**Stewart told the court that the only time he saw her get dressed was in the morning when they both woke up and she was getting ready to leave. The trial counsel had questions about those events:**

Q. Was she completely dressed?

A. When she was leaving she was--woke me up and said, "hey, I need to go," and I--that's when the conversation came up about how she was going to get home and how I needed to get to my car, how we were going to do that; what was the quickest way--and we were both getting dressed simultaneously together at the time.

Q. Did she appear that she was in pain in any way?

A. No, sir.

Q. She didn't complain about abdominal pain?

A. No, sir.

Q. Didn't complain of pain in her buttocks and thighs area?

A. No, sir.

Q. Didn't complain about pain in her anus area?

A. No, sir.

Q. And you asked her for her cell phone number?

A. Yes, I did, sir.

Q. And she gave it to you on the Marriot stationary?

A. Yes, sir, she did.

Q. And you asked her if it was the right phone number?

A. I did not, sir.

Q. But she saw you have your cell phone right there, isn't that correct?

A. We--initially we were both trying to put in the cell phone number--
Q. So she saw you with a cell phone, yes--
A. Yes, sir.
Q. --or no?
A. Yes, sir.
Q. And then you gave her money, after you had sex with her, so that she could get back to her place?
A. To pay for the taxi-cab ride for her, sir.
Q. And this is somewhere between 9:00 and 9:30?
A. Yes, sir.

The cross-examination ended there, and Judge Kuhfahl asked if any panel members had questions. Several of them did, but most simply asked for Stewart to restate something he had said earlier.

One question had to do with the speakers for his 15-inch MacBook laptop: "Does your laptop have external speakers hooked up to it, or is it just the built-in speakers?" Answer: Built-in only.

Another question—"Did you ever call Ms. Heinrich any time after 23 August?"—yielded an affirmative reply from Stewart who explained that he tried to call her "a couple of days later" to "See if she wanted to go out to See-Studio again on Wednesday."

In answers to separate questions, he went on to explain that Heinrich never answered the phone, that he never saw her later and that he could not remember whether or not he left a message on her answering machine.

Asked if he ever heard Heinrich say "no," "nein" or "stop" while in the hotel room, Stewart again said, "No, sir."

Asked if she ever returned his call, he said she had not.

Shortly after the questioning of the accused sergeant ended, Heinrich took the stand for the second time—this time as the trial's final witness—just before 3:30 p.m. August 19, 2009.

The assistant trial counsel began the final direct examination of Stewart's accuser, Heinrich. Below is the transcript of that exam as taken from the Record of Trial:

Q. Ms. Heinrich, when you left the club with Sergeant Stewart, did you decide and tell him to go--that you were going to go to his place because you wanted to be alone with just him?

A. No, that is not true.

Q. In the morning, when you left his hotel room, did you see a tattoo between his shoulder-blades that he told you was his wife's name?

A. No, that's not true.

Q. Did Sergeant Stewart tell you in the morning that he was married?

A. No.

Q. Did you drink a vodka and Red Bull at the See-Studio that night?

A. When I was 15 years old I tried vodka for the first time and since then I've never touched it again.

Q. Why haven't you touched it again?

CDC: Objection, relevance.

ATC: I'll withdraw the question, Your Honor.

MJ: Sustained.

Q. Did Sergeant Stewart ever tell you that his full name is Kelly Anthony Stewart?

A. No, that is not right, he only said Antonio, he never completely introduced himself.

Q. When he said that his name was Antonio, did he say that was his nickname only or was that his true name?

A. His real name.

Q. When you left the See-Studio with Sergeant Stewart in the taxi, did you and him both agree that you needed to stop at a gas station to get drinks because his mini-bar was out of beverages?

A. No, that's not true.

Q. When you were in the taxi-cab driving from the See-Studio to the Marriot Hotel with Sergeant

Stewart, were you kissing him during that entire taxi ride?

A. No, that's not true, I sat in front. He was sitting in the back. There was only one kiss and that was at the See-Studio when he kissed me.

Q. You did not turn around in the front seat of that taxi, lean over, and kiss him while he was sitting in the back seat?

A. No, I did not turn around. I was buckled in, I mean, I didn't--I couldn't have even done it--it wouldn't have even been possible.

**[The witness turned her head and looked over her left shoulder.]**

Q. What type of taxi did you take--

MJ: One second, the witness, when she was testifying moved her head over her left shoulder.

Q. What type of taxi did you take from the See-Studio to the Marriot Hotel? Was it a car or a van?

A. It was a normal, regular car. I believe it was a Mercedes.

Q. So not a van?

A. It was definitely not a van.

**Near the end of her testimony, Judge Kuhfahl asked the question, "Ms. Heinrich, was it an old taxi or fairly new taxi that took you to the Marriot that night?"**

**"I can't say for certain, but I believe it was a Mercedes, the old 'C' class," she replied, reaffirming that she recalled being in a sedan-style vehicle that wasn't a van.**

**Later, Heinrich answered more prosecution questions, including the following, about what took place inside the hotel room:**

Q. When you were at the Marriot Hotel in Sergeant Stewart's room, did Sergeant Stewart perform oral sex on you?

A. No, that's not true.

Q. When you were at the Marriot Hotel in Sergeant Stewart's room, did the sexual activities start by Sergeant Stewart laying you gently down on the bed on your back and then him getting on top of you and starting vaginal sexual intercourse?

A. No, that's not true.

Q. After Sergeant Stewart took a shower in his hotel room, did he come out of that shower and come directly over to you on the bed and begin to consensually kiss you on the mouth?

A. No, that is not true. We only kissed one time, that was at the See-Studio on the dance floor when he kissed me.

Q. In Sergeant Stewart's hotel room when he came out of the bathroom after the shower, did he come over to you and you and him begin to engage in consensual vaginal intercourse?

A. No, that's not true.

Q. Did you ever take a shower in Sergeant Stewart's hotel room that morning?

A. No, that is not right--it's not true. I also had my boots on the whole time.

Q. In the morning, after you had woken up and gotten your clothes on, did Sergeant Stewart give you money to pay for your taxi ride back home to your house?

A. No, that's not true.

Q. That morning, did you and Sergeant Stewart talk together about leaving that hotel together in a taxi?

A. No, that's not true.

Q. That morning, did you and Sergeant Stewart discuss trying to put your cell phone number into his telephone, but not being able to complete that?

A. That's not true. I never saw his cell phone, I had to write down my number on a piece of paper on his desk.

ATC: No further questions, Your Honor.

MJ: Defense?

CDC: Yes, Your Honor.

**CROSS-EXAMINATION**
**Questions by the civilian defense counsel:**

Q. The apartment you lived in on 22-23 August 2008, was it an apartment that you lived in by yourself?

A. No, it's a shared living.

Q. So that many people--several people have their own bedrooms but there are common rooms to the apartment?

A. No, it's not right--well yes, the kitchen and the bathroom they're shared, it's three apartments and upstairs in my apartment there is only one other person living there.

Q. Did you never see the name of a woman between his shoulders, or just not in the morning?

A. In the evening I saw the tattoo but I didn't know it was a female name.

Q. Is it your testimony that the entire time you were in the room at the Marriot you never took off your boots?

A. That is true; and the socks neither.

Q. What time of boots did you have on?

A. Army boots, they went up like this.

**[The witness gestured to just below her knee with her right hand.]**

CDC: The witness pointed to just below the knee, indicating how high the boots came up. Thank you, Your Honor, no further questions.

ATC: No redirect, Your Honor.

MJ: Members, any questions for this witness?

**[LTC Yarman, CPT Buchanan, and SFC Roberts, gave an affirmative response, all other members gave a negative response.]**

MJ: Apparently so.

**[The bailiff retrieved the questions and gave them to the trial and civilian defense counsel to review, then gave them to the court reporter to mark it as Appellate Exhibits XXV to XXVII, who then gave them to the military judge.]**

MJ: Appellate Exhibit XXV is a question from Lieutenant Colonel Yarman.

**EXAMINATION BY THE COURT-MARTIAL**
**Questions by the military judge:**

Q. Ms. Heinrich, was it an old taxi or fairly new taxi that took you to the Marriot that night?

A. I can't say for certain, but I believe it was a Mercedes, the old "C" class.

MJ: Sir, does that answer your question?

**[LTC Yarman nodded in the affirmative.]**

MJ: Apparently so. Appellate Exhibit XXVI is a question from Captain Buchanan.

Q. Ma'am, did Sergeant First Class Stewart ever call your phone, either your home phone or your cell-phone, from the time you left in the morning?

A. I don't know that, I had several calls from an unknown participant, so I don't know whether, you know, whether that was him or not.

Q. Do you recall how long after the 23rd you received these calls?

A. Maybe five days--a week later.

Q. And this was on the same phone number that you had given to Sergeant First Class Stewart?

A. That he called?
Q. Yes, it was on the phone number that you gave him?
A. Yes, that was the phone number.

Captain Buchanan was satisfied that his question was answered, no more questions were raised and Heinrich was temporarily excused and left the courtroom.

No more witnesses were called that day and, as was the case on the first day of the trial, no physical evidence was presented during the second day of the trial.

# Day Two: Closing Arguments

At 4:06 p.m. on August 19, 2009, Judge Kuhfahl reviewed the charges for and issued instructions to the panel members and allowed attorneys to present their closing arguments.

In reviewing the charges, the military judge told members of the court-martial panel that, in order to find the accused guilty of each offense, "you must be convinced by legal and competent evidence beyond reasonable doubt."

He proceeded to remind panel members of each of the offenses that accuser Heinrich alleged had took place August 23, 2008, at or near Sindelfingen, Germany: two specifications of rape; two specifications of abusive sexual contact; two specifications of forcible sodomy; one specification of assault consummated by a battery; one specification of kidnapping; and one specification of communicating a threat.

He followed that by making four key points and then elaborating on each:

> First, that the accused is presumed to be innocent until his guilt is established by legal and competent evidence beyond a reasonable doubt;
>
> Second, if there is reasonable--that if there is reasonable doubt as to the guilt of the accused, that doubt must be resolved in favor of the accused, and he must be acquitted;
>
> Third, if there is a reasonable doubt as to the degree of guilt, that doubt must be resolved in favor of the lower degree of guilt as to which there is no reasonable doubt; and

Lastly, the burden of proof to establish the guilt of the accused beyond a reasonable doubt is on the government. The burden never shifts to the accused to establish innocence or to disprove the facts necessary to establish each element of each offense.

By reasonable doubt it is intended not a fanciful or ingenious doubt or conjecture, but an honest, conscientious doubt suggested by the material evidence or lack of it in the case. It is an honest misgiving generated by insufficiency of proof of guilt.

Proof beyond a reasonable doubt means proof to an evidentiary certainty, although not necessarily to an absolute or mathematical certainty. The proof must be such as to exclude not every hypothesis or possibility of innocence, but every fair and rational hypothesis except that of guilt. The rule as to reasonable doubt extends to every element of the offense, although each particular fact advanced by the prosecution, which does not amount to an element, need not be established beyond a reasonable doubt.

However, if, on the whole--if, on the whole evidence, you are satisfied beyond a reasonable doubt of the truth of each and every element, then you should find the accused guilty.

Bear in mind that only matters properly before the court as a whole should be considered. In weighing and evaluating the evidence you are expected to use your own common sense, and your knowledge of human nature and the ways of the world. In light of all the circumstances in this case, you should consider the inherent probability or improbability of the evidence. Bear in mind you may properly believe one witness and disbelieve several other witnesses whose testimony conflicts with the one. The final determination as to the weight or significance of the evidence and the credibility of the witnesses in this case rests solely upon you.

You must disregard any comment or statement or expression made by me during the course of the trial that might seem to indicate any opinion on my part as to whether the accused is guilty or not guilty since you alone have the responsibility to make that determination. Each of you must impartially decide whether the accused is guilty or not guilty according to the law I have given you and the evidence admitted in court, and your own conscience.

**Without taking a break after wrapping up his instructions to panel members, Judge Kuhfahl allowed attorneys for both sides to present their closing arguments. Below is the text of Captain Bashore's closing argument as it appears in the Record of Trial:**

TC: Mr. President, members of the panel, over the last two days the government has proven beyond a reasonable doubt that the accused is guilty of forcible sodomy, forcible rape, committing abusive sexual contact, kidnapping, communicating a threat, and assaulting Ms. Greta Heinrich at the Sindelfingen Marriot.

It was 22 August, Ms. Heinrich was full of life. She goes out with her friends. They go to the café and then they go to the See-Studio. They have a great night of dancing. She has some friends that come and go. Her friend Jasmine is there. Her soon to be boyfriend Rudy is there. They're having a great time. And then her life changes; her life changes forever when she met the accused on the dance floor.

This whole case means nothing if the government did not prove that the accused was the man who did the acts alleged against him. While he's admitted to you that he is the one who actually was with her that night, we're still going to walk through that piece, and I'll explain why in a minute.

Ms. Heinrich explained to you where his room was in the Marriot Hotel. She explained to you and Detective Lorch that they came out of the elevator and they turned left. She also explained it was on the right side. And Detective Lorch was able to narrow that down to four rooms, and Ms. Heinrich told you it was either the third or the fourth room on the right.

Ms. Heinrich had also described to Detective Lorch, earlier, the layout of the room. And the reason that was important is because the rooms were a mirror image; one bathroom was against the next room's bathroom and vice versa. And Detective Lorch was able to narrow that down to two rooms, 533 and 537. And he contacted CID and he got the rooms--the pictures for those people who stayed in that room.

And that was the accused and Colonel Myers. He then talked to the general manager and he got the sign-in log. And you'll notice there's a signature on that sign-in log. That signature is the signature--is the signature of the accused, and you'll get to take back Prosecution Exhibit 23, which is an NCOER of the accused, and you'll be able to look at that signature and compare it to this one. And the reason that's important is his name is wrong, it says Kelly Steward instead of Kelly Stewart. And Detective Lorch told you why that delayed some of the process of identification. But it also has his birth-date on it, 12 January 1973. That birthday, along with the signature, beyond a reasonable doubt that that's the accused. And you also saw the bill from the Marriot that said the accused was in that room, 533, on the night of 22 August 2008.

You also heard about what Ms. Greta Heinrich talked to you about about [sic] the accused. That he had a German mother. That he speaks German. And you'll be able to take back his ERB which shows German. Some of the defense's own witnesses acknowledged that the accused speaks German. It also shows that his middle name is Anthony and he told her his name was Antonio, a reasonable derivative of Anthony.

She was able to identify that he had nipple piercings, not a common thing amongst the average man.

CDC: Objection. Objection, argument of facts not in evidence, whether it's common or not.

MJ: Counsel--excuse me, panel you will not consider that last statement by trial counsel. There has been no evidence introduced at this trial as to whether or not it is common or uncommon for males of the general population to have nipple piercings.

Are there any--

TC: Did you--

MJ: Excuse me. Are there any questions about that?

**[All members indicated a negative response.]**

MJ: Trial Counsel, carry on.

TC: The accused had two nipple piercings. Detective Lorch testified that he took the pictures of those nipples and he saw them and they were pierced.

The accused also had unique tattoos, tattoos that ran from the top of the shoulder to the elbow. And Ms. Heinrich identified him having a skull, an eagle, and a screw. She also identified the word, "quick," she remembered it was quick something and it was on his pectoral muscle. That's exactly where the accused has a tattoo that says "quick-draw."

And you heard from Dr. Dittmann and Mr. Betting and they testified that they saw his tattoos as well underneath that t-shirt. And they also gave consistent testimony to what Ms. Heinrich said about the clothes that he was wearing.

And finally, Mr. Betting and Ms. Heinrich can identify the accused.

But why is that important, knowing that the accused came in here today and told you he was with her?

It's important because the accused saw the evidence and the only reasonable story that he could tell the panel was that he [sic] consented and it was a consensual--or consensual sex. He couldn't come in here and tell you I don't know Ms. Heinrich, I've never seen her. Or he couldn't come in here and--

CDC: Objection, Your Honor. The government is implying that the accused has a burden to come in and say anything at anytime about this case.

MJ: To the extent that the trial counsel's comments inferred any obligation on the accused to come in and defend himself or to disprove any of the elements, the panel will disregard that comment.

And trial counsel, please don't comment on the accused's right--Constitutional Rights.

TC: Yes, Your Honor, that is not what I intended.

I'll move on.

So after Ms. Heinrich meets the accused, they start to dance. They dance and the accused acts like a gentleman. He kisses her hand. He thanks her for the dance. They go their separate ways. They come back and they dance some more. And throughout the evening he talks to her. He gives her a false name, he tells her his name is Antonio, and you heard from witnesses that say he's known as Kelly, not as Antonio.

And after knowing Ms. Heinrich for only approximately an hour, he asks to be alone with her. And she came in here and admitted she was good with that. She was okay with a one-night stand. But on one condition, and that condition was that they go back to her place. A place where she felt safe. She felt safe because she had roommates. If she needed help, she could get it. And she told the accused that, "I want to go back to my house." And the accused agreed. They picked up their coats. They talked to their friends. And then they exited the club.

And then they get into the taxi-cab, and that's when the accused changed and he takes control. He puts Ms. Heinrich in the front seat. He sits in the back seat. And immediately upon getting in that taxi-cab he starts to talk. And he talks to the driver and he's telling the driver he wants a Red Bull at a gas station.

And Ms. Heinrich testified and she told you the general layout of Böblingen and Sindelfingen. She identified where the club was. She identified where her home was. She identified where that closest gas station was at approximately 3:30 or 4:00 a.m. on the morning of 23 August.

And when the taxi came around and it was coming to the gas station, she didn't think anything of it, there was no need to because they were going to the gas station. But when they got close to that gas station, the accused waved the driver on and they kept going, all the way up into Sindelfingen where the Marriot was.

**[The trial counsel pointed at Prosecution Exhibit 4 throughout.]**

TC: Ms. Heinrich testified she--although she objected, she was ignored as the accused held a conversation with the driver. And the accused was talking to the driver and he was telling him how he'd been watching Ms. Heinrich all night and how she knew she could get anybody in the club she wanted. He was talking her up. And he told the driver he was divorced. Just another step to ensure that he would get Ms. Heinrich back into his hotel room.

And when he got to the Marriot, she didn't understand why they were there. She didn't even know that he was living at the Marriot. She didn't understand that. And the accused explains why they were there; that he lives there; that he just wanted to get a drink, he wanted to get that Red Bull. So she goes across the street with him, she thinks they're getting Red Bull and going back home. She goes up to the fifth floor, but what did she testify to, she said that when she got to that doorway she hesitated, she was apprehensive. And the accused beckoned her in. He said, "You don't have to be afraid. I won't do anything to you. I'm a man. A real man." You don't have to be afraid. I won't do anything to you. And that's exactly what he ended up doing [sic].

I'm going to talk a little bit more about this--these specific specifications and the elements, but it's a little different. Kidnapping is not just a van [sic] clubbing somebody on the head, dragging him in the--dragging him in the van and you get a ransom call the next morning. UCMJ defines kidnapping with the term inveigle, and inveigle means to trick or to make false representations to get someone to go to a place. And the judge just read you an instruction and that instruction is exactly what we have in this case. And he said, "A person who entices another to ride in a car with a false promise to take the person to a certain destination has inveigled that passenger into the car."

She thought she was going to her house. She gets in the car. The accused immediately takes control of the driver. Changes where they're supposed to stop. Changes why they're going where they're going. Promises to just get the Red Bull to come down-stairs. And then he does just the opposite. And he holds her.

And when he holds her and he detains her, he's committed kidnapping and should be found guilty of Specification 1 of Charge II.

Now after he gets Ms. Heinrich into the room, you heard from her about how he positioned her.

**[The trial counsel pointed to Prosecution Exhibit 12 throughout.]**

TC: And he positioned her at the foot of the bed. And fairly quickly he ordered her to get undressed. He says, "Get undressed." And as soon as Ms. Heinrich says, "Not this way my friend," she was expecting a little bit more than that, she gets slapped. The accused slaps her upside the back of the head; the right ear.

The accused instantly starts to apologize, "Sorry, sorry." And he tells her how beautiful she is and he talks her back up and he convinces her to stay. Her having no idea what was about to happen. And how did she--how did she--her words, "since I was fighting back, I thought he understood that he could not do this to me." She gets undressed. She told you, she willingly took her clothes off. But what happened immediately upon taking her clothes off? The accused takes her, he turns her around, he pushes her on the bed, she has problems catching herself, the accused grabs her hair, pushes her shoulder down, puts his knee into her buttocks to get her down on the bed, and then he shoves his penis into her anus. And up to this point there had been no discussion, even by the admission of the accused, of anal sex or permission to have anal sex. Ms. Heinrich testified how she tried to fight back but she had no chance. She screams from pain. She falls over on the bed and goes into a fetal position. And after she recovered from that pain, she testified how she went to the bathroom, she thought she was bleeding, she thought she had to vomit.

She comes out of the bathroom with the intent to leave and she tells the accused she's going to leave. But the accused had already committed forcible sodomy, very violent forcible sodomy, and the evidence shows beyond a reasonable doubt he should be found guilty of Specification 1 to Charge III.

And I ask you also to look at some of the other evidence. Colonel Smith, he talked about it being normal that a person may not bleed after forcible anal sodomy. And Ms. Haug's testimony, how Ms. Heinrich had trouble, difficulty, sitting down in her cab on her ride home.

So Ms. Heinrich leaves the bathroom and she goes to return to her clothes, but while she was in the bathroom, the accused took her clothes and put them on the far side of the room. So now Ms. Heinrich has to go through the accused to get to her clothes, to get dressed, to exit the room. And as she is going to do that she tells him, "That is not okay. I am leaving now." And when she tells the accused that he turns violent again and he grabs her by the throat. What does he say to her? "You're not leaving. You're first to blow me one and you will swallow." As he does this, he grabs her head, grabs her hair, pushes her shoulder down and pushes her head down to his penis. And he forces his penis into her mouth and makes her give him oral sex.

And when the accused did that, he committed forcible sodomy again, this time the oral type, and as a result should be found guilty of Specification 2 of Charge III.

Now Ms. Heinrich told you the accused went to take a shower and she testified and told you how she stayed on the bed, how she was in pain, how she was humiliated, and how she couldn't move. Testified how that shower was approximately two minutes. And as you're looking at the pictures of the hotel room, look how small it is. Look how small that hallway is compared to how close the bathroom is. She testified that bathroom door was left open during that two-minute shower that the accused took. When the accused comes back out, she's laying down. He moves her, puts her on her side and he lays behind her. She testified that he held her head and he tried to put his penis in her vagina and she told you that he was partially successful. But she also told you she resisted. She resisted, she said she--she blocked it. Said he could not conduct further penetration. When he put his penis inside of her vagina without her consent and by force he committed rape. And he did this act while hitting Ms. Heinrich in the head, the buttocks, the thighs, further demonstrating the force that he was using and as a result should be found guilty of Specification 1 of Charge I.

Then the accused probes Ms. Heinrich's vagina and anus, and he did not have consent to do either one of these. When he probed her vagina with his fingers, in the UCMJ that is also classified as rape. When he probed her anus that is classified as abusive sexual contact. He did both of these acts without consent and the force that he'd been using and thus should be found guilty of Specification 2 and Specification 3 of Charge I.

And as he's doing these acts, she testified how he grabbed her breasts; that's abusive sexual contact when it's done without consent. And not only did he grab her breast, he bit it. She told you how she screamed, it was so painful, and how later it swelled up. Ms. Heinrich did not consent to this grabbing or biting. And what did the accused say to her when he was doing these acts? Showing the power and the control that he sought during this whole entire incident, he said to her, "I gave it to you the way you needed it. You needed it hard." He also talked to her--he had taken control as the male and the female had to be totally submissive to his needs and his wants. He told her "normally you have the control of sex." Only the second thing he had said in English to Ms. Heinrich. Normally you have the control of sex; this time the accused did. And when he did that--when he did that act, when he grabbed her breast, when he bit it, committed abusive sexual contact again and should be found guilty of Specification 4 of Charge I.

Communicating a threat; throughout the night he said various things, but one of the things that he said was, "Do what I say and I'll be good to you, otherwise you know already." You may have to look at the surrounding circumstances to put that whole phrase into context. "Otherwise you know already." What had already happened to Ms. Heinrich? She'd already been physically and sexually abused. Sodomized and raped. Assaulted. Otherwise you know already was very clear. Not done with a friendly tone. It had meaning and that meaning was conveyed to Ms. Heinrich. The accused becomes angry because Ms. Heinrich will not perform additional sexual intercourse. He grabs her throat and he forces her to lick his testicles. And she tells you she would do anything to get out alive at this point. She told you she licked his testicles because of the force he'd been applying to her. Then the accused goes to a new deviant low, a low that she is not willing to go to and she would do anything she possibly could to prevent it. She mustered all of the energy she had left and she refuted it with all she had when the accused tried to force her to lick his anus. And she told you how she fought. And how was she repaid when she fought back from that? She was slapped and the accused made her give him oral sex once again.

And when he forced her mouth on his penis again he committed forcible oral sodomy again and thus should be found guilty of Specification 2 of Charge III.

Once the accused decides that he's done, how does he react? He thumps his chest and says, "That was really good," and then he's done with her. Ms. Heinrich was just happy to survive this, she was just happy this was over.

Let's talk about lack of consent; the law does not require that she continuously say no. No. No. No. No. She has to manifest--she has to make it clear to the accused that she did not consent to these acts and she did that. After the first assault she said "I don't know what kind of stuff you're into, but I don't get off on that." Immediately telling the accused where he was going, was wrong, and she didn't like it.

And when he flipped her around, and he pushed her down, he shoved his penis into her anus, there was no consent; shown by the force that he applied. There was never permission. Never was it asked. Never was it discussed. And then she screamed when he did it. And she was asked the question and she said that she said, "No," when he did that. Then she goes into the bathroom, and when she comes out of the bathroom she said, "That was not okay. I'm leaving now." Clearly indicating that what was going on was wrong and she didn't like it, and the accused repays her by grabbing her throat and forcing her to commit additional sexual acts on him. And then when he bit her nipple she screamed in pain. And he did all of these things while physically and sexually assaulting Ms. Heinrich. Pushing her down. Holding her. Making threats. Making her serve him.

And the judge read you an instruction, and that instruction said, if it was futile for Ms. Heinrich to continue to resist, the law does not require her to keep fighting and scratching. She gave it all she had. A Special Forces soldier was much stronger, more skilled and powerful than she was.

And the last charge was the assault consummated by a battery. It's been discussed how the accused slapped her in the face, the back of the head, the buttocks, and the thighs. And you heard from Ms. Heinrich which we'll talk about in a minute, testifying how she came out walking strangely and she had difficulty getting in and out of a cab, that she had difficulty sitting in a cab. All consistent with Ms. Heinrich's testimony that she was physically, sexually assaulted, and because of this he should be found guilty of Charge IV and Its Specification.

These last few slides are quite possibly the most important slides that tie it altogether. You heard Ms. Heinrich's testimony. Ms. Heinrich said that Ms. Haug was her taxi-driver that morning. And Ms. Haug said that she had never seen Ms. Heinrich before. Ms. Haug doesn't have a dog in this fight; she's just the taxi-driver sitting in front of the Marriot on a Saturday morning. But what she testified to corroborates what Ms. Heinrich testified to. Don't let the defense convince you this is a "he-said, she-said case," it is not. Ms. Haug saw how the--how Ms. Heinrich looked when she came out of that hotel and that's very, very significant. She talked how she looked liked she was drunk at first, she was walking so strangely. And then she quickly realized that she wasn't intoxicated. She talked to you how she had difficulty entering the taxi, even though the average adult does not have trouble. She talked to you how she sat on one of her sides and every time that she would hit a bump she heard Ms. Heinrich moan in pain. You don't moan in pain, you don't have problems walking, you don't have problems getting into and out of a taxi, because of normal consensual intercourse.

CDC: Objection, no evidence on that part that there is--that the government just argued.

TC: It's a reasonable inference from the facts, Your Honor.

MJ: Which fact are you referring to?

CDC: That the government is suggesting that you don't have trouble walking after normal sexual intercourse. There is no evidence to support that argument.

MJ: Panel members, you can use your own common sense and the ways of the world to determine whether or not such an inference should be drawn.

TC: Ms. Haug also testified the way she looked at--the way she looked, she didn't look well rested. She didn't look cleaned up. She didn't have perfume on. She didn't engage in normal conversation, instead she just kind of stared out the window. And then, again, she had difficulty exiting the taxi when she got to Ms. Heinrich's house.

You also heard from Dr. Dittmann, who described Ms. Heinrich's change. She noticed a change after 23 August. She stopped going--going out so much with her friends. She didn't go back to the See-Studio with Ms.--with Dr. Dittmann, even though she had been before with her multiple occasions. She talked to you about her changed appearance, her cutting her hair, changing the phone number.

Ms. Heinrich testified, she told you about some of the ways she had changed. She talked to you about always being afraid. Having trouble sleeping. She also testified, starting in early December, she was in therapy. Weekly therapy until the end of Jul--end of June when she moved to a new place as a new employee.

You also heard from Detective Lorch and Detective Lorch described Ms. Heinrich's reaction when he took her into the hotel. She had to walk through the same corridors that she had to walk with the accused that night. She had to walk into a room that looked exactly like room 533. He also testified how she reacted that first time he showed her a picture of the accused.

Now Ms. Heinrich has been open with some very unfavorable facts. She told you she went with a strange man. She told you, knowing that you may hold it against her, that you may not think highly of her but she was going to go have a one-night stand. She told you she went into his room without actual force; she wasn't pulled and thrown in from the doorway. She admitted that she got undressed on her own after that first assault. She talked to you about the bleeding from the anus. She said she thought she was, but she didn't. If she was going to come in here and come up with a story to try to convince you of something that didn't happen, knowing that it could not be proven true or false whether she had bled or not, why would she come in here and say, "I felt like I was bleeding and, in fact, I was bleeding." She didn't do that.

Same for the shower. Why would she come in here and tell you that there was a shower, knowing that you would say, "Well why didn't you run away? You could have escaped." Why would she not have put that in her--why would she not have taken that out of her story? So the whole thing was, all combined, she couldn't ever escape because he was always grabbing her. Why so elaborate? Rape is rape. She could have come in here and said, "I got in there, I wante--I didn'--I decided I didn't want to do it and he put his penis in my vagina and that was rape." But no, her story is much more detailed than that. She testified for four hours in one shot, not including what she did today, telling you about the details of those facts.

And that's important. Because if she was going to come up with a story, she would have come up with something much better.

I ask--I also ask you to remember Colonel Smith's testimony. He testified--there was a question about the THAMAR, the therapy sessions, and whether they could have ingrained in her head the statements that she was giving. Colonel Smith testified the two statements that she gave police in November, before she ever went to THAMAR, were consistent with what she told you all yesterday. Before she ever went to an appointment with a therapist to help her get over the mental issues she was having because of these assaults.

He also testified about delayed reporting, that it's not uncommon. Sixty-percent don't report at all. And a third of those who do report are delayed reports. So it's not uncommon. It doesn't mean "Ahh, she didn't report it right away, she must not have been raped; she must be making it up; she must have some motive. Some motive that we don't know, but some motive." That's not what that means. He said one-third at a time, that's what the research shows.

And he testified about the false motive allegation, and he also testified there's three primary allegation motives--false allegation motives that are in the research. And he did not believe any of those three applied to this situation.

He also talked about the urinary-tract infections. While having a urinary-tract infection does not go to whether the sex was consensual or non-consensual, he said a cause of urinary-tract infection is going from the anus to the vagina. Ms. Heinrich had not had a urinary-tract infection since 2001. And within a week of this incident she had a urinary-tract infection; just another piece of corroboration that the events happened the way Ms. Heinrich says they happened.

He also testified that it is common for a victim to just want to get clean, to feel dirty, to want to get home and take a shower.

And lastly, he testified that Ms. Heinrich's actions are consistent with how other rape victims might act.

Gentlemen, you've heard all of the evidence. That evidence clearly shows that the accused is guilty. Two specifications of rape; two specifications of forcible sodomy; two specifications of abusive sexual contact; one specification of kidnapping; one specification of communicating a threat; one specification of assault consummated by battery. And the government is confident that when you return to that verdict--to that chamber and you deliberate, that you will return a fair and just verdict of guilty.

Thank you.

**Immediately following the government's presentation, civilian defense counsel Court offered his closing argument, the text of which appears below as taken from the Record of Trial:**

CDC: Thank you, Your Honor.

Mr. President and members of the court, on 23 August 2008, a 28-year old German woman, in full possession of her faculties, agreed to go to a hotel; walked in voluntarily into that hotel with a man she had met about an hour ago; two people went upstairs in an elevator; went quietly into the room; stayed in that room for four--three to five hours, depends on what estimates you believe; and then the woman left.

Two people, and only two people in this world, know what happened in that room, and you heard both of them. You heard both of them testify under direct examination and under cross-examination. And your decision is not who to believe, because that would mean that the defense has a burden to convince you of something, your duty is to determine, having heard both people tell you what happened, whether you can now believe Ms. Heinrich beyond a reasonable doubt; that's the true burden. The classic phrase "he said, she said" implies a burden for the defense to convince you and that is not the law.

The government has tried to tell you with their slick power point why you should convict. Ninety to 95-percent of what they argued was based on what Ms. Heinrich said. They had at the end a few things, a few ideas, of why you might decide to credit her testimony, and I'll talk about their slide in a minute.

Why should you credit what she says? Merely because she said it? Because she has some reactions some way that other people react other ways; Dr. Smith. What supports what she says sufficiently that having heard Sergeant Smith [sic] you can believe her beyond a reasonable doubt; and that's the bottom line.

You know, from the government arguing why you should believe her, that she walked awkwardly and sat uncomfortably and moaned softly in the cab the next morning, at whatever time it was 8:30, 11:00, somewhere the next morning, and because of that the government says you should believe she had forcible sex. The defense submits to you that an active night of sex can cause pain even in voluntary consensual activity, to where walking may be uncomfortable or sitting may be uncomfortable. The defense also submits to you that someone who wears army boots, high up to the knee, and dances in them for hours the night before may very well have pain walking. Feet pain, nowhere else. But nonetheless, that is one fact that the government has submitted as why you should believe her.

The government says "she screamed loudly in pain" as a proof of a lack of consent, there is absolutely no evidence to support that statement other than what she said. She screamed loudly when her nipple was being bit. It swelled up it was so painful. Where is there evidence to support that assertion by Ms. Heinrich? There is none. Not only do you know from what you heard that there is none, but Dr. Smith told you that he knows of no scientific evidence to support anything she has said. Now it is true you do not have to have that, and the government asked you that in voir dire whether you would require scientific evidence to convict, and there is no such requirement, but at the same time you should wonder, "Why is there no scientific evidence?" And there's only one answer to that, because Ms. Heinrich did not report this.

Not only did she not report this--

**[The alleged victim, Ms. Greta Heinrich, departed the courtroom causing a delay in the argument.]**

CDC: Not only did she not report this to the authorities, she didn't report it to anyone. She went to an old family doctor, two, three, four days later, because of a stomach complaint that was a urinary-tract-type infection. And she wants you to believe that a doctor, who is getting that kind of complaint, makes no physical examination. None. She's got this great pain in her breast but she doesn't tell the doctor, "I have a pain in my breast, I need some help." She doesn't go even for an STD test, according to what we know, although based on what Sergeant Stewart told you, no protection was used. She doesn't say, as a reason why I might have a urinary-tract infection, someone put something in my anus and then it went into my vagina, be it a finger or a penis is irrelevant, it's a transport mechanism. She doesn't say that knowing that could be a cause. She's going to a doctor to get a diagnosis, but she doesn't say that. She's back several times to that doctor before she goes to report it. The doctor never sees--no one ever sees any black and blue marks, any swollen breasts. There is no scientific evidence to support it. She has no bleeding in the anus. The government says, "Well, gee, why wouldn't she say she was bleeding all over the place," because she went to a doctor four days later who probably would have noticed that if you're talking about a urinary-tract infection. Be that as it may, we have nothing to support, concrete, objectively, what she says.

We have the fact that she was seen leaving the hotel between 8:30 and 11:00 the next morning with the cab driver. That's a fact. But that is a neutral fact because she doesn't say anything to the cab driver. She doesn't make any complaint other than, I hurt. And she doesn't even say that, it's just the physical walking and the light moaning as she goes over bumps. The defense would submit that sometimes if you've got a headache from having been up all night, that you might have bumps--pains in your head when you go over bumps.

Dr. Smith is the government's other support for Ms. Heinrich, and Dr. Smith basically told you that some common myths are not true, but that doesn't really mean anything. If they report it right away or report it later or don't report it all, that doesn't mean that it did or didn't happen, it's just that some people don't report right away. About one-third of those who report, report later, although he and I had a long discussion about what "delayed" really means. I think all of us could agree that 10 weeks later is delayed. So his statement of, "If you don't report it right away that doesn't mean you were raped," the reverse isn't true, "If you wait 10 weeks it means you are," is not what he was saying. He's just saying some people right away and some don't. Just like in voir dire you agreed that what some people would do, other people wouldn't. All that's saying is that people are different and people react differently. But you can't read from the different reaction that something did or didn't happen, it's just people do different things.

The idea that her behavior changed afterwards, the testimony in support of that, in addition to her saying that, is at odds. Her very good friend Dr. Dittmann, and you could see from the way Dr. Dittmann interacted on cross-examination that she has absolutely no use for the defense in this case, you know where her loyalties lie. She said that her friend changed a bit and didn't go out as much; Mr. Betting said, "No, I didn't notice any change." He didn't see her all that often, but when he did he saw no change.

Now the government is trying to attack Mr. Betting for a sexual reason as well, but I'll get there in a moment, by saying "Well Mr. Betting obviously is upset with Dr. Dittmann for breaking off the relationship." And because he's upset with Ms. Dittmann, then he's going to go lie about Ms. Heinrich. The defense believes that you might conclude that that's a stretch too far in terms of bias on his part against her.

He said that she asked him to forget something, that she was apparently happy leaving the club. Why would she ask him to forget anything? What's she trying to hide? She of course says that didn't happen, "I didn't do that." So there you have a concrete contradiction between basically two government witnesses. You've got her saying, "I never asked him to say that. I didn't ask him to forget that." And you've got him saying, "Yes, she did." Why would he be lying? Because Ms. Dittmann broke up with him? You saw him testify, you saw his recollection. He said [the civilian defense counsel snapped his fingers] "It was on this date; it was on this date." He remembers what happened. He's got it down. Why would he be lying? No reason. Why would she lie? Why would she ask him to cover that up? No reason, really. She'd already acknowledged she went voluntarily, so why ask him to? It doesn't make sense for her to do that. On the other hand, maybe that's part of her psychological makeup? We know that she's been in therapy before; four months in '04-'05. Now there's nothing wrong with being in therapy, a lot of people need it and come out better for it, and that's fine. However, we only have her word that she was there for a burnout syndrome as opposed to something else; whatever burnout syndrome means in that context. So we know that there--that she's had some kind of psychotherapeutic problem in the past and she now goes back into psychotherapy again once she's made the report she says.

We were trying to talk about what the government has provided to cause you to believe her. Dr. Smith's testimony included the fact that he didn't know that she'd been in therapy, the fact of the delay, the fact of behavior change, all of which have been explained as not proving one or the other they're just sometimes something people should think about.

Why else should you believe her? Well, she did cut her hair she says in November after she's reported it. She looks the same way for 10 weeks afterwards; she's not trying to change her appearance. She changes her phone number, but not until after she reports it. The phone number she gave a "rapist" under pressure, under duress, but she doesn't change it right away, and it's **[the civilian defense counsel snapped his fingers]** that easy to change cell phone numbers, everyone knows that.

He tried to call her he said. She confirmed that she got some calls from a number she didn't recognize. No concrete evidence that that's him, but it makes some sense. Does she then cancel the phone feeling, "Oh God, this guy's trying to call me"? No. She keeps the phone and that number for another eight/nine weeks after that.

So these changes in attitude, what do they really mean? Or changes in behavior, what do they really mean? They mean that 10 weeks later she cut her hair after she reported this to the police. And did the police say why, you know, "Why do you still have your hair long if you're worried"? Who knows, but she did it later. That's the government's basics on why to believe her.

On their important facts about why to believe her they add that, well, she was open about unfavorable facts. Let's look at the unfavorable things she said to see how unusual it was.

She admitted that she left with a man that she didn't know. Well she had to, her friends saw her. Both Ms. Dittmann and Mr. Betting knew that, so admitting that is not something that's unfavorable, it's a fact you can't get around.

Admitted she wanted a one-night stand; she had to, how else is she going to explain going to the hotel? He didn't drag her out of there by her hair from the See-Studio.

Admitted she went to his room without actual force. Well she had to, otherwise if she's being drug into a room in a hallway of the Marriot Hotel at four in the morning, she's going to scream and people are going to wake up. And no one did, so she had to acknowledge voluntarily going into the room, there's no choice.

She admitted that she voluntarily undressed. If he'd torn the clothes off of her there would have been torn clothes that would have been seen by the cabbie in the morning. She had no choice but to indicate that the clothes were not forcefully removed.

Admitted she wasn't bleeding, as just pointed out, if she had tried to contend she was the doctor wouldn't have supported that, so that's not an unfavorable fact that you have to admit.

The issue about the shower? That's the one point that she may not have had to admit.

Why elaborate--why develop an elaborate story asks the government? Recall, she was in that room for somewhere between four and five hours. Four to five hours of being in that room. A lot of things have to happen normally, particularly if, on the other hand it's consensual and you sleep for a number of hours, you've got to explain that time. So you've got to have a whole bunch of violence and different things over time. Maybe that's another reason for the shower, to fill some vacuum. And then she suddenly realized, "Oops, bad answer" so it's so short.

Two-minute shower? Gentlemen, you have the pictures in the diagram, you remember her testimony that this is not just a stall shower. You walk in, it's actually a tub shower, you've got to draw the curtain, get in, run the water, do those things, dry off. Whether it was two minutes or five minutes, however long it was--

**[The civilian defense counsel retrieved Prosecution Exhibit 7 from the court reporter and held it up for the panel to view.]**

CDC: --however long it was, her testimony was that she was lying on the right side of the bed that's in

Prosecution Exhibit 7. Now she says she was lying in a fetal position, but she was lying on that side within hands reach of a telephone which goes right down to the reception desk at the Marriot, 24/7. All she's got to do is pick it up and say, "Help, I'm being held hostage. The man's hurting me. Please come."

**[The civilian defense counsel made a clicking sound as if hanging up a phone.]**

CDC: That's all it took. Now, okay, Dr. Smith said sometime victims won't report it right away. Sometimes they aren't going to make those things happen. Okay, sometimes they won't, but here, where you've got the immediate opportunity to put your hand out, you're not trying to crawl out a window, you're not trying to run out the door, reach out your hand and pick up the phone. Defense submits that that doesn't add up in a story of an evening of violence.

What else did the government say supports her? That Colonel Smith said her story has been consistent. The defense recalls the testimony and here it's up to you, that Dr. Smith was talking about her version didn't change apparently after she got therapy starting in November, assuming she got therapy beginning in November and not earlier, or didn't go to anybody earlier.

The government said that it's not uncommon for delayed reporting. We talked about that already. The fact that it's not uncommon doesn't mean it happened, it just means that sometimes a third of the people don't report right away. But two-thirds do.

No apparent motives for the common false allegation, but of course Dr. Smith on talking about that did not know about the prior psychotherapeutic treatment.

It's possible to obtain a urinary-tract infection from anal and vaginal sex, true. It's possible if you've got a history of it that you'll get it again, true. It's possible from normal sexual intercourse for some women to have a urinary-tract infection, true according to the doctor. What does that show?

A desire to get clean occurs, okay, but it's not everybody who has that. Obviously it's not, or two-thirds wouldn't go immediately and report it. And the fact that her actions are consistent with how some may act doesn't mean she was raped, because her actions are also inconsistent with how others act, as he also acknowledged.

That's why you should believe her testimony beyond a reasonable doubt.

We've already talked about a bunch of reasons why you shouldn't. Mr. Betting, no scientific evidence, no reporting to her doctor, no corroboration of the supreme loudness of the noise and her screaming, remember Detective Lorch was unable, although he checked various places, to find anyone who confirmed that that room was that loud, even though the room was on to an interior courtyard.

Other parts of her description of what happened in her version also should raise a question of "Does that make sense?" Her description, for example, of being forced to attempt to lick the anus. Went through that in some great detail. Please describe that? He's got--he's on his back spread-legged, somehow though he's got one hand on her shoulder and another hand in her hair pushing her toward his anus. Defense just asks you to conceptualize that and think how do you even do that physically?

Now, what speaks on the other side? Even though there is no requirement for the defense to convince you to believe Sergeant Stewart, what speaks to his recitation being credible?

Just credible, I'm not going to say beyond a reasonable doubt, because if his recitation is credible, we submit, that means you must have a reasonable doubt about hers.

Why in the world does he need to force himself on a young woman who is willing to go to his room to have sex with him? Why? She's there voluntarily. She wants to have a one-night stand. Why is he doing this, is he some sort of "closet sadist"? Is that the government's theory? She's willing to have sex with him. It's his room. People know it's his room. He's been there for weeks. He's still going to be there until the 20th or 29th of August, it's in the reports, it's in Prosecution Exhibit 17, the dates he was there. It's his place.

What else supports that his version is credible? He told his wife that he cheated on her. And members of the panel, you've had the opportunity to observe Sergeant Stewart, and much of his testimony was an extremely professional in disputing things the government was talking about; being respectful but saying, "No, sir, that's not what I said," or "yes, sir," or "no, sir." But when he was asked about when he told and why he told, he wasn't that tough guy anymore. He told his wife upon the delivery of their child in November, long before he was a suspect in this case. He was confessing to his wife his sin. He was concerned that his wife might die in that operation. He'd seen her on an operating table before. And as you can see from Prosecution Exhibit 1, and have heard from other people, he's a medic. He understands the dangers. And he didn't want the chance that his wife would die without him coming clean to her. He didn't have to do that. He wasn't under suspicion of anything at the time. This had happened months ago. Months ago. That suggests a degree of credibility, defense submits, of Sergeant Stewart.

He tried to call her later. Again, no direct corroboration for that, we don't have her phone records, but she acknowledged in the window of time getting several calls, he said he called twice, from an unknown number. Why would he call her again if he has raped her and forcibly sodomized her?

He also was asked about anal activity on his part. And he again wasn't the hard, tough, cool SF NCO. He explained why that's just not part of his repertoire, again, it had to do with his wife and what happened to her and why he's concerned. That also speaks to the likelihood that he did not do anything anally with Ms. Heinrich. It would have been very easy for him to get up here and say, "Yeah, we did all of the things she said, but they were just consensual," he could have said that, but he said, "No, no, that didn't happen at all and here's why."

The defense submits that that adds some credibility by definition. He's disputing not only that it was consensual, but some of the actual things that she is alleging occurred, says, "That didn't happen and here's why." You're not getting someone, as the government was implying, he's just trying to go along with the flow and say everything was cool, no.

The government has another opportunity to get up here and speak to you and they will have a chance to attempt to respond to the comments that have just been made, and that's fine, and that's fair, because our system does present the burden to the government. They have the burden to prove beyond a reasonable doubt that the offenses occurred. There is no burden on Sergeant Stewart to get up here and expose himself to you, but he did, he told you exactly what happened. There are some discrepancies between the two of them, even on minor points, what kind of cab it was, okay. It's a year ago. He had no reason to even think about this case and to remember that other than reporting it to his wife until the end of January when the cops picked him up.

But if he is trying to kidnap her, why let her sit next to the cabbie? Next to a door she can get out whenever she wants? When she can tell the cabbie, "Wrong direction, I want to go here." Why not have her, as the gentleman, have her sit in the back while he sits up next to the cabbie and says, "Go this way. Go that way."? No, that's not what--he let her sit in front because it was more comfortable and it was a little dirty in the back he said. So there's some dispute about what type of cab it was, was it a van, was it a seat van, was it new or old; it was an older one. Okay, so there's a discrepancy there.

She denies that she wanted to have drinks because that would contradict her statement that she always intended to go to her house; her house where there are other people living there, there are some common areas, and there's somebody living on the same floor she does, another person. Basically what she told him, there are other people there and I don't want to be known as a one-night stand person. That's why she's now saying "I wanted to go home but we couldn't."

You have the issue before you, when the government gets up here again, they will probably point out, "Well, the defense made a lot of Sergeant Stewart's testifying to you, remember he is a trained SF guy." He's a US soldier, who, like all US soldiers, are trained what to do in the event they're captured by the enemy. You're not the enemy. You are what he is defending. You are the United States military system. He took an oath to tell the truth and he got up there on the stand. Your decision will be, based on everything that I've heard including his, was the government's evidence enough to convince me beyond a reasonable doubt that Sergeant First Class Kelly A. Stewart is a sadistic rapist, because that's what they're alleging. Or is Ms. Heinrich, for her own reasons, reporting this as a rape. Her own reasons being possibly revenge because he didn't really call her a second or a third or a fourth time; possibly being that in here in the German system she may believe that if he is convicted, may believe, that if he's convicted she can get some civil damages out of it--

TC: Objection, Your Honor, facts not in evidence.

CDC: It's acknowledged as speculation, Your Honor, it's within the common knowledge that there may be ways--civil suits--

MJ: Panel, again, I will allow you to use your own common sense and the ways of the world in determining whether or not a proper inference should be drawn.

CDC: Was she seeking attention? The defense cannot present you with that answer. But as you also agreed, during the voir dire in response to a question, all panel members agree that they understand--that they believe that the burden is not on Sergeant Stewart to prove a motive to lie, but rather the burden is on the government to convince you she's not.

This may be one of those cases where you go back and you think, "I'm not sure what happened. I can see it both ways. I can understand each one and each one could be true." You might be thinking that, the defense doesn't agree with that, but you might. But even if that's your conclusion, by definition, you have a reasonable doubt, because this is not a case of balance or balance. This is a case of proof beyond a reasonable doubt and it's the defense's submission that the evidence you've heard over the past two days have not proven that the government can show this beyond a reasonable doubt. In fact, we believe it's just the opposite. But we don't have to prove that.

The government has the burden. They have not met it. Based on all of the evidence you have before you, Sergeant First Class Kelly A. Stewart should be found not guilty of all charges and specifications.

Thank you.

**Following Court's closing statement, Captain Bashore took the government's final stab at convicting Stewart via rebuttal:**

TC: Gentlemen, I will be brief on rebuttal.

Look at the facts. Look at what can be corroborated. Look whose side of the story can be corroborated. Ms. Greta Heinrich's can, by a person who had no part of this case whatsoever in Ms. Haug. She testified she didn't look clean, didn't look like somebody that had just take a shower, certainly. Look disheveled, looked like she was in physical pain, just moments after leaving the Marriot Hotel.

The accused mentions Mr. Betting and whether or not Ms. Heinrich told him to lie. And the defense got it right, it doesn't make sense. Ms. Heinrich came in here and told you she went willingly. Why would she tell her friends boyfriend to come in here and say something otherwise. That just doesn't make sense at all. When she didn't even ask her own best friend. A friend that's more likely to keep that inside if she was going to ask somebody to come in here and lie for them. And it doesn't make sense why she would do that anyway. She came in here and told you all kinds of facts. Many of those weren't helpful. She stayed after getting slapped, knowing in hind-sight, that doesn't make sense. She didn't have to tell you that. She could have made a different story.

Shout--she didn't have to fill three plus hours with multiple rape and abusive sexual contact and sodomy stories. She could have said he made her lay there for two hours. Saying that the shower was filling up time? Two minutes? Ms. Heinrich could do better than that if she was going to come in here and tell you a false story.

I ask you to consider the accused's testimony. While the defense has no burden, the accused did testify, and you can consider that testimony. Some of the things that he said, taking his weddin--his wedding band off because he was afraid he would get robbed in Germany? How he was the gentleman and put her in the front seat of the taxi, he sits in the back and then they make out the entire ride up to the Marriot? That doesn't make sense. If you're going to make out with a woman, you put her in the back with you. It just doesn't make sense.

Lying about the vodka drink. Ms. Heinrich testified she hasn't drank vodka since she was 15. On top of that, the accused said she had drank Red Bull, well if she had drank Red Bull he had Red Bull, why did they need to go somewhere else to get more--more types of drinks? He told you he didn't offer her anything, but she didn't want beer. Doesn't make sense.

He said she didn't look like she was in pain when she left his room. He told you she had showered and Ms. Haug testified to something the exact opposite.

And isn't it ironic that he tries to hide behind his wife and her medical issues to get sympathy from the panel. There's no corroboration--

CDC: Objection, Your Honor.

MJ: Again, panel members, I once more remind you that the defen--that the accused has no burden whatsoever to present any evidence or any corroboration of any kind. The burden is always and shall remain on the government to prove every element of every offense, to include corroboration.

Are there any questions about that?

**[All members indicated a negative response.]**

TC: I ask you to consider how the accused wouldn't even answer simple questions. I ask you to consider when the government would ask the accused questions, trying to get answers, how he would look towards the defense table. It's very important to consider those facts.

Lastly, I want to talk about motive. Who has the motive to come in here and lie? What possible motive does Ms. Heinrich have? That the accused didn't call her? The accused says he called her, but that may have been her motive for two and a half months later seeking revenge, a year-long process to get to trial today. That doesn't make sense. There's absolutely no evidence of a possibility that Ms. Heinrich would gain financially from this. There's absolutely no evidence that Ms. Heinrich has any motive to come in here and fabricate this story. She didn't even know his name; Antonio, an American soldier, that's all she knew. Instead, she's changed her life-style, she's been attending therapy classes for nine months, and what's her motive?

The government would proffer that the accused has a motive, because he's facing very serious charges. And the government has proven beyond a reasonable doubt, a reasonable doubt, that the accused committed the offenses as charged and would ask that you return a verdict of guilty of all charges and their specifications.

Thank you.

**At 5:40 p.m., closing arguments ended.**

# Day Two: The Verdict

**Following the closing arguments and some administrative sessions involving only himself and attorneys for both sides, Judge Kuhfahl offered some final instructions to the panel of 10 soldiers who would render a verdict in the case of United States vs. Kelly A. Stewart:**

> The influence of superiority in rank will not be employed in any manner in an attempt to control the independence of the members in the exercise of their own personal judgment. Your deliberation should include a full and free discussion of all the evidence that has been presented. After you have completed your discussion, then voting on your findings must be accomplished by secret, written ballot, and all members of the court are required to vote.
>
> The order in which the several charges and specifications are to be voted on should be determined by the president subject to objection by a majority of the members. You vote on the specifications under the charge before you vote on the charge.
>
> If you find the accused guilty of any specification under a charge, then the finding as to that charge must be guilty. The junior member will collect and count the votes. The count will then be checked by the president, who will immediately announce the result of the ballot to the members.
>
> The concurrence of at least twothirds of the members present when the vote is taken is required for

any finding of guilty. Since we have 10 members, that means seven members must concur in any finding of guilty.

If you have at least seven votes of guilty of any offense then that will result in a finding of guilty for that offense. If fewer than seven members vote for a finding of guilty, then your ballot resulted in a finding of not guilty bearing in mind the instructions that I gave you about voting on the lesser included offenses.

You may reconsider any finding prior to its being announced in open court. However, after you vote, if any member expresses a desire to reconsider any finding, open the court and the president should announce only reconsideration of a finding has been proposed.

Do not state:

One, whether the finding proposed to be reconsidered is a finding of guilty or not guilty; or

Two, which specification and charge is involved.

I will then give you specific further instructions on the procedure for reconsideration.

As soon as the court has reached its findings, and I have examined the Findings Worksheet, the findings will be announced by the president in the presence of all parties.

**Judge Kuhfahl concluded his instructions with a call for questions any panel members might have had. After none were raised, he excused the 10 panel members shortly before 6 p.m. to begin their deliberations and offered instructions to Stewart as to his rights following the announcement of a verdict.**

**Two hours later, panel members came out of their deliberations to ask for a copy of the initial report Heinrich made to the German police in November 2008. Less than a half-hour after that, they took a one-hour break for dinner and then returned to their deliberations.**

Three more hours of deliberation followed until, at 11:28 p.m., the panel members returned to the courtroom.

"It was getting late at night," Stewart said, recalling what he saw when he as he watched panel members return. "Based off a couple of the jurors and their body language, I could tell that I was screwed... because three of them came out and they had a very disgusted look—but not at me, more for me.

"You can tell if someone's pissed at ya or if they're fearful for ya. Three of 'em walked out, and they had that fearful look for me, and I was like, 'Holy cow,' and I lean over and I tell my lawyer, 'Mr. Court, I don't think things are going good.'

"One of the guys, the second senior guy that was there, kind of had a smile on his face—a kind of smirk smile—and he looked over at Captain Bashore and Captain O'Malley. That really sealed the deal for me."

Lieutenant Colonel Denny informed Judge Kuhfahl that a verdict had been reached. In turn, the military judge reviewed the Findings Worksheet and informed the panel president of a problem with the way they had indicated their findings.

"On a couple of the charges, there appears to be what--what I assume to be an indication of your finding," he said. "However, as I instructed you, or as is listed on the findings worksheet, once you make a finding as to a particular specification or a charge, you must line out all of the inapplicable language. So for example, if a specification has the option of "Not Guilty," "Guilty," "Guilty of lesser included" and you choose, for example, "Not Guilty," then you would line out all of the other options, to include the "Guilty"or the "Not Guilty, but guilty to a lesser included offense.

"Second, as I instructed you, if you find—you will make a finding as to both, first the specification, and then the charge," he continued. "If you find the accused guilty of any specification, then he must also be guilty of the charge above that specification. So please make—please ensure that you annotate it on your findings worksheet, not only for each specification, but then for each charge.

"And third, if you are choosing to make a finding by exceptions and substitutions, at the end of that particular offense you must also make a specific finding of "Not Guilty," or "Guilty," to the excepted language and to the substituted language," he concluded.

After Lieutenant Colonel Denny acknowledged that he understood the instructions, Judge Kuhfahl sent the jury to its deliberation room to fix the charge sheet at 11:33 p.m.

"Right there, that already told me I was found guilty of something," Stewart said, recalling the night when his life changed forever. None of the four charges were ones of which anyone would want to be found guilty.

During that intermission, Stewart called his wife and told her that he wouldn't be coming home that night. He also called his bank and transferred all of the money in his bank accounts into his wife's account "...because I already knew what I was gonna do."

Seven minutes later, the jury returned with a corrected Findings Sheet which Judge Kuhfahl asked the colonel to read to the court.

Lieutenant Colonel Denny announced that Stewart had been found guilty of aggravated sexual assault, inveigling (a form of kidnapping defined as using flattery to accomplish an objective), sodomy and assault consummated by battery.

Less than 39 hours after it had begun, the trial portion of the court-martial came to an end and, due to the late hour, Judge Kuhfahl opted to end the proceedings for the day and resume with sentencing in the morning. It was 11:45 p.m. on August 19, 2009.

Incredibly, Judge Kuhfahl did not issue an order requiring that Stewart, now convicted of sex crimes against a German national, be confined under guard during the night before his sentencing.

# DAY THREE

# Day Three: 15 Reasons to Proceed

**At 8:02 a.m. August 20, 2009, civilian defense counsel Court advised the court that his client, the now-convicted soldier, Stewart, was unaccounted for and did not appear in court as previously instructed. During the next four hours, Judge Kuhfahl conferred with attorneys and heard from a number of witnesses in an effort to decide whether the court should proceed with sentencing in Stewart's absence.**

**Captain Greg O'Malley called Army Sergeant First Class Detrick Hampton, Stewart's good friend and co-worker at the International Special Training Center (ISTC), as his first** witness:

Q. Do you know Sergeant First Class Kelly Stewart?

A. Yes. I do, sir. I have known him since September of '08, sir.

Q. How do you know him?

A. We are instructors together at ISTC, sir.

Q. Have you been present with Sergeant First Class Stewart during this court-martial?

A. Yes. I have, sir.

Q. What have been your--why are you here at this court-martial?

A. Sir, I am here to support him as a friend, as a fellow NCO soldier, sir.

Q. How did you get up to Vilseck, Germany?

A. We came together, sir. We departed Germany on this--last Monday, of course, with a rental vehicle.

Q. Whose rental vehicle is that?

A. It was in Sergeant First Class Stewart's name, sir.

Q. Where was your lodging in Vilseck?

A. It was at Kristall Inn, sir.

Q. How many rooms did you each have?

A. Just one, sir.

Q. Did you each stay in the same room?

A. Yes. We did, sir.

Q. Last night after the court adjourned [sic] around midnight, where did you go?

A. We went back to the Kristall Inn, sir. Of course, sir, he took it very hard--the verdict. We talked for a couple of hours. He talked to his family. He talked to me, sir; and my understanding, sir, was we were coming here today for his sentencing, sir.

Q. You say that to your understanding. What are you basing that off of?

A. Because, sir, we talked about--last night--of him coming here--specifically of what will he do and the only option of which he could do in my eyes as well as his eyes was come here and take their verdict, sir, and I would support him as a friend, sir, no matter what.

Q. How late did you and he stay up?

A. We were up until approximately 5 o'clock this morning, sir.

Q. Okay. Did you hear any comments that he made to his wife regarding coming here tomorrow?

A. Yes.

Q. Coming here today, excuse me.

CDC: Objection, Your Honor, privilege still applies.

ATC: Your Honor, the privilege doesn't apply if a third party is present to hear that communication.

MJ: Overruled.

CDC: As long as it's only what he is saying, not what the wife said back.

ATC: I'm not asking for that, Your Honor.

**Questions by the assistant trial counsel resumed:**

Q. Please answer the question.

A. Just basically, sir, he told his wife that he loved them and he would be here tomorrow for his sentencing, sir.

Q. Okay. Did he make any comments to you that he would not be here tomorrow?

A. No. He did not, sir.

Q. When was the last time you saw Sergeant Stewart?

A. It was approximately 6:45ish, 7 o'clock, sir, this morning.

Q. And where were you at?

A. I was lying in bed next to him. I mean, we are in different beds, of course, sir, but next to him, sir. I do understand Kelly had a problem sleeping, which is understood; and when I rolled over, I saw Kelly, and I knew I had to get some type of sleep before court tomorrow; and that was the last time I saw him, sir.

Q. Okay. And where was he located that last time you saw him?

A. In the other bed, sir.

Q. Okay. Was he awake or asleep?

A. He wasn't asleep, sir. He was definitely rolling over; and he had a problem sleeping, which I can understand, sir.

Q. What was he wearing at that time?

A. A white T-shirt and briefs, sir.

Q. Okay. When was the next time you woke up?

A. I woke up at around, I want to say--before 7:30, sir. I woke up, brushed my teeth, shaved real quick. When I woke up, I noticed Kelly wasn't there. I was sure he was outside. He's got a lot going on right now in his life. I got dressed; I walked outside, sir; no Kelly outside the room. I walked downstairs--no vehicle or Kelly. I kept walking around the area--maybe he went somewhere else. I attempted to call him. I went to the front desk, and then I came here, sir.

Q. How many times did you call him?

A. Only once, sir.

Q. Okay. And your purpose of going outside was to look for him?

A. My purpose of going outside was to look for him at first, sir, because he wasn't in the room and he wasn't outside the front door--that he might be at, sir.

Q. After you went to the front desk, then what did you do?

A. After I went from the front desk, sir, it was approximately, I want to say, 9 o'clock or close to 9 o'clock, sir. It was, like, 8:45; and I knew that we had to be here--or Sergeant First Class Stewart had to be here at approximately 8:45; so I walked from the Kristall Inn to here. At that time, I received a call from Settle; and I was right here at the court; and I told them I could not find him. I informed my chain of command at that time what was going on.

Q. You alerted them that he was--you couldn't find him?

A. Yes. I did.

Q. Okay. Did you notice in your hotel room you were sharing with Sergeant Stewart if his wallet was still present?

A. No. It's not, sir.

Q. What about the car keys, were they still present in the hotel?

A. No. They are not, sir.

Q. What about his two cell phones; were they present?

A. No. They are not, sir.

ATC: One moment, please.

**[The assistant trial counsel conferred with the trial counsel.]**

ATC: No further questions, Your Honor.

## CROSS-EXAMINATION
### Questions by the civilian defense counsel:

Q. Sergeant Hampton, just for the record, would you, please, spell your first name?

A. My first name is Detrick, spelled D-E-T-R-I-C-K.

Q. Thank you. Sergeant Hampton, when you woke up this morning and discovered that you could not find Sergeant Stewart, did you look to see what kind of clothing he might have had on when he left the room?

A. When I first noticed that he was gone, sir, of course, I finished shaving, brushed my teeth, and when I walked outside I saw he was not out there. I did open up the door because I thought maybe he had left without me. I really did.

Q. What do you mean "opened the door"?

A. Opened his wall locker and see was any clothes in there. I noticed that his uniform was gone, sir.

Q. When you say "uniform," do you mean his Class A Uniform?

A. His Class A, sir.

Q. The one that he had been wearing here in court?

A. Yes, sir.

Q. And the one he would have had to come to court today?

A. Yes, sir.

Q. Did you notice if any other clothing was missing?

A. No. I did not, sir.

Q. What, if anything, did you notice about footgear he might of had on if he had on footgear?

A. When I noticed his uniform was missing, sir, I immediately thought maybe he got dressed and walked out here; but as I looked down, I noticed that his boots were still there which I felt at that time was kind of very odd because, of course, he needed his jump boots--part of his Class A's, sir.

Q. Did you see his beret still in the room?

A. No. I did not, sir.

Q. Are you aware--what other footgear did you see in the room, including the--aside from the boots?

A. I noticed that he had--his flip-flops were still present as well as some tennis shoes were also still present, sir.

Q. Other than those three sets of footgear, boots, flip-flops, tennis shoes, did you know if he had any other footgear in the room?

A. Not that I know of, sir.

Q. Did you notice if any bags, or packages, or containers were taken from the room--things to carry things in?

A. No, sir.

Q. What was still in the room in that category?

A. His suitcase, sir, which was still in the room. I know the suitcase is there because I brought it up to the room, and that was the only luggage in which I knew of him having.

Q. Did you notice if he left money in the room?

A. Yes. He did, sir.

Q. So somewhere between 6:30 and 7:00 was the last time you had eyes on?

A. Yes, sir.

CDC: Thank you, Your Honor. I have no further questions.

MJ: Government?

**REDIRECT EXAMINATION**
**Questions by the assistant trial counsel:**

Q. Sergeant Hampton, you mentioned that there was money left in the room. Was this pocket change coins or was this folded bills?

A. Pocket change coins, sir.

Q. Okay. You don't know how--approximately a value of that pocket change?

A. No. I do not, sir.

ATC: No further questions, Your Honor.

MJ: Defense, any questions on that?

CDC: No, Your Honor. Thank you.

**EXAMINATION BY THE COURT-MARTIAL**
**Questions by the military judge:**

Q. Okay. Sergeant Hampton, when did you come up to Vilseck with the accused?

A. Monday, sir, approximately at 1300, sir.

Q. Since Monday, did the accused ever take the rental car and leave on his own?

A. No, sir.

Q. Was there only one set of keys to the rental car?

A. Yes, sir.

Q. You indicated that last night after you got back to the hotel room the accused took the verdict very hard.

A. Yes, sir.

Q. What do you mean by that?

A. Sir, he--he just felt like his life was over, sir. He just--he was worried about his family. He was worried about, of course, what the verdict--what the sentence was going to be, sir.

Q. He told you specifically he was worried about the sentence?

A. Yes, sir.

Q. What did you mean when you stated he asked what could he do?

A. Of stating of--last night conversation?

Q. Yes.

A. We talked about, sir, of--he was very worried, of course, of his sentence and we just talked about, you know, of course, he has friends and we were going to be there to support him--so whatever he could do, sir, about him coming here, sir--I was worried about him hurting himself, sir, really. And I'm sure that maybe was going through his mind, and I was worried about him, sir. And that's the reason, again, why I stayed up so late with him because I was worried about him, sir. He did take it very hard as I said earlier.

Q. Did he discuss with you any other options or any options other than coming to court today?

A. No. He didn't, sir; but, of course, I have been knowing Kelly for awhile; and if I put myself in that seat, it would go through my mind also, sir, so I was worried about it.

Q. You said you tried to call him this morning?

A. Yes. I did, sir.

Q. And did he answer?

A. No. He did not, sir.

Q. What time was that?

A. It was--I have to look at my telephone to be precise, but it was approximately 8ish.

Q. Have you had an opportunity to call him since Monday when you arrived to Vilseck?

A. Yes, sir.

Q. Did he answer on those other occasions?

A. Yes. He did, sir.

Q. I didn't understand something you said. You said about 0845 you received a call from SATO was it?

A. No, sir.

Q. Who was it that you said you received a phone call from at zero----

A. Oh, it was from Settle, Sergeant First Class Settle.

Q. Oh, Sergeant First Class Settle. Okay. Do you know whether or not Sergeant First Class Stewart brought any Class A loafers with him?

A. Not that I know of, sir.
Q. Do you (know) what types of civilian clothes he brought up with him?
A. The only thing which I saw was Tuesday, sir. I never looked in his suitcase, but I do know he had civilian clothes, sir.
Q. Did you look to see whether or not the civilian clothes were still present?
A. Yes. I did, sir.
Q. Were they present?
A. The ones in which I've seen him wear prior--yes, sir. They are.
Q. When you woke up this morning and noticed that the accused was gone, did you notice any evidence of a fight or a break-in in the room?
A. No, sir.
Q. Was everything pretty much the way you left it when you went to bed?
A. Yes, sir.
Q. Did you hear anything between the time you saw him and the time you woke up which would have indicated a fight or a struggle?
A. No, sir.
MJ: Counsel, any questions based on mine?
ATC: Yes, Your Honor.

**REDIRECT EXAMINATION**
**Questions by the assistant trial counsel:**

Q. Sergeant Hampton, when you called him this morning, did his cell phone ring or did it go directly to voice mail?
A. Directly to voice mail, sir.
Q. Have you ever called him in the last couple of days and had a call go directly to voice mail?

A. No, sir.
ATC: No further questions, Your Honor.

### CROSS-EXAMINATION
### Questions by the civilian defense counsel:

Q. Sergeant Hampton, you told the military judge that Sergeant Stewart was worried about the sentence, what it would be. You said something about, "I would think that too," or something like that and I wasn't clear what you meant.
A. Sir, we both have families; and one of the things in which I felt that he was worried about--it's just my feeling, sir--is he was worried about who is taking care of his family. That is what I am worried about, sir; so my worry about if I would go to jail, sir, was to take care of my family and I am sure is what his worry was, sir--to be more precise.
Q. You indicated that you were concerned that he might hurt himself.
A. Yes. I am, sir, and I still am.
Q. Was that based on something he said or just you knowing him.
A. On how he took it, sir, and on me talking to him last night. And I am worried about him, sir, and his Class A's are gone, and I'm worried.

**On that note, Sergeant Hampton was excused without further questions, and Army Master Sergeant Barry J. Beilhart, the noncommissioned officer in charge of Military Police operations (a.k.a., "the provost sergeant") at U.S. Army Garrison Grafenwoehr was called as a witness for the government.**

**Sergeant Beilhart answered Captain O'Malley's questions about the steps his office took after being notified of Stewart's unauthorized absence from the legal proceedings. Those steps included sending a "Be on the Lookout" order on Stewart and his**

**vehicle, a black Audi Q5, to U.S. and German law enforcement offices and sending a team to search the Kristall Inn where Stewart and Sergeant Hampton had been staying and questioning Sergeant Hampton about Stewart's whereabouts.**

**Daniel Lorch, the officer in charge of the eight-man investigation unit at the German criminal police office in Böblingen who had testified previously, was recalled as the government's next witness. Like Sergeant Beilhart, he informed the court as to the actions his office had taken upon being notified of Stewart's absence from the courtroom.**

**In addition, Detective Lorch reported that his people had the numbers for two mobile phones owned by Stewart and were working with the appropriate phone companies in trying to locate him via the signals from those phones. In addition, they learned from Army Criminal Investigation Division agents in Stuttgart that Stewart had called his wife, Freija, sometime between 7:30 and 8 o'clock that morning.**

**Judge Kuhfahl received updates from various persons about unsuccessful attempts to locate Stewart before moving on to hear testimony from other witnesses around 12:30 p.m.**

**First to take the stand as a witness for the defense was Command Sergeant Major Richard K. "Spike" Klein, the senior enlisted soldier at the ISTC:**

Q. Command Sergeant Major, let's try to cut to the chase. You know Staff Sergeant [sic] Stewart?

A. I do. Yes, sir.

Q. About how long have you known him?

A. I arrived in the unit on February 10th of 2009. He was currently assigned to the unit in August of 2008 so approximately six months.

Q. We have heard a lot of testimony about the type of unit and what it is. We will go past that. Do you know if Sergeant Stewart has been on missions where he required other identities?

A. Yes, sir. He has; and yes, I do know that.

Q. Do you know if he has received any kind of threats or threatening messages to him or his family since he has been at Pfullendorf?

A. On one or two occasions, yes, sir, he has minimally discussed that he has had contact with entities or organizations that could possibly be a threat to him or his family since he returned from rotations either in Iraq of Afghanistan.

Q. Are you aware whether in Afghanistan or Iraq posters have been found with pictures of SF operatives with rewards for their elimination?

A. Yes, sir.

Q. Do you know directly whether that has ever occurred with Sergeant Stewart?

A. No, sir. I do not.

Q. Did you speak with Sergeant Stewart last evening after the announcement of the verdict?

A. Only briefly, sir, whenever we were in the room with yourself and then momentarily after you left the room.

Q. So then that would have been your last personal contact with him?

A. Yes, sir. The last personal contact was shortly after midnight after we were adjourned after our discussions and your explanation in layman's terms what he was convicted of.

Q. When you departed that room, did you have any reason to believe he would not be here today?

A. I did not, sir.

Q. When you departed that room, did you have any fear for his personal safety?

A. I think professionally, sir, I did not. Personally, as I look back on, the only comment that he made as I shook his hand and hugged him was, "Sergeant Major, please take care of my wife." In that instance, other than that, no, sir.

Q. You're aware--were you sitting here when Sergeant Hampton testified earlier today?

A. Yes, sir.

Q. So you're aware of what was--what Sergeant Stewart apparently has in the way of clothing?

A. Yes, sir. I am.

Q. Does that cause you any concern?

A. It does; and the reason for that concern is is that one, the uniform and the beret are a definite symbol of pride and integrity with our force and to only take that uniform without the boots and the beret and whatever civilian clothes that he might have been wearing or not wearing does cause concern.

Q. In what way, Sergeant Major?

A. I think primarily because if an individual were to decide to take his or her own life in that instance that that would be the last piece of dignity that they would take with them in the sense of wearing this uniform since that is the only uniform that he currently has with him.

CDC: Thank you. I have no further questions, Your Honor.

ATC: No questions, Your Honor.

**EXAMINATION BY THE COURT-MARTIAL**
**Questions by the military judge:**

Q. Command Sergeant Major Klein, when the accused talked to you about these threats, how long ago was that?

A. It's hard to put an exact time-frame on it, sir, but being in-depth with his case pretty much since I've been in the unit as of February I can only say possibly April, May time-frame. It's really hard to say, sir. I can't place a date or even a direct month as to when that conversation took place.

Q. When did you arrive here in Vilseck for this trial?

A. Sergeant First Class Settle and I drove the TMP vehicle up on Tuesday, arrived here approximately 1200 hours at the Tulip Inn Hotel in Amberg.

Q. Since your arrival on Tuesday and the last time you saw the accused, did he make mention of any of these threats to you?

A. Which threats are those, sir--with any organizations or----

Q. Yes.

A. No, sir. He did, however, voice true concern about the release of his name and photographs to, you know--through any media channels based on this court-martial.

Q. Was that just a general concern based upon his job?

A. No, sir. I think it's more specific with the system and infrastructure with which he's associated with as far as the release of his name and photograph not just his job at ISTC.

MJ: Any questions based on mine?

ATC: No, Your Honor.

CDC: Yes, Your Honor.

**REDIRECT EXAMINATION**
**Questions by the civilian defense counsel:**

Q. I realize that there are obvious limitations, Command Sergeant Major. Are you suggesting that while he has been here in Germany he's had not only the job at the ISTC but also some other function within the organization?

A. No, sir. Absolutely not. He's only been a part of ISTC in the capacity of a Special Forces soldier teaching in the survival division, both sniper operations and survival operations, and working the S-3 operations office.

Q. Then can you clarify what you meant with other systems and other operations involving him when you answered the military judge a minute ago?

A. Right. I specifically am talking about the infrastructure and the system of which he has operated in rotations in Iraq and Afghanistan that would lead him to have concern for his identity in some sort of media stream should it happen to be released.

Q. And are you aware, Sergeant Major, having been here the past three days whether there is media presence at this court-martial?

A. Absolutely, sir.

Q. And there is?

A. Yes, sir.

**Command Sergeant Major Klein was excused and, shortly before 1 p.m., Judge Kuhfahl conferred with attorneys from both sides to discuss what they knew about Stewart's absence to this point. A few minutes later, he offered a recap of that knowledge to those in the courtroom—the panel members were absent—and proceeded to offer 15 reasons why he had decided to proceed with sentencing:**

"One, the accused was informed on 28 July 2009 at his arraignment that he could be tried in absentia if he voluntarily absented himself from these proceedings;

"Two, the accused specifically admitted that he understood that he could be tried in absentia at that said arraignment;

"Three, the accused was also informed on 28 July that he needed to keep his defense counsel and chain of command apprised of his whereabouts throughout the trial;

"Four, the accused stated that he had no questions concerning his obligations;

"Five, at approximately 0015 this morning the accused was convicted of one specification of aggravated sexual assault, one specification of kidnapping, two specifications of forcible sodomy, and one specification of assault and battery;

"Six, the accused was present at 0015 this morning when I informed all parties to the court that the court would be in recess until 1000 hours this morning;

"Seven, the accused took the findings of the court very hard and was emotionally distraught about his future;

"Eight, the accused was present in his hotel room with Sergeant First Class Hampton at approximately 0700 this morning;

"Nine, at approximately 0730 the accused was absent from his hotel room. The accused's rental car was also missing from the hotel as well as the accused's Class A uniform;

"Ten, there were no signs of a break-in or a struggle in the accused's room when Sergeant First Class Hampton awoke at approximately 0730;

"Eleven, between 0730 and 0800 the accused contacted his wife who also resides in Germany;

"Twelve, Sergeant First Class Hampton attempted to contact the accused via his cell phone, but the accused's cell phone went directly to voice mail. Sergeant First Class Hampton also made attempts to locate the accused around the hotel but could not find him;

"Thirteen, efforts have been made by both MPs and local German authorities to find the accused, to include lookouts for the accused's vehicle, placing a flag on his ID card, and attempting to triangulate the position of his cell phone. While there has been a ping on one of cell phones, those efforts to date have not resolved in actually locating the accused;

"Fourteen, efforts have been made to locate the accused at the Vilseck medical clinic. No evidence has been located indicating that the accused has sought medical treatment between the court's recess at 0015 this morning and present, which I note for the record is now 1255. There is also no evidence that the accused--or excuse me--yes--that the accused has sought treatment in any local German hospital surrounding the Vilseck military installation; and

"Fifteen, there is no evidence before this court that anyone has seen the accused since 0700 this morning.

"As such, in accordance with Rule for Court-Martial 804(c)(1) this court holds that the government has demonstrated by a preponderance of the evidence that the accused, Sergeant First Class Kelly Stewart, has voluntarily absented himself from this court-martial and that this court-martial may proceed in the accused's absence."

**One minute later, the sentencing phase began without Stewart.**

**Four individuals—Heinrich, Army Lieutenant Colonel (Dr.) Marshall Smith and two of Stewart's ISTC colleagues—were called as witnesses.**

**The transcript of Heinrich's sentencing phase testimony appears below as taken from the Record of Trial:**

**GRETA HEINRICH, civilian, was recalled as a witness for the prosecution, reminded of her previous oath, and testified through an interpreter as follows:**

**DIRECT EXAMINATION**
**Questions by the assistant trial counsel:**

Q. Ms. Heinrich, as you know, Sergeant First Class Stewart has been found guilty of several offenses against you. How have these offenses that he has been found guilty of affected you?

A. I am very scared.

Q. Scared of what?

A. I am scared. I am scared to be with people. I am scared of men and scared of soldiers.

Q. Why are you scared to be with people?

A. I have to think the whole time that you are not able to see--you know, look at people and see to what they are capable of doing.

Q. How has this affected you regarding men?

A. I have no contacts to men anymore.

Q. Why not?

A. Because I couldn't bear it if something like that happened to me again.

Q. Have you been engaged in any dating relationships with any men since this attack?

A. No.

Q. How have these crimes that have been committed against you affected you with--regarding to soldiers--you mentioned soldiers; what did you mean by that?

A. Soldiers are actually there for our protection, but this soldier used his physical power against me.

Q. Has your opinion changed regarding American soldiers?

CDC: Objection, Your Honor, assumes facts not in evidence. We don't know what the opinion was before.

MJ: What was the objection again?

CDC: Effectively assuming facts not in evidence. We don't know if she had an opinion before and the government assuming whatever it was has changed.

MJ: Was the question has it changed her opinion?

ATC: Yes, Your Honor.

MJ: Overruled.

The questions by the trial counsel resumed as follows:

Q. Please answer.

A. Yes. He was the first American I met; and he, of course, influenced my opinion.

Q. Negatively or positively?

A. Negatively.

Q. Has that affected your ability to interact with other American soldiers?

A. Yes.

Q. How so?

A. There's always places, localities where there is American soldiers like, for instance, the Irish pub. I am scared. I cannot, you know, have normal contact.

Q. Has your social life changed as a result of these attacks?

A. Yes.

Q. How so?

A. I was always with people a lot of times, but that's not this way anymore. I now spend a lot of time alone or with friends.

Q. Why do you spend so much time alone?

A. At home because that's where I feel safe--safer.

Q. Have your sleeping--your ability to sleep been affected by the actions of Sergeant First Class Stewart?

A. I dream of him every night.

Q. How has that affected you?

A. I at the most sleep three hours a night.

Q. Is that because of the dreams you have regarding Sergeant Stewart?

A. Yes.

Q. While you are awake, how often do you think of the attack?

A. When I have a lot of work, then it is easier; but when I am on break or when I am, you know, in the evening home or, you know--it always comes back. It comes back while I am driving in my car or while I am going for a walk.

Q. How do you feel when you think about the attack?

A. It hurts.

**[Pause.]**

A. I cannot understand that a person does something like that to another person. I just can't understand that.

Q. Have you had any problems eating since the attack?

A. Yes. I had a lot of disturbances in my eating pattern. Right after the attack I was eating a lot. I kept eating, and then I stopped and didn't eat at all anymore. Now, I am slowing getting back, getting my weight back to where it was and, you know, getting better.

Q. How do you feel when a man looks at you with interest?

CDC: Objection, calls for speculation as to whether the man is looking at her with interest.

MJ: Overruled.

A. Most of the time I can't bear it if men look at me.

Q. How do you react?

A. Either really harsh verbally, you know, so I--so that they leave me or I'm leaving the situation.

Q. In the days after the attack, how much pain were you in?

A. A lot.

Q. How long did it take for that pain to go away?

A. Eleven weeks.

**[A noise of a cell phone ringing is heard in the gallery.]**

Q. Have you changed your appearance to the public--the clothes that you wear?

MJ: Let me stop you here before you answer the question. Let me remind all personnel in the gallery to either turn off all your cell phones or to exit the courtroom. Thank you.

A. Yes. I cut my hair off. I mean, somebody that didn't know me before--that knew me before would not recognize me. I look totally different with long hair.

Q. Why did you cut your hair?

A. I am trying to build a new identity for myself, and I don't ever want again that anyone can hold me by my hair.

Q. Why do you want to build a new identity for yourself?

A. Because nothing was left after this night. Nothing of my personal--my life was left after that night.

ATC: No further questions, Your Honor.

**CROSS-EXAMINATION**
**Questions by the civilian defense counsel:**

Q. Ms. Heinrich, shortly after you went to the German police, you got a German attorney involved in this case, correct?

A. That's right.

Q. It was a male attorney, correct?

A. Yes, but he's an expert. The counseling place for sexual violence has given me his name.

Q. And you initially planned on this case being tried in--you initially expected this case would be tried in German court, correct?

A. That's correct.

Q. And in German court you could have acted as the adjunct prosecutor in the case, correct?

A. That's correct.

Q. And a German court could have also given you a financial recovery as part of that trial, correct?

A. I don't know. My attorney was paid for. I didn't have to pay for him.

Q. The question is whether you would have been able to receive financial damages, perhaps, as a result of the German court decision.

A. You think you can make this up with money, with whatever amount? I don't need any of his money.

Q. The question was whether you would have been able to get money based on the German court decision.

ATC: Your Honor, the government objects. We don't understand what rule of evidence or sentencing that is relevant to these proceedings.

MJ: Overruled. You may answer the question.

A. I don't know.

Q. What charges do you believe the jury found Sergeant Stewart not guilty of doing?

A. I don't know. I didn't understand everything when it was read out.

Q. Did the government not tell you what charges he was acquitted of?

A. Rape--the straight pure rape--that's what he was acquitted of. That's what I was told.

Q. You were not told that he was found not guilty of grabbing your throat and choking you with his hand while inserting his fingers into your anus?

A. They didn't, but I don't understand the question.

Q. You were not told that he was not guilty of that offense?

A. No. I asked what he was found guilty of.

Q. So you did not know he was found not guilty of placing your breast nipple in his mouth and biting it?

A. No. I didn't, but I don't understand the question.

Q. How do you feel that he was found not guilty of those points?

A. I know that he is guilty.

Q. So you disagree with what the jury said?

A. I accept the decision of the panel.

Q. But you don't agree with it?

A. I don't understand the question.

Q. You do not agree with the findings of the jury, do you?

A. My answer is that I know he is guilty, but I accept the findings of the panel.

Q. Prior to the 22nd of August 2008, did you believe that you could look at someone and tell what they were capable of doing?

A. I am not a person that can look into other people heads, but I am a person that really liked people and contact with people. That's why I worked in the social field for 10 years, but now----

Q. You told the government that you don't want to be around people now because you can't see what someone else can do, correct?

A. With strange or foreign people rather.

Q. Before the 22nd of August, you also could not see what strange people were capable of doing, could you?

A. That's true, but I answered the question already.

Q. Prior to 24 August 2008, how often did you have dating relationships?

A. Always again.

Q. Now and again?

A. Every three months. What do you mean by "date"? Did you mean a date or do you mean a relationship?

Q. The government asked you about a dating relationship.

A. My last relationship was in 2007.

Q. Do you judge all people in a group by the actions of a single person?

A. I try not to do that. I also try not to think the same of all Americans, but it's very difficult because of what happened to me.

Q. So you do judge all people in a group by the actions of a single person?

ATC: Objection, asked and answered, Your Honor.

MJ: I'll allow the answer.

A. I did answer the question already.

Q. Do you judge all soldiers by the action of a single soldier?

A. No. The husband of my girlfriend is a soldier.

Q. You commented that there are pubs where Americans go and that you're scared to go to those pubs. Is that what you're saying?

A. Partially, but I will go in with friends so that I will lose my fear.

Q. So you do still have a social life?

A. My friends I still have, yes--and my family.

Q. The people who have been sitting here with you for the past three days, correct?

A. Also, yes. I mean my immediate circle of friends.

Q. You told us when you testified before that you had been in therapy from December of '08 to June of '09 absent three weeks of vacation, correct?

A. That's correct.

Q. Are you still in therapy?

A. No.

Q. You said that in July you moved to the Allgaeu for work, correct?

A. That is correct.

Q. And you are still working there?

A. Yes.

CDC: Thank you, Your Honor. No further questions.
MJ: Government?
ATC: Yes, Your Honor.

**REDIRECT EXAMINATION**
**Questions by the assistant trial counsel:**

Q. Ms. Heinrich, who referred you--who told you that you should get an attorney?
A. The counseling place has told me that.
Q. And what type of counseling place is that?
A. THAMAR--that's a counseling place for people that suffer from sexual attacks or sexual violence.
Q. Was it your idea to get an attorney or was it Thamar's?
A. They advised me of it.
Q. What about the polizei, did they tell you anything about getting an attorney?
A. They said it was advisable, yes.
Q. And who paid for this attorney?
A. The government pays in Germany in case of murder of rape, that's what was explained to me.
Q. Did you have a conversation with me last night after midnight regarding what----
CDC: Objection, Your Honor, improper questioning, improper leading, advising the panel--the witness of evidence not in evidence--just a totally improper way to ask a question on direct.
ATC: Your Honor, this goes to the defense questioning regarding what she was told regarding what offenses he was found guilty of. They refer to----
MJ: Okay. Then just ask her that.
Q. Were you told about what offenses the accused was found guilty of?
A. Yes. That's right.

Q. Were you told that Sergeant Stewart was convicted of aggravated sexual assault for placing his fingers inside your vagina?

A. I only know about the oral sex, the anal sex, the kidnapping, and the assault.

Q. That's all you can recall?

A. I can't remember anything, I mean, it was a lot of different impressions last night. I can only recall that of the straight-out rape he was found not guilty.

ATC: No further questions, Your Honor.

CDC: No redirect [sic], Your Honor.

MJ: Panel members, any questions.

**[All members indicated negative responses.]**

MJ: Permanent or temporary?

ATC: Permanent excusal, Your Honor.

**[The witness was duly warned, permanently excused, and took a seat in the gallery.]**

TC: Your Honor, the government calls Colonel Smith.

CDC: Your Honor, the defense does not believe that R.C.M. 1004--1001(a)(4) permits this testimony.

**[Pause.]**

CDC: I'm sorry. B, Your Honor, (B)(4).

MJ: You're talking specifically about evidence in aggravation?

CDC: Yes, Your Honor.

MJ: I read it as stating includes but is not limited to evidence of financial, social, psychological, and medical impact. What are you saying falls outside that scope?

CDC: We do not believe that this witness will be able to talk about that specifically with regard to this witness. We believe it to be more generic and therefore hypothetical or prospectively possible as opposed to directly relating.

MJ: Well, Trial Counsel, any information brought out from the witness has to apply directly to, obviously, the victim. Do you understand that?

TC: Yes, Your Honor.

MJ: Continue on. If there is an objection made on the question or answer, Defense, you are entitled to object.

**Following Heinrich's testimony, Colonel Smith was recalled as a witness for the government. While under direct examination by Captain Bashore, he faced questions about the accused woman's mental health and the likelihood that her delay in reporting the alleged attack by Stewart was due to Post-Traumatic Stress Disorder. Asked to provide specifics of her symptoms, the colonel offered the following:**

The traumatic experience and her response to the experience meets criteria one for PTSD that I mentioned before and then the nightmares that she described pertaining to the assault. She talked about avoiding certain things, certain places because of fear. She described some anxiety symptoms that she gets when she's in certain situations that remind her of either soldiers or being around other people. She mentioned that she isolates herself because she doesn't trust to be around some people that she doesn't know, people that are not her close friends. She talked about her social life--how her social life is affected and her ability to have relationships--significant--to develop a significant relationship, especially with men.

**Questions by the civilian defense counsel followed:**

Q. Doctor, you spoke with her for two to three hours a couple of months ago and then you have watched her in trial, correct?

A. Correct.

Q. And you did not look at her medical records for the treatment she had in 2004, 2005, correct?

A. Correct.

Q. So you don't know if she had PTSD symptoms back then, do you?

A. Correct.

Q. You know that she has been in treatment--psychotherapeutic treatment from December to June, approximately--December '08--June '09, correct?

A. Correct.

Q. And you know she completed that treatment according to her own testimony, correct?

A. Correct.

Q. Isn't completing treatment something which acts affirmatively to diffuse PTSD?

A. Well, completing--ending treatment and completing treatment are two separate things. People--from my experience, people that have PTSD sometimes can stop coming to their appointments. It doesn't mean that they are effectively treated.

Q. All right. Doctor, she indicated she finished her treatment. Okay? We may play words about whether she stopped going or completed; but if one ends treatment and does not continue with other treatment, isn't that an indication that the person believes he or she is treated?

A. It's possible.

Q. Thank you. All the symptoms she described were just that, self-described symptoms, correct?

A. Correct.

Q. Do you have any concrete evidence to support nightmares?

A. No.

Q. Did you talk to anybody who lived with her that said she wakes up in the middle of the night screaming?
A. No. I did not.

Not surprisingly, the trial counsel's single question during redirect tried to counter the defense's intent to show Heinrich's PTSD had been "cured." When Captain Bashore asked the colonel to answer whether or not PTSD is a short-term or lifelong type of problem, the defense objected and Judge Kuhfahl sustained that objection.

After Colonel Smith stepped down, the defense recalled Sergeant First Class Greg Settle to the witness stand.

Asked what kinds of things Stewart did that impressed him, Sergeant Settle said spoke volumes.

"First of all, he has always been knowledgeable on topics in which we train our students in," he said. "If I ever had a question, he would probably be the first person I would go to in order to get an accurate answer.

"He is an excellent wingman as far as accomplishing missions, as far as getting training done, making sure things are ready to role because we do work in a somewhat difficult environment given the nature of the NATO background and the difference between countries and how they choose to go about business. So it's always good to have a reliable person at your, you know--next to you.'

Asked if he would want Stewart on his team if he was to go into combat, the sergeant said he would.

"I know what he's capable of," Sergeant Settle explained. "I know of some of the things that he has done downrange in very, very tight situations and that is a characteristic that you don't find in everybody, even in Special Forces—in operators across the board. He is among the best and second to none."

Sergeant Settle's testimony ended with him answering, "Definitely," to a question about whether he thinks Stewart had "rehabilitation potential."

Command Sergeant Major Klein was recalled as a witness and answered several questions via which he provided a powerful character reference for Stewart.

In addition to the courtroom testimony, panel members reviewed information about the accused soldier as they considered their sentencing options. It came in the form of a packet, commonly referred to by soldiers as a "Good Soldier Book," that contained 76 separate documents attesting to his noteworthy accomplishments while in the Army. In addition, it contained dozens of letters written on his behalf by family members, friends and colleagues.

At 2:23 p.m., Judge Kuhfahl gave everyone in the courtroom a break until 3 p.m. At that time, the final stage of the sentencing phase would begin. In addition to his individual freedom, all of Stewart's pay, benefits and other allowances were on the table.

Judge Kuhfahl admonished panel members to take their work seriously:

> Members of the court, you are about to deliberate and vote on the sentence in this case. It is the duty of each member to vote for a proper sentence for the offenses of which the accused has been found guilty. Your determination of the kind and amount of punishment, if any, is a grave responsibility requiring the exercise of wise discretion. Although you must give due consideration to all matters in mitigation and extenuation, as well as to those in aggravation, you must bear in mind that the accused is to be sentenced only for the offenses of which he has been found guilty.

Afterward, Judge Kuhfahl delivered instructions orally that were backed up by paper copies of the same. Among their options, according to the judge, was this: "...if you wish, this court may sentence the accused to no punishment."

**Final arguments followed, beginning with those of the government's Captain O'Malley which appear below as taken from the Record of Trial:**

ATC: President of the court, members of the panel, this case is about the violent rape of a young, German girl.

CDC: Objection, Your Honor. He was acquitted of rape.

MJ: Sustained. Counsel, he was not convicted of that offense.

ATC: Yes, Your Honor--violent forcible sodomy of a young, German girl. This is not a case of a simple misunderstanding of two consenting adults going home and there being a mistake or some kind of misunderstanding as to consent. That is not why we are here today. This case was about violence--about brutal, sexual violence perpetuated on the victim, Ms. Heinrich.

Sergeant Stewart used his size, his muscle, and his mind to help him commit these crimes against Ms. Heinrich. His crimes totally demeaned, dehumanized, embarrassed, and destroyed the person Ms. Heinrich was as she entered that hotel room. She discussed how she's a new person now, that the person that entered that room no longer exists because of what Sergeant Stewart did to her. She is building a new identity, a new person. She's changed her appearance. She's changed her hair. She's changed her behavior because of his actions, because of his violence and what he did.

Everything Sergeant Stewart did was to break her down, both physically and mentally. He struck her with his hands in the face, head, all of the parts of the body. He forcefully rammed his penis inside her anus. He forced her head down to his genitalia and then forced his penis inside her mouth. He probed her vagina with his fingers. That is what he did to that young woman. Every major orifice were [sic] violated in some means, in some manner--incredible force by Sergeant Stewart.

He took total control. Once they stepped foot outside the See-Studio, Sergeant Stewart took control. Right when they got in the taxi cab he took control--talking incessantly, telling the taxi driver where to go, drowning out what she wanted to do; but he was also placating her saying, "You're beautiful. You're so pretty," so she would not react so much to this ride completely away from where they were supposed to go--completely away from her house.

Once they got outside the Marriot, again Sergeant Stewart was using his mind. He convinced her, "We're just going in to pick something up," so he convinced her inside the hotel. Once inside the hotel, they are outside the room. She still does not want to enter; but he convinced her again, "Don't worry. I am a real man. You have nothing to worry about." Then she enters that room, that door closes, and that Greta Heinrich never appeared again from that room. A different woman emerged that next morning from that hotel room.

Everything that happened in that hotel room after that door closed was calculated and with the proper means of beating down Greta Heinrich, beating down her will to resist, beating down the person who she was. It started off with a strike to her head [hitting left palm with right fist]. Once he convinced her to stay, right in to forcible anal sodomy. She was in so much pain you heard she couldn't even move. She couldn't even do anything. What does the accused do then? He forces her face down onto his penis to give him oral sex, forces his fingers inside her vagina.

You heard that she made him--he made her feel like scum. She was ashamed and embarrassed of all the brutal sexual violations of her body, and she felt dirty by what he did. Sergeant Stewart took everything from her that night.

You've heard Colonel Smith talk about how she has the symptoms of PTSD. Ms. Heinrich said her relationships with men are different--her relationship with her friends--where she goes out--who she is. Everything has changed. Something as simple as a choice of whether to have short hair or long hair has now been taken away from her because she said she will never let anyone use her hair against her again, so now she has short hair. You saw her hair--how short it is. Every aspect of her life has been affected.

Now, the judge has mentioned several sentencing factors or principles that you should consider when crafting your sentence. I will briefly go through each of those. The first is punishment of the wrongdoer. Sergeant Stewart deserves to be punished for his brutal sexual acts. He has forever changed Ms. Heinrich's life. Now it is time for his life to be forever changed. He violated our code. His heinous actions scream out for punishment, scream out for justice. Ms. Heinrich has screamed out for justice. There must be justice. There must be a reckoning for his actions--for the brutal violence. As I said, this is not a case of a simple misunderstanding between two adults as to consent or maybe there was too much alcohol involved. This was control. This was planned. This was incredibly violent. A severe punishment is required--a long term in confinement.

Another principle is specific deterrence. Specific deterrence is the principle that what sentence can this court craft that would specifically deter Sergeant Stewart from ever doing the same or similar offenses again. A strong sentence can teach Sergeant Stewart a lesson. You have heard the testimony of his actions that night. He didn't care. He didn't have a thought for her. To get through to that type of person you must have a long term in confinement, a reduction to E-1, a total forfeiture of all pay, and a dishonorable discharge. Anything other than a strong message, a strong sentence will not reach Sergeant Stewart.

He treated her as less than human. He took what he wanted without a care for how it affected her physically and how it would affect her mentally for the rest of her life.

Now, protection of society from the wrongdoer--another sentencing principle--society must be protected from a brutal, violent rapist.

CDC: Objection, Your Honor.

ATC: Excuse me, brutal, violent sodomist.

MJ: Sustained.

ATC: Excuse me. Sergeant Stewart is a danger to society. He's a danger to his fellow soldiers. He's a danger to Army families.

CDC: Objection, Your Honor. There's no evidence he is a danger to soldiers--none. It's not even a proper inference.

ATC: Your Honor, the facts before the courts are--is that he's committed brutal, violent acts against another person.

MJ: Panel, I advise you to remember the facts as you remember them and to apply whatever inference you think needs to be applied to those facts in determining your sentence.

ATC: Sergeant Stewart is a danger to women in general. Society, especially women, must be protected from this type of action. A long term of confinement will do that.

General deterrence and preservation of good order and discipline are two more of the sentencing principles. General deterrence is what sentence can this court craft that will send a message to the Army community as a whole that this type of crime or similar crime is not allowed. Only a strong sentence--long term of confinement and a dishonorable discharge--that will be recognized by the military community. A reduction to E-1, a total forfeiture of all pay--the military community understands what that means. This will send a message--not in our Army. Brutal sexual violence against women is not allowed in the Army.

Not only is that the general deterrence message, but that will assist in the preservation of good order and discipline inside the force--that every soldier that hears of this strong sentence will know that's not allowed. There is a line, and you can't cross it. If you do cross it, you face severe punishment.

Finally, rehabilitation of the accused--of the wrongdoer--these brutal acts of violence that he has perpetrated on Ms. Heinrich--penetrating her different orifices without a care, without a thought for her--make it appear very difficult or a low probability that he can rehabilitate himself from these actions, but this court's sentence can assist him in that process of rehabilitation. An extended period in confinement where Sergeant Stewart can sit in his cell, think about what he did, reflect on his actions, reflect on who he is, who he was, and who he should be--away from all the distractions of the world, everything else--he has himself in there to decide who he is, what he did, what he did to the victim, Ms. Heinrich, how he has forever changed her life, and then he can think about what he can do for himself to possibly come back from the edge of the cliff of that brutal, sexual, violent sodomist that we heard the evidence here today.

Because of the nature of these crimes, their brutal nature, the effect on the victim, how they were perpetrated--with plan, with intent, and with such a high level of violence--the government asks for sentence of confinement of 15 years, a dishonorable discharge, a reduction to Private E-1, and a total forfeiture of all pay and allowances.

Thank you.

**Waiting until after the assistant trial counsel finished, Judge Kuhfahl offered the following advice to panel members:**

Members, to the extent that government counsel may have indicated that the accused was convicted of rape or was a "rapist," those references were completely improper. As I am sure you know, the accused was acquitted of those offense; and your duty in this sentence proceeding is to determine an appropriate sentence only for those offenses which you have found him guilty.

**Defense counsel Court delivered his closing argument next:**

CDC: Colonel Denny, members of the court, the government just got up here and gave you a very impassioned argument for a particular sentence. As the military judge will tell you, that recommendation is the recommendation only of a single counsel. It does not mean that that is what is appropriate. One could even suspect that that argument, given it's obvious mis-references, as the judge just told you, was probably written out and planned long ago. It may not have anything really to do with what your conclusions were.

The defense, however, does not believe it has the luxury of coming up here and saying "x" is an appropriate punishment. Why? Because, as you know, there are various types of punishment possible and no matter what the defense were to suggest in one particular area, one of you might be thinking of doing less; and so I've asked you to harm my client, which I cannot do. I don't have that luxury.

I can only--the defense can only talk to you, as did the government, about the principle reasons for sentencing. There are the five. The four types of punishment that you have, which can be broken down into basically job, in or out of the service, position, rank, financial, and freedom--those types of punishments. And add to that mix the three--the triumvirate of lodestars that the military judge will talk about--that is, the sentence should address the ends of good order and discipline, the needs of the accused, and the welfare of society. And try and take all of those things, mixing and matching and figuring out what's appropriate.

Given your lengthy deliberations last night, I almost hesitate to make this comment, but then you had the easier choice. It was yes or no--nine different times, lesser included but nonetheless yes or no. Now you each individually have to decide on a scale from no punishment, as the military judge told you could be proper, all the way up to the maximum taking each of those steps in between.

Talking about the reasons for a sentence, we use a sequence the government walked through. Punishment of the wrongdoer, members of the panel--because of his actions and your findings Sergeant First

Class Kelly Stewart now has federal felony convictions for five serious sexual offenses. Nothing is going to change that, unless he can find enough money to buy a pardon in the future. He has now those five convictions, which will stay with him for the rest of his life, which will affect his employability, which will affect every aspect of his life. It may affect his ability to go fishing and use a knife to cut bait, to have firearms, to vote. Please do not misunderstand. The defense is not suggesting that federal convictions are punishment. They are not. They are society's recognition of wrong doing, but they have criminal aspects of which you all are aware. And they stay with you.

In addition, because of the nature of these offenses and what you all know from the paper you can easily conclude that some or all of these will require registration as a sex offender for the rest of his life.

ATC: Objection, Your Honor. The government requests an instruction on jury nullification regarding felony and sexual assault registration.

MJ: Jury nullification applies to findings, so what exactly are you talking about?

ATC: Your Honor, it's goes to sentences--that these things have already been imposed, therefore, no punishment is necessary--or may be potential ramifications of these trial, therefore, no punishment--further punishment is necessary.

MJ: Panel members, where there may be some disagreement or confusion between the recommendations of counsel and the instructions I have given you, you will follow my instructions as I have given them to you.

Are there any questions about that?

**[All panel members indicated negative responses.]**

MJ: Apparently not. Please continue.

CDC: Thank you, Your Honor.

The defense would only point out that no punishment is an authorized punishment. I am not certain what the objection was; but, in any event, what the defense is saying is the fact that he has been convicted of these sexual offenses will cause those defects. And we ask you to consider those, again, not as punishment but as punitive effects because they will have very long term effects on him. Everywhere he goes he will register as an offender.

How much more punishment is needed for the sake of punishment? The government says, effectively, he needs to be punished as retribution for what he did to Ms. Heinrich. Now, retribution is not listed as one of the reasons for a sentence, so the government is there trying to slide in hurt him because he hurt her as a retribution.

Specific deterrence, that is, deter him from doing this ever again. All right. That is a valid consideration and should be given its due weight; but, as a practical matter, there is no way to guarantee at any time that any offender will not re-offend short of capital punishment and we fortunately aren't there. As a practical matter, you could sentence someone to life and he could still, in that confinement facility, reoffend; so what you have is the government saying for specific deterrence send a message to him, teach him a lesson. Okay. You need to do that. The question becomes what will teach him that lesson, and that's what you have to determine.

Knowing what you know about the offenses, about what he was convicted of, what he was not convicted of is to the side, and about him as a person, something the person totally ignored--you know a lot about Kelly A. Stewart. You heard about him from Major Grow a few nights ago, from Sergeant Major Klein, and Sergeant First Class Settle. They've told you about the Kelly A. Stewart they know; and in addition to that, you'll have some heavy reading [holding up DE A].

Defense Exhibit A is a packet commonly known as a good soldier book about Sergeant First Class Stewart. Defense Exhibit A is here. Because of its size and the number of panel members there are two other copies to be used around to speed up your review. That will tell you much more about Kelly A. Stewart and give you a better picture of who this person is who in a four hour period on one night in his life did criminal misconduct for which you have convicted him and figure out based on that what needs to be done to deter him from doing it again.

Protect society--that's a buzz word for put him in jail--fair enough. Obviously, this is an offense that affected a member of the German community--one time, one night. You have no evidence that it's anything but that. The government implies that he is going to go do this again when they say put him away for a long time so he can't do it again. There's no real basis to believe it will happen again. However, for deterrence of him there may be a reason to put him in confinement. Again, the government is trying to argue protect society, put him away, he's a danger to society. Where is the evidence before you of anything like recidivism? Where is there anyone who's going to say Kelly Stewart is likely to do this again? There isn't. There's just the opposite.

There is evidence of his ability to be rehabilitated. Those people who knew him longer and better than anyone else in this room said he has rehab potential again. I would serve with him again. I trust him again.

I want to work with him again--Command Sergeant Major Klein, Sergeant First Class Settle.

The ends of good order and discipline and general deterrence--general deterrence is normally the send a message kind of thing--tell everybody what happens when you do it. Okay. There is some benefit to that. That makes sense. However, how is that going to occur? How is that going to occur with your sentence? At most, Stars and Stripes will put it in an article at most; and it will be read, maybe, one time by people who don't know the facts, who just know the conclusion and know the sentence. How will that deter people from this conduct if they don't know what it was?

Second point, once it's read the paper goes into the old paper pile and the memory goes out the window because in a week no one is going to remember that anymore. Even if each of you chose to go back to your respective units and put it out in formation, the defense would probably be willing to wager a fair amount of money that in a month no one is going to remember what that was all about; so this general deterrence idea is not really smart. Besides, there's a fundamental, philosophical, logical flaw in general deterrence because people who commit offenses don't expect to get caught or they wouldn't do it. So how do you deter someone who doesn't expect to get caught by telling what happens if he does get caught? General deterrence is probably not a good argument for any kind of particular sentence.

Preservation of good order and discipline--same kind of problem with that. How are you going to make sure that this is known for the preservation of good order and discipline in the future? Don't get the defense wrong. We're not saying well, gee, because you can't do anything don't give him any punishment.

All we are trying to do is ask you to analyze the reasons for punishment so you can understand what effect your sentence will have in fulfilling any of those.

The government put it last, rehabilitation potential, because that's the really positive thing in the whole batch--to fix him and make him be a productive member of society; and when we speak of society, members of the panel, please, remember we are dealing with two separate societies--two societies--one, the military society of which you are all members and he is currently, and the second is the civilian society to which he will return at some point unless you give him life without the possibility of parole which is not what the government is asking which is really excessive in this case.

At some point he will return to civilian society, so we also have to consider his rehabilitation in that society, his ability to function in that society. And there one has to recall that he will come into that society with conviction, registration, probably bad paper if you choose to discharge him, and the label of a con. And if you do what the government says and sentence him to 15 years, he will be over 50 years old at that point. How is he going to function in society; how is he going to be able to do anything in the civil society? What will that sentence do for his rehabilitation in that society? If you think it will, then you should do that; but we ask you to consider that long term consideration when you decide what is appropriate for the ends of good order and discipline, the needs of the accused, and the welfare of both societies.

Obviously, you have the wide range discussed. You have evidence before you of the type of person he is from Prosecution Exhibit 1, his ERB. You can learn, as you already know, that he is married. He has two children. Obviously, your sentence will affect them.

We ask that you merely consider that not as any kind of excuse but just in keeping in mind your sentence does not only affect him. It has larger ramifications.

As stated, you have lots of options. Will a long period of confinement serve those ends we discussed? The defense submits the government is requesting too much, but we can't tell you what is right because we don't know. We are not the triers of fact. We don't know, for example, how you, either collectively or individually, concluded kidnapping had been proved, whether you concluded that kidnapping was inveigling into the car, whether the kidnapping was keeping her in the hotel room, or a bit of both. We just don't know which is why we can't tell you what you should think, regardless of the government's own position.

You should also, of course, consider how the evening developed. Please don't misunderstand this argument. The defense is not blaming Ms. Heinrich for what happened, but it usually takes two people to make a criminal misconduct. And if her habits have changed, one would hope that the habit of going with strangers to hotel rooms has also changed. The whole evening developed and ended in four hours, and those four hours of his life are in your hands for determination as to the future. You've heard from her the affect it had on her, but you also heard from her that she doesn't really accept your complete findings. She believes you were wrong. She didn't want to say that. She says, "I accept it, but I know what happened." That's the same thing as saying, "They're wrong. He did do those things of which he's been acquitted." And so when you analyze her testimony in terms of what it means to you in sentencing, please, keep that in mind.

That's where she's coming from in her argument. She hasn't accepted. She says it; it's pretty easy to say, but she doesn't really accept your findings. She thinks you're wrong. She thinks it's much worse than you said it was; and accordingly, her reaction is much worse than to what you found him guilty by the same percentage. Please keep that in mind in coming up with your sentence which, the defense believes, will be the fair sentence that a conscience of the community, which you represent, should be but it will not be to send him away for as long as the government says.

Final point--when thinking about loss of liberty, be it restriction, hard labor without confinement, or confinement--when thinking of those things, please, don't fall into the trap of thinking in terms of years because then you have small numbers. Please think in terms of the way people live, day-to- day. "How short are you?" "Twenty-four and a wake-up." Think about your liberty limitation, if you choose to give any, in the concept of days. Okay? You can sentence a person in days. You'd make a large number of days. You can sentence a person to 365 days, which is one year. You can multiply it out. The government is asking for well over 15,000 days. Sorry. I did the math wrong. You can do the math if you choose.

My point is think in terms of the way people live if you decide to limit liberty. You all have been downrange. You know what I am talking about--how long you got left--you know what a short-timer's calendar is. When you think about it remember too that each day will be a day--if it's adjudged in confinement--will be a day waking up in a cell, not being able to do what you want, go where you want, eat what you want, see what you want. Each day is under control. That's why we have confinement so that people are made to think about things, as the government pointed out; and that's the purpose of it.

> But think about how many days it will take to do that. If you feel that 15 times 365 is the right number, then do that; but it you think that 1,000 days for 4 hours is reasonable, then you can say that. If you think 2,000 or 5--pick a number that you think is appropriate for Sergeant First Class Stewart, the offenses you found him guilty of, the ends of good order and discipline, and the welfare of society.
>
> Thank you.

After Court finished, Judge Kuhfahl offered some final pre-sentencing instructions and asked panel members if they had any questions those instructions. Noteworthy among the handful of questions asked was one posed by Sergeant First Class John Alam.

"When determining the sentence," he asked, "are we determining the sentence based off a fact that he is guilty because he has been charged?"

"You are to sentence the accused on the offenses of which you found him guilty in yesterday's closed session deliberations," Judge Kuhfahl replied. "By the court's calculations, that was one specification of aggravated sexual assault, one specification of kidnapping, two specifications of forcible sodomy, and one specification of assault and--assault consummated by battery. You are not to sentence the accused on any other offense for which he was charged which this panel ultimately acquitted the accused of."

The military judge asked Sergeant Alam if his response answered his question satisfactorily, and the sergeant said it did not.

"I understand that he's--what I--I guess, collectively if the group decided that Sergeant First Class Stewart was guilty of that charge, then we--then I would determine my vote off of the collective decision that he was guilty," Sergeant Alam said. "Suppose, hypothetically, I said--I was one of the voters to say, 'No. I don't think he was guilty.' Do I take that into consideration as I determine what his sentence should be or should I just determine that Sergeant First Class Stewart is charged--he's guilty and now I make the determination based off of that?"

"Whether or not he has been charged is irrelevant for your consideration," Judge Kuhfahl replied. "The fact that he has been found guilty of the offenses----is a relevant consideration. Whether or not you particularly voted on a finding of guilty or not guilty is a consideration that you alone may consider."

After a handful of other questions were asked and answered, panel members were reminded of their duties and released to begin their deliberations behind closed doors at 4:10 p.m. on August 20, 2009.

Meanwhile, other arguments were made in the court of public opinion.

In a *Stars & Stripes* article published on the day of sentencing, Detective Lorch expressed his views about Stewart's status in no uncertain terms:

> *"He should have had a guard. He was found guilty last night," Lorch said. "Under German law, we would have thrown him in jail from the beginning and brought him to court in handcuffs. Here he walks around as a free man. He's found guilty, and he walks out the door. It's ridiculous."*

Stewart's accuser had her say in the same article.

> *"He's an angry animal and not a human," said the 29-year-old victim, standing outside the Vilseck courthouse Thursday morning after learning he had disappeared. "I* know how dangerous he is. It's impossible to believe that they left him alone last night."

Members of the court-martial panel, however, reached their conclusion without reading that article.

One hour and 16 minutes later, the panel had finished its work. Members of the panel returned to the courtroom, the court was called to order and, per Judge Kuhfahl's direction, Lieutenant Colonel Denny announced the sentence to the court:

PRES: This court-martial sentences Sergeant First Class Kelly A. Stewart:

To be reduced to the grade of E-1;
To forfeit all pay and allowances;
To be confined for eight years; and
To be dishonorably discharged from the service.

# Day Three: 'I Wasn't Going to be That Dog'

"So, they find me guilty. It's late at night. In an instant, my whole life got flushed right down the toilet," said Stewart, recalling the verdict that changed his life just before midnight on August 19, 2009. "I am smart enough to know that my life is screwed. The rest of my life. No matter what. My life is done.

"Clearly, I felt that I was shafted, and I knew there was no way to fix it," he explained. "This is an analogy I use. It might come across as messed up, but this is my analogy, and this is why I chose to do what I did.

"I was not going to have everybody do prison time with me," said Stewart, recalling his thoughts after a court-martial panel found him guilty of sex crimes against a German woman and handed down a sentence that included a reduction in rank, from E-7 to E-1, forfeiture of all pay and allowances, eight years of confinement and a recommendation for dishonorable discharge upon release.

"I wasn't going to go to prison and have my kids have to go through having their dad in prison and my wife having to stand by my side and go without a husband for years—and, at that time, I didn't know the length of the years," said Stewart, a Special Forces combat medic and Level One-trained sniper. "I didn't know the length of my sentence; I just knew that I was found guilty."

That's when he made a decision.

"I never thought I was going to prison," Stewart said. "When I got back after (being convicted), I had a reality check in the hotel room" at the Krystal Inn, the on-post hotel where he was staying near the court building where his trial was taking place at Rose Barracks in Vilseck, Germany.

About the only plans he made took place during the last intermission in the courtroom before his guilty verdict was announced. After calling his wife and telling her he wouldn't be coming home soon, Stewart also called his military-friendly bank, USAA, and transferred all of the money in his account into his wife's account.

"I already knew what I was gonna do," he recalled.

Back in their room at the Krystal Inn, Stewart and his buddy, Sergeant First Class Detrick Hampton, laid in their beds and talked most of the night until Sergeant Hampton fell asleep around 5 a.m. Less than an hour later, Stewart began to implement his hastily-crafted plan.

Careful not to wake Sergeant Hampton, Stewart got up out of his bed about an hour later, put on his Army Combat Uniform and low-quarter shoes and collected a few items—including a combat knife and a rubber band—he thought he might need. Oddly, he left his black Army jump boots in the room.

Quietly, he walked out of his second-floor room at the Krystal Inn where, even after he was found guilty, he was not kept under guard—an indication, perhaps, that some in the Army still didn't think he was as dangerous as the charges, eventual conviction and news media coverage of his case might have indicated. He had, after all, never been deemed a danger to others or a flight risk.

Because he had not planned to go away for a long time, Stewart didn't prepare by gathering lots of clothes, money and 16 passports. Instead, he ensured only that he had enough money for gas to go where he needed to go to take his own life. And with three combat tours in Iraq and other stints in Kosovo and Macedonia under his belt, he knew enough about medicine to make it happen.

Once outside the hotel room, Stewart walked the short distance to a staircase in the center of the building, down a single flight of stairs and through an open-air hallway out to the parking lot where his rental car, an Audi Q5, was parked.

He drove the SUV a short distance to the Shoppette—the name the Army and Air Force Exchange Service gives its convenience stores located on military installations—where he purchased a laundry list of items: three 50-count bottles of Tylenol caplets, one 72-count package of Sominex tablets, two 16-ounce bottles of Gatorade Riptide Rush, some writing paper and a couple of pencils.

"I thought about how other people have killed themselves, and they generally either hurt or make a display for other people, but I didn't want to do is be found dead somewhere where some kid was gonna see me (and) I didn't want to get drunk and drive down the road and do something irresponsible where I could injure someone else or another family," he said. Instead, he tried to pick an out-of-the-way place close by, in the woods, where he knew only an adult would find him. In the end, he opted for a wooded park area at a nearby training range.

After leaving the Shoppette, he knew he had to reach his destination by 6:30 a.m., the time at which the perimeter road that encircled two Army posts and the training range in between them would close so troops could use it for physical training (i.e., "PT").

Immediately after pulling off the road and parking his car near a trail, Stewart drank about a fourth of the contents of each Gatorade bottle. Next, he used the flat surface of a tree stump and the flat edge of a large combat knife to methodically crush 150 Tylenol tablets (500 mg) and 50 Sominex tablets. Finally, he scooped the now-powdered medicines into the bottles and shook them up.

From his experience in hospital emergency rooms, he knew the crushed tablets, when swallowed, would have a much more toxic effect than coated tablets designed to reach the stomach before their contents were released. In addition, the sleep medicine would simply make it easier for him to endure his passage from life to death.

Next, he used a 12-foot length of CAT-5 cable that he had had in his room at the Krystal Inn to make a hangman's noose on an A-frame-style deer stand he found in the woods only a kilometer or two away from the court building.

"I measured the CAT-5 so my feet wouldn't touch the ground," Stewart explained. "There was a base I could stand on to get my neck in the noose, but the base was high enough that, when I passed out, my feet wouldn't touch the ground."

At one point before he put the noose to work, a German forest marshal working on the German-American post drove by, saw Stewart in his vehicle and exchanged pleasantries with him. Upon learning from Stewart that he was "just waiting on doing some training here," the forest marshal drove away.

In retrospect, Stewart said, "I think that was my divine intervention, telling me, 'Don't do it, stupid.'" But he didn't listen.

As soon as the forest marshal left, around 9:15 a.m., Stewart began consuming the drink in a process he compared to a Selection event—one of the grueling steps he survived en route to the SF Qualification Course. In other words, consuming the drink—and keeping it down—was very difficult.

Trying to hold it down was difficult. Every once in a while, he found himself throwing it back up into the bottle, because it burned so much on the way down.

"Everybody says, 'I'm gonna kill myself," he said, "but, to really do it and be successful is an event in itself."

Why Tylenol, Sominex and Gatorade? It was part of his plan.

"In SF, we have this acronym called a PACE plan—Primary, Alternate, Contingency and Emergency. Everything that we do has a four-step plan in there...a redundancy thing...

"I had a PACE plan, but it wasn't very good," he said, noting the fact that he had survived.

"The Tylenol was, I guess, the primary thing," he said, explaining that he had seen enough Tylenol overdoses in emergency rooms to know that it was an effective, but very painful technique.

"The alternate was the sleeping medicine."

"The CAT-5 cable was the contingency."

Consuming the toxic cocktail took close to 40 minutes.

"Basically, when I started feeling myself get drowsy, I knew it was time and kind of stood up in this little A-frame deer stand, and I had the CAT-5 cable," Stewart said. "I had it double-knotted, and I used a Prusik knot." Similar to a slip knot, it was invented by an Austrian for mountaineering and climbing purposes.

While waiting for the drugs to take effect, Stewart wrote one letter each to his wife and daughters, to his parents and extended family, to members of his SF team, to Judge Kuhfahl and to the members of the court-martial panel. After writing the letters, he put a rubber band around them and placed his Tag Heuer wristwatch, his wedding ring and the money he had had in his pocket on top of them next to his vehicle. Accompanying those items were instructions for whoever found him to make sure the letters were delivered and the watch and ring were returned to his wife.

It was approaching 10:30 a.m., the time the court was set to convene, and Stewart realized people would start looking for him soon. Before he could worry too much about being discovered, however, the drugs began to take effect.

"I get drowsy (and) I realize, 'Hey, it's time,' and said some prayers, because I knew I was gonna black out," he said. "I had to work my way over to where this hangman's noose was, because I had to basically kind of climb a little bit on it so that, when I passed out, (it) would catch me" as the contingency and emergency elements of his PACE plan. That was the last thing he remembered.

When he woke up, it was dark—probably the middle of the night, but he wasn't certain—and he wondered if he was dead. Noticing he had stuff all over himself that hadn't been there before, he realized he was not.

"I don't remember what it was," he said, "but I had stuff all over my face." Including ants.

"I had to remember, 'Oh, I was going through a court-martial.' You know, I was basically having to go through a restart and figure out where the hell I was at."

Stewart had had a similar experience two years earlier in Iraq while serving as the lead gunner on a gun truck during Operation Iraqi Freedom.

In the turret manning the main gun, he was knocked out briefly after his vehicle was struck by an Explosively-Formed Penetrator, a special type of shaped charged designed to penetrate armor effectively at standoff distances. The blast went through another vehicle, which took the brunt of the explosion, as his vehicle was passing it on a road.

"I remember waking up there, feeling like I was in Sleepy Land for a long time (before) realizing, 'Oh, I'm in Iraq, and I'm in a gun truck,' but there was that little restart that I had to go through.

"That's kind of how I felt here. I was restarting. It was dark."

After realizing he had failed in his suicide attempt, he thought to himself, "Oh man, I survived? What am I going to do?"

"I tried standing up and I fell down and landed on my face," he said, explaining that the medicines had left him with virtually no muscular control throughout his body.

"Every time I'd stand up, I'd take two steps and, bam!—I'd fall down on my face (when) I was trying to walk over to where the vehicle was."

Stewart wasn't sure how long it took for him to stand, step and fall his way to the vehicle where he could see what time it is and think of what to do next. Once he made it to the car and turned the dome light on, he realized he had dry blood all over his face, coming out of his nose and mouth. In addition, the noose formed out of the length of blue CAT-5 cable was still hanging around his neck.

"That's really kind of what saved me, I guess," Stewart said, noting that it likely broke when it couldn't support his weight—approximately 178 pounds on a 5-foot, 8-inch frame.

"So then I'm sitting there thinking, 'Man, what do I do now? I need to come up with a plan, because I know everybody's looking for me," he said, noting that he was still "puking a little bit of blood" every few seconds.

Stewart wondered to himself, "What am I going to do?"

The Czech Republic border was some 50 minutes to the east, but Stewart thought officials would be looking for him at border crossings, so he decided he needed to "buy time" and allow the Tylenol to do the job he knew it was going to do.

In 15 years of doing medicine—including working in some major hospital's emergency room each year for the past 12 years—Stewart had seen many Tylenol overdoses, but had never seen someone survive taking an amount as large as the one he had taken. People who survived after having their stomachs pumped did so because the pills they took were in tablet form and had not yet been absorbed by the body. That's why he crushed them and used the electrolyte-based Gatorade to further accelerate the absorption process.

Though concerned about his ability to drive and not wanting to injure anyone else, Stewart decided he would drive until such time as he was too impaired. Passing troops as they began their morning exercise, he followed a perimeter road for about eight miles around the outskirts of the training area until he reached the main gate and drove off the post at Vilseck.

Once he reached the Autobahn, he drove west to Stuttgart and changed vehicles at the Panzer Kaserne Family Housing complex before continuing toward Switzerland. Though he would not elaborate on the source of the second vehicle, a mid-'90s BMW, he did say it wasn't stolen.

"I can tell you, unequivocally, that not one team member, not one guy in the Army helped me do what I did," Stewart said, referring to the change in vehicles. "No one helped me evade."

Border crossings be damned at this point, Stewart decided to enter Switzerland. Once across the border, he phoned his dad, retired Chief Master Sergeant John Stewart, a man with experience working in high-stress scenarios.

"Hey, here's the deal, I don't care what anybody else says, dad, I'm telling you the truth," the younger Stewart told his father, thinking no one would ever believe him because he was found guilty. "I don't feel like I have a chance anymore."

He went on to share with his dad an analogy about a dog.

"People have a dog, and they love that dog, and they take care of that dog," Stewart told his dad. "Over time, that dog gets old and grows with the family and everybody's grown attached to him. At some point, that dog gets old and can't take care of itself. It pees on itself and is kind of laying around.

"As a family, you have to take care of that," he continued. "You pull your carpeting out, because the dog can't control its bowels.

You don't want to put the dog down, because the dog still wags his tail, the dog's still there.

"Periodically, you get this love out of him, but the dog's not living a great life, because it's old and it's just time for the dog to pass.

"The majority of people cannot put that dog down," Stewart continued, "because they don't want to have to put their dog down (and) because they love that dog. Then that dog lives and suffers, and everybody else around that dog suffers, because they have to cater their lives around that dog. You don't go on trips. You don't do all these things."

Stewart told his dad he had made the decision that night that he wasn't going to be that dog and apologized.

"At that point, that was the worst, physically, that I thought I was at, but it actually got worse," Stewart said.

Having seen death on a lot of faces, including sick people and those mortally wounded in combat, Stewart knows what death looks like. He felt as if his time was near. All he was doing was throwing up blood. There was no food and only a little Sprite, in his system. He could no longer eat.

Stewart's throat was so burned from the toxic portion of the Tylenol that, he suspects, he aspirated when he hung himself and that caused blood to come up through his nose.

Fortunately, Stewart's dad wasn't ready to give up on his only son and he started telling him about a lady who had come forward with information about the accuser that had the effect of offering an ever-so-slight glimmer of hope to light Stewart's otherwise-dark world. Her name was Inga Queren.

Queren, a 17-plus-year civilian employee of the U.S. military who had served as the victim/witness liaison during the court-martial, had made a statement to Command Sergeant Major Richard "Spike" Klein that the accuser in the case had perjured herself on the stand and that she (Queren) was willing to make a statement to that effect to the court.

Upon hearing that news from his dad, Stewart called Command Sergeant Major Klein whose plane had just arrived at an airport in England.

"I called his phone and he's like, 'You know, you need to turn yourself in, man,'" Stewart recalled. "'It's the right thing to do. What you're doing is wrong. All you're doing is embarrassing the regiment. That's not the kind of person you are. You don't need to run. I believe you're innocent, and you need to turn yourself in the best way you can, because they're looking for you.'"

Command Sergeant Major Klein told Stewart he didn't want to know where he was, only that he was going to turn himself in. With that knowledge in hand, he told Stewart, he would coordinate with someone to meet him.

"Of course, the Germans really wanted me bad," Stewart said, "and to parade me around in a German police car and make them look good. And I wasn't gonna let that happen."

Without getting into details, Stewart confirmed that he spent more than 40 hours "on the lamb" and used his extensive Special Forces training to avoid capture.

Eventually, however, he drove back to Stuttgart and turned himself in to Sergeant Hampton, the friend who authorities questioned after Stewart disappeared, believing he had helped the convicted soldier escape from the hotel where he was not placed under any sort of confinement or watch. Their rendezvous location, a Volkswagen/Audi dealership, was only a short distance from the entrance to Patch Barracks.

"Spike told me that Detrick was catchin' a lot of heat and that they were berating him for letting me go," Stewart said, "so I made a point to turn myself in to him for nothing more than I felt bad for putting him in that messed-up situation.

"If Detrick had known what I was gonna do, there's no way he was gonna let me do it. Even what I chose to do, I would never let another SF guy go through that willingly. I mean, it's just not going to happen."

Stewart explained that Command Sergeant Major Klein coordinated with officials at the Army Criminal Investigation Division so that he could turn himself in at the checkpoint at Patch Barracks in Stuttgart and, after that, he would be driven directly to the provost marshal's office a half mile past the checkpoint. No guns were drawn. Nothing like that took place.

"It showed me that people had some respect for me early on and that they thought it was kinda bullshit, too," Stewart said.

As soon as he and Sergeant Hampton arrived at the gate at Patch Barracks around 10 p.m. the night of August 22, 2008, the local-hire security guards looked at the soldiers' IDs and waived them through after Detrick explained that he had already talked to the guard's boss and was taking Stewart to the provost marshal's office. That was a sign that it was a well-coordinated operation.

After their vehicle entered the post, a CID car pulled in behind theirs, following them during the half-mile or so to the provost marshal's office, but without flashing lights and sirens or anything else to draw attention to the two-car motorcade.

Once at the provost marshal's office, Stewart was met by a couple of military policemen (MPs).

"No one puts me in handcuffs, there's no rush, no draw," Stewart said, "and they're like, 'Hey, come on in, Sergeant Stewart.'"

Once inside, Stewart walked up to the desk sergeant who was positioned behind a protective glass window, pulled out his I.D. card and said, "My name is Sergeant First Class Kelly Stewart, and I'm here to turn myself in."

## 'Monkey in a Cage'

"There was a lot of speculation that I ran because of my punishment," said Stewart before noting that such speculation was wrong. After all, at the time when he ran, he had not yet learned what his punishment would be. "All I knew was that I had been found guilty."

At the provost marshal's office, Stewart put his wallet in the little tray slot beneath the window and was told someone would be with him in a second. He had just turned himself in after being found guilty of sexual assault of a German woman, fleeing the temporary quarters where he was not staying, and failing in a suicide attempt.

A short while later, a couple of MPs arrived along with the provost marshal, Lieutenant Colonel Shawn Driscoll, who Stewart said apologized to him while explaining that he was just having to do his job.

"Listen, I'm not mad at you man," Stewart said. "Do what you need to do."

After that, the MPs gave Stewart a light pat down and allowed him to tell Sergeant Hampton goodbye before he was taken to a holding cell in the back of the provost marshal's office where he was strip-searched.

The cell was square with bars on one side and a sitting-height concrete slab built into the floor and the wall served as a bed. Having no toilet or sink and no sheets or pillows or anything like a regular long-term cell might have, it was clearly intended for short-term stays (i.e., "the drunk tank").

"It was kind of cold in there. I was shivering from being sick and kind of throwing up there," Stewart said. "Of course, they had a guard on me 24/7."

Showing some compassion, one of the guards brought Stewart a police jacket to use as a blanket.

"They didn't have to do that," he said.

None of the guards assigned to watch Stewart overnight were disrespectful to him, he said.

"No one's really saying anything to me," he said. "I'm kind of like a monkey in a cage at this point."

"The next morning, when it's daylight, two guys from my unit show up," he continued, noting that the pair had been tasked to escort him to the military prison at Mannheim—known officially as the U.S. Army Confinement Facility Europe—and had brought him the uniforms and other items he was required to have while in confinement.

En route to Mannheim in a Mercedes Transit van, Stewart said he was "feeling like crap in there, but I'm not saying anything to anybody."

"When we get to Mannheim, they're barking and yelling at ya, you know," he explained, comparing his new environment to the one new soldiers find at basic training. "Of course, I could care less what they have to say, because, you know, they're just a bunch of young kids yellin' at ya and I don't care, because I'm feeling like trash, and it's getting worse."

After going through an inventory process during which his keepers determined what he could and could not keep, Stewart was signed for—meaning he no longer belonged to his unit, the International Special Training Center—and taken to the Special Housing Unit (a.k.a., "The SHU") of the Level 1 prison.

The SHU is where all new people go when they arrive at Mannheim, usually spending five to 10 days there while being processed and having their levels of custody determined. Most proceed to general population after that, but the Death Row and life-sentence guys stay put.

"I get there, and they put me in a cell. The cell is 6 by 8. It has 144 blocks in it—not that I ever counted it," he said, chuckling. "It's got a sink and a toilet kind of built in there, and they bring you your food three times a day."

Stewart wore an orange jumpsuit while in the SHU, because he was a "max" inmate who was locked down 23 hours a day. His typical meal included ham slices, cabbage, milk, juice and an apple delivered in a little styrofoam container.

Though extremely hungry, Stewart's throat hurt so bad from his acetaminophen overdose that the only thing he could get down was some Kool-Aid, he said. That would turn out to be only one of his health concerns.

While taking a mandatory shower as part of his initial in-processing, a guard assigned to keep an eye on Stewart noticed he was urinating blood and wrote it down in the notes he turned in at the end of his shift. Later the same day, Stewart's life nearly came to an end.

"They've got me under 24 hour observation," he said. "I've got a dude sitting in a chair right outside my cell and, (because) I couldn't eat any of the food, I laid down to go to sleep.

"The next thing I remember is being carried down the long hallway there by a bunch of cops," he explained, adding that he remembers the commandant of the facility being there along with one the senior guard on the shift, an Air Force technical sergeant—first name unknown, last name "Luzinski."

***[Editor's note:** From this point forward, I refer to this sergeant as "Sergeant Luz" (rhymes with ooze)]*

"I've got blood on my orange jumpsuit, so I'm realizing things can't be good," he continued. "They put me into another Mercedes Transit and take me over to a university clinic there in Mannheim. It's a German hospital—one of the better hospitals there... (and) it's a teaching university hospital."

Again feeling like a monkey in a cage due to the orange jumpsuit and an entourage of cops, he said, "The only thing I didn't have was a dolly and a mask like Hannibal Lechter."

While Stewart was in the German hospital, it was impossible for him to use the bathroom while wearing the orange jumpsuit—which opens in the front—and being constrained by a double set of handcuffs, a belly chain and leg restraints. Rather than unshackle him while he went to use the latrine, however, Sergeant Luz got a pair of EMT scissors and cut a hole in the crotch of the jumpsuit so he could urinate. Then he was transported to Landstuhl.

Fluent in German, Stewart was aware that the German doctors and nurses had called for a lot of blood work to find out why his liver was failing and his eyes and skin color were indicating severe jaundice.

"The Germans were telling the cops that I had hepatitis and was diabetic and was having diabetic (symptoms) indicative of kidney failure," Stewart said, "but I didn't meet the requirements of a diabetic." At the same time, however, he exhibited the symptoms of both diabetes and hepatitis but had neither.

Sometime during a conversation between the police officers escorting him at the jail and the folks back at his unit, someone mentioned Stewart had overdosed on aspirin.

The German doctors responded, saying that an aspirin overdose would not produce the symptoms they were seeing. Then one of the cops told the doctors it was acetaminophen, the generic name for Tylenol, and not aspirin. That changed everything.

"Laying down, I remember seeing the 'lightbulb' go on on this doctor's face and realizing that what they had been doing during the last couple hours was wrong.

Panicking because they had eaten up some time, they began hooking up bottles and IVs and then another bad thing happened: Stewart had an allergic reaction to a drug the German doctors used and went into anaphylactic shock.

"(There's) nothing like being double-handcuffed and (having) your feet shackled and strapped to a bed (while) going into anaphylaxis," Stewart said. "I've seen a lot of people go through it, but being conscious and going through it is very difficult.

"It just started off as being real tight in the chest," he continued. "The next thing you know, it felt like somebody put lighter fluid on me and caught me on fire.

"I couldn't breathe at all, and everybody was kind of panicking around me, trying to give me medication to stop what was happening."

Soon, the Germans said they didn't have a doctor who could treat him, that he was probably having liver and kidney failure and was probably going to die. Their message to the American cops: "We need to get him out of here."

"Of course, I'm understanding what the Germans are saying and what they're telling the cops," Stewart said. "They're kind of underhanded, saying, 'We can't treat him here. We need to send him over to Landstuhl,'" the U.S. Army's largest hospital in the Europe.

"What they're saying in German is, 'We need to get him out of here, because he's not going to survive,' and they didn't want that (outcome) in their hospital."

The cops are rushing around trying to figure out what to do and decide to put Stewart in a German ambulance and drive him to Landstuhl Regional Medical Center.

One cop was in the back of the ambulance with Stewart and two paramedics. Another cop was in the front seat of the vehicle. Plus, each of the police vans escorting them—one in front, one behind—was full of regular MPs and prison guards (MPEs), all wearing Army Combat Uniforms, making it hard for Stewart to tell them apart in the condition he was in.

Arriving at Landstuhl surrounded by cops, Stewart once again felt like a monkey in a cage.

"Initially, when everybody shows up and this ambulance shows up, they're thinking it's a wounded soldier, and all of these people are wanting to come out at Landstuhl and help," Stewart said, "and then they realize, you know, it's just a piece-of-shit prisoner. You could just see the disgusted looks on their faces.

"And then, of course, the cops are saying, 'Ah, he's the escaped Special Forces rapist that's in all the newspapers,' so, you know, that's kind of the treatment that you're getting."

From the Emergency Room, Stewart was moved to the intensive-care unit and was put on a steady diet of fluids.

"They were basically treating my symptoms, because there's no quick fix for a Tylenol overdose," he said.

After two days—perhaps more, but Stewart could not recall with certainty—hospital officials decided to send Stewart to

Walter Reed Army Medical Center in Washington, D.C., where he would be treated by doctors specifically trained in dealing with the kinds of liver and kidney issues he had. Unspoken by the same hospital officials, however, was the likelihood that no one at the hospital relished having an SF soldier convicted of sex crimes in their midst.

One person, however, ensured Stewart received good care at Landstuhl. He was the SF liaison at Landstuhl whose job it was to assist sick or wounded SF members and their relatives.

"The guy that was there knew me from Special Forces and treated me with great respect," Stewart explained, adding that the same level of respect was extended to his wife and kids, arranging for them to have a place to stay, etc.

"To this day, what they did for my family was just awesome and shows that I still have their loyalty."

Stewart went on to describe the scene as he was loaded into a bus converted into an ambulance that would transport him to a nearby airfield for his medevac flight back to the United States.

Upon seeing him in cuffs and shackles, the 30 to 40 people assembled near the hospital's exit had excited looks on their faces, thinking they were about to load a wounded hero into the back of a "mercy" bus. Their looks turned to "pure disgust," Stewart said, when they realized he was a prisoner and that they had volunteered their time to help someone like him. Still, they loaded Stewart and another man—both of whom were hooked up to machines—into the back of the bus.

"I don't know who he was, but he was missing both of his legs and one arm, he's intubated and, basically, in an induced coma," Stewart said. "(He) was injured either in Afghanistan or Iraq."

Once inside the bus, Stewart didn't really want anyone to talk to him or be near him, and he told medical staff to take care of the wounded man.

"I'm feeling like shit that they're trying to take care of me and here's this great American that's been injured and, at this point, I couldn't have cared less about my life."

Arriving at the ramp where one of the Air Force's largest cargo aircraft, a C-17, was waiting, Stewart had a repeat of his earlier experience—people disgusted that they had to help him.

Inside the C-17, there were wounded people as well as military family members flying "Space A" (i.e., space-available status) back to the States.

"Of course, I'm over there with all these cops," Stewart said. 'I'm a prisoner."

While en route to Walter Reed, Stewart was assisted by a male nurse who was a former SF medic-turned registered nurse contractor. That man, Stewart learned later, worked an extra 12 hours after his shift to help his brother in arms with his liver and kidneys issues. Especially after seeing Stewart's wife and children, he wanted to help him live.

In addition to the nurse and Space-A passengers on the flight, eight armed guards kept their eyes—as well as handcuffs and shackles—on Stewart for the duration of the flight to Bolling Air Force Base.

Soon after landing and having another bad experience with people seeing him in his orange jumpsuit, Stewart found himself on another converted patient-transfer bus—this one white with red crosses—traveling on a busy road inside the Beltway with the siren blaring.

When people saw and heard it coming, they believed it was carrying wounded soldiers and pulled over to let it pass. They were only half right.

"Here I am feeling less of a man again, because, you know, people were honking horns and giving thumbs up and saying 'Thank you' as you're going down the road... and I'm a prisoner. It's really for the other guy; it isn't for me."

Upon arrival at Walter Reed, the scenario Stewart has already experienced twice in one day replayed itself again before he was given a room and placed under guard, round-the-clock, by two shifts of two guards at a time.

Amidst all that, however, another SF liaison showed up at the 102-year-old hospital to let the soldier know he had arranged places to stay for both his dad and his wife. In addition, a guy from Stewart's unit showed up as an observer whose job it was to relay information back to his bosses, Colonel Schurr and Command Sergeant Major Klein, in Germany.

"Once I was up there, everybody and their mamma came by to see me," Stewart said, noting that he thinks the attention he received was due, in part, to news that had surfaced weeks prior to his arrival about poor treatment of wounded vets. The staff, he said, was "very touchy-friendly."

The soldier had to tell his story 10 or 15 times, because most of the people who came into his room in the ICU did not know many details.

That went on for a couple days, and then Stewart's wife showed up with his youngest daughter and his dad and sister showed up as well. The Army had flown them in from Germany, thinking Stewart was going to die.

After a couple days passed, Stewart had not died and Army officials were trying to determine whether they were going to send him to a federal medical prison in Springfield, Missouri or to the U.S. Military Disciplinary Barracks at Fort Leavenworth, Kansas. Doctors at Fort Leavenworth reviewed his medical records and decided they could treat him—and, if necessary, provide dialysis—so the Army decided to ship the convicted soldier to them.

A short while later, Stewart learned from Sergeant Luz that he was going to be handcuffed and shackled, put into a wheelchair and would be on his way to Fort Leavenworth immediately.

"As I'm being wheeled out," Stewart recalled, "my wife, my daughter, my dad and my sister are right there, and I don't even get to say goodbye to them." Stewart's dad protested vehemently and wanted to know who ordered such treatment, but it was all for naught.

"They take me out in a set of hospital clothes, double-cuffed up with some socks—no shoes, not in uniform," Stewart said, "and they put me in a civilian van, which they rented, and then drove me to Quantico, Va.

"Of course, they took me to a rental car place, because they had one rental car and had to drop off another one," he said. "So I'm out in public... with these guards and one dude from my unit, and I'm in hospital clothes, all cuffed up."

They drove him to the well-known Marine Corps base at Quantico, Virginia, near Washington, D.C., where he would join Army Private Bradley Manning (a.k.a., "The Wikileaks Guy") who was a temporary "guest" at the facility.

"I've got a full beard going on now," Stewart said, noting his appearance was in stark contrast to the very professional Marines surrounding him, "and here I am showing up in hospital clothes, no shoes on, cuffed up with a beard."

Immediately, the guards took issue with his appearance.

"You can't come in here with a beard," they told him. "We're going to have to shave your beard off."

Realizing that was a minor issue in the overall scheme of things, Stewart responded, saying, "Do what you need to do."

Unfortunately, the Marines' battery-operated clippers didn't work very well, so they decided to skip the shave and continue running Stewart through the in-processing at the jail. While running through their checklist, they found he had nothing with him but his hospital gown and socks.

"You can't come into prison like this," one guard told Stewart.

Realizing the prisoner wasn't really responsible for his lack of gear, the guards provided him a pair of hospital pants, prison shorts and a t-shirt.

Because of the type of prisoner Stewart was, they put him on 24-hour watch where all he had was a small, padded blanket (a.k.a., "Samurai suit").

"If you're suicidal or if you're a violent person, you can't hurt yourself with it," Stewart explained, "and that's all you get."

No bedding, no toiletries and none of the items his unit buddies had, per Army regulations, brought from his home in Germany to the prison at Mannheim, the only U.S. military confinement facility in Europe.

Stewart spent three days at Quantico. While there, he ran into a Marine guard who, he said, "treated me like a human, treated me like a soldier and had professionalism. He didn't cater to me. He just did his job and was very professional."

Though drawing a blank on the Marine's name, he remembers what he looked like and what he did.

"This guy was 6-foot 5, Native American guy, big hands. Real big guy," Stewart said, noting that the guy made sure he got bed sheets he could use as a towel as well as a bar of soap, because regulations required that prisoners shower once a day.

The Marine also went above and beyond by calling over to Stewart's unit in Germany and getting all of the phone numbers Stewart needed—including those of his wife, his dad, his lawyers, etc.—and made it a point for his prisoner to be able to call his wife and speak to her for 30 minutes.

"I'll never forget that," Stewart said, adding that, although he understands some people might say he shouldn't expect much as a prisoner, he expected to be treated professionally.

A couple of days went by, and Stewart found out he would be moving again. This time to Fort Leavenworth.

"I'm in a hospital gown again. No shoes," he said. "They put me in the minivan, and they take me to Dulles Airport."

When the group—including an observer from Stewart's unit—arrived in front of the airport terminal in the minivan, an airport cop told the Sergeant Luz he could not park the minivan curbside. The sergeant's response generated a lot of attention at the airport.

"I've got an escaped convicted rapist in this vehicle," he said. "I need some assistance to get him down to one of your detention cells prior to the flight."

"The next thing ya know, I've got TSA (and) Homeland Security out there, and they're putting me in a wheelchair, wheeling me through the airport down to their detention cell in front of everybody," Stewart explained, "and I'm in a hospital gown with no shoes on, double-cuffed up with Army guys in uniform and one Air Force guy.

"I'm a monkey in a cage again," he continued, "and every TSA and Homeland Security person that is somewhat important in the airport wants to know about this escaped Green Beret slash convicted rapist."

Around 10 o'clock that morning, Stewart's handlers asked if he was hungry. He told them he was, and they got him some food.

A short time later, a TSA officer appeared and told Stewart they would take him to the search point, search him and then load him aboard the aircraft before everyone else boarded. He thought things were looking up, but was wrong.

"They wheeled me out, and we get up there to the security checkpoint," Stewart said. "Of course, the TSA people there clearly weren't briefed.

"They were like, 'Well, we've gotta wand him,'" Stewart recalled. "Now, think about wanding someone who has two sets of metal handcuffs on. How do you do that?"

Recalling that he had to stand up in his hospital gown, Stewart vividly remembers all of the people in the airport passing by, seeing these people in uniforms and saying, "Thank you for your service. Thank you for your service."

"And here I am, standing in double-handcuffs and hospital clothes with a Chuck Norris beard, and they're just scared of me," Stewart said, adding that he felt bad because he knew the scene probably frightened some people, especially little kids, at the airport.

Before boarding his flight, the TSA folks told his handlers they needed to see if Stewart had any bombs on him. They proceeded to swab the soles of his feet and the palms of his hands until they were confident he had not somehow smuggled a bomb out of his prison cell at Quantico and transported it to the airport while double-handcuffed and under escort.

Finally, they got through the security checkpoint and to the gate, only to find the back half of the aircraft loaded with passengers.

"So much for not parading me around," Stewart said.

On the plane, some of the last eight seats that were supposed to be reserved for Stewart and his escorts had been taken by a young mother with two kids, including one in a car seat-style carrier.

What Sergeant Luz did next shocked Stewart.

"Ma'm, you need to get up and get your kids out," the sergeant said as if he was talking to a prisoner. "These are our seats!"

The mother, obviously frightened, grabbed one of her children while holding the other in his carrier and quickly moved them all to another section of the aircraft.

After Stewart and his escorts took those seats, Stewart felt as if all of the people on the plane were glaring at him, but there was little he could do to improve the situation.

Before the aircraft could take off, an issue related to Stewart's restraints had to be tackled.

A female flight attendant told Sergeant Luz he would have to remove Stewart's leg cuffs before the plane could depart and chided him for not coordinating with the airline in advance about his prisoner. Though the sergeant argued with her and cited his regulations that called for the restraints, she won the battle.

His pride hurting, Sergeant Luz began warning Stewart that there was a federal air marshal aboard the flight who would shoot him if he tried to escape.

Thanks to his training and experience, Stewart had already spotted the FAM two seats in front of him when his sidearm was exposed as he reached up toward the overhead bin. "He wasn't hard for me to find."

The aircraft finally left the ground and, upon arrival in Kansas City nearly three hours later, Stewart was placed in a wheelchair again and wheeled out of the airport.

Then his chief handler panicked.

Instead of taking advice about how to get to the rental car place—and eventually to Fort Leavenworth—from two E-5s and an E-4 who were familiar with the Army post after having served there, Sergeant Luz put everybody into two taxi cabs and told the drivers to take them to the rental car place. According to Stewart, it was almost as if the guy expected a helicopter to swoop down and whisk his prisoner away in some sort of bizarre SF-coordinated rescue attempt.

"Twenty-seven dollars later, we're going into Kansas City, and we've passed a bunch of these rental car places right there at the airport," Stewart said, noting that the two-car convoy eventually turned around to find one of those rental car outlets.

"I'm standing in front of this huge rental car place in Kansas City...just out there in the open," he said, visible to countless people coming and going as he stood there in hospital clothes with no shoes on. Again, he was like a monkey in a cage.

A short while later, Stewart found himself sitting in another minivan en route to Fort Leavenworth.

"As far as I know, there's never been another prisoner other than myself—and I've talked with some old heads that have over 10 years in that prison and guards that have been prison guards for over 15 years," Stewart said, "and they've never seen anyone show up at Leavenworth in a set of hospital clothes. Ever. Without any shoes on. That's how I was transported by the guys from Mannheim."

With multiple violations of Army Regulation 190-47, having to do with the treatment of prisoners during transport, behind him for now, Stewart experienced his first taste of professionalism in a military prison.

As soon as he arrived inside the arrival area (a.k.a., "Welcome Center") inside the prison, he was approached by an E-6 who seemed to have experience greeting new arrivals at the facility—a new building completed in 2002 to replace its aging predecessor.

"I know things have been kinda crazy for you," he told Stewart. "We're not gonna do anything crazy. Just have a seat for me, okay. Just relax over here."

After he sat down on a concrete bench, he noticed a big mural on the wall bearing the message, "We hold the key."

*[**Editor's Note:** Stewart didn't find out why he was taken to Quantico until several months later when two of the guards who had been assigned to his security detail ended up working at Fort Leavenworth. They told him they took him there for two reasons: they wanted to attend a Redskins football game, and it was a three-day weekend.]*

# 'Double-Max' Guy

When Stewart arrived at the U.S. Military Disciplinary Barracks at Fort Leavenworth, Kansas, a few weeks after being convicted of and sentenced to eight years confinement, he expected life inside its gray walls to be similar to what he found inside military prisons in Germany and Virginia. But it wasn't. The differences began with his first impression of the place.

After Stewart arrived at the infamous facility a few miles north of the Kansas City metropolitan area, he found the soldiers who greeted him there seemed to have some common sense. In short, they were upset with the fact that Stewart had been transported halfway across the country, through airports and aboard aircraft, while wearing only a hospital gown and socks. As a result, the E-6 in charge of the "welcoming committee" began chewing the Sergeant Luz's ass.

"Where's this form at? Why doesn't he have his clothes? Why did you transport him this way?" he yelled, making things a bit uncomfortable for everybody else around.

"You can't do this! This is wrong!" the sergeant told Sergeant Luz before pointing over to Stewart and asking some rhetorical questions: "You took him through an airport looking like that? Are you serious?"

"Of course, (Sergeant Luz's) saying, 'My unit told me to do this, blah-blah-blah....'" Stewart said. "It was real quick, because he didn't care."

After the heated discussion, the Fort Leavenworth sergeant signed the paperwork via which he accepted Stewart from Sergeant Luz and then turned to his prisoner.

"I apologize for the way you've been transported," the E-6 said, "and, I'll tell you right now, the way you were transported was wrong. I can't believe it, and I apologize.

"I would be pissed if I was you," he continued, "but we're not them so, please, with my staff, be professional. Show them professionalism, and we'll show you the same professionalism back."

"Listen, you guys didn't put me in prison," Stewart replied, "and I have no animosity toward you." And that's the way Stewart said he feels toward 99 percent of the guards he encountered, because they didn't put him in prison or do anything bad to him.

During the in-processing experience, Stewart received shorts, t-shirts, shoes and socks, shower shoes, toiletry items, toothbrush—"everything I need," he said. After that, his real prison experience began.

"Then I'm walking down the long hall," Stewart explained. "There's this huge hall in Leavenworth that everybody walks down, kind of like in "The Green Mile"—and there's a change of shifts."

A "cease inmate movement" order had been issued, so Stewart was the only prisoner on the move. That meant other inmates had the opportunity to see Stewart.

In full beard, double-handcuffs, a belly chain and a body cuff connected to two leg restraints, his appearance contrasted stark with the way most prisoners arrived (i.e., wearing one set of handcuffs and one set of leg restraints).

"I'm looking overly zealous," Stewart explained, recalling other prisoners' comments: "Ah, man, double-max."

"Everybody thought a double-max guy had to be in there for a big murder or something else," Stewart said, because very few people arrive at the prison in the manner he did unless they were violent during transport or something like that. Stewart had been neither.

The manner in which he arrived, however, turned out to be helpful in the long run.

"Believe it or not, that kind of helped me with my credibility a little bit," Stewart said. "They're like, 'Man, look at that dude.'"

After walking the big hallway, Stewart was taken to the reception area inside the SHU. Having a couple sides to it, he said, "it's a prison within a prison."

The SHU consists of four blocks: Reception, Level 2, Level 1 and Death Row.

Though the prison is relatively new, having replaced an older structure in 2002, some things from the old building carried over to the new one. And to the SHU.

The old prison had the SHU downstairs, so everyone at the prison still refers to leaving the SHU as "coming upstairs"—even though that's, technically, not the case.

Most prisoners spend their first 30 days at Fort Leavenworth in Reception, going through in-processing, getting their affairs in order and being briefed on things such as finance, medical, social services and legal. In addition, they get their prison uniforms and phone accounts and attend classes about prison life taught by other prisoners.

Something prisoners learn eventually is that the guards in Reception are, according to Stewart, "overly nice to you, because they're trying to get you to let your guard down and say things.

"While you're down there in Reception, they're recording all of your conversations," he explained. "They're getting intelligence on you, seeing if you're going to talk about some of your old crimes. They use that as an assessment."

And the recording doesn't end at Reception.

"Everything in Leavenworth is recorded," Stewart said, explaining that there are huge microphones in every cell that inmates refer to as their "phones."

After Reception, non-Death Row prisoners end up in Level 1 ("max custody"), Level 2 or General Population.

Level 1 involves spending 23 hours each day in one's cell as a result of having either done things wrong in prison or committing crime(s) appropriate for placement in that section. Level 2 is for less-serious crimes or in-prison behavior that still warrants separation from the general population. Everything is based on a point system.

Each of the blocks has a cell known as "The Fish Bowl." Made out of thick plastic walls, it's a bit larger than 8 foot by 10 foot. It has slider doors with two cup slots and features a closed-circuit video camera that records a prisoner's every move.

"They usually put people in there who are suicidal," Stewart explained, but they also put double-max guys like himself in there. The list of others who "qualify" for the room includes folks who've done something wrong and have to be extracted from their cell so that a cell inspection can take place.

Stewart was placed in "The Fish Bowl," because he was a double-max prisoner.

About the second day he was in there, the door opened unexpectedly and he walked out of the unusual cell and started eating with other prisoners who were in the common area around it. When one of the guards asked him why he came out of his cell, he told the guard, "I don't know. My door opened up."

The guard then called up to the control room and was told the prisoner was being allowed out.

"I think they made a mistake, because I was supposed to be on max," Stewart said, adding, "and mistakes do happen in prison."

Describing himself as "kind of nonchalant," Stewart said he had a couple of people from the prison's mental health unit come down and tell him he's probably going to be locked down on max for a couple of months, because he had escaped and would get high-risk points in his assessment.

Stewart told them he was never in custody prior to the so-called "escape," and they expressed surprise.

"I said, 'I was never in confinement. It's not like I broke out of prison,' and I explained my situation."

Based on the law, they couldn't give him high-risk points, Stewart said, because he had not been in a confinement status when he escaped.

Surprisingly, Stewart's knowledge paid off. He was able to keep his risk number lower than it otherwise might have been and, as a result, was able to move into the general population much sooner than he might otherwise have.

The first week he was at Fort Leavenworth, Stewart was approached by a guard who had gotten an email from one of his buddies in Germany.

"He walked over to me while I was in my cell and said, 'Hey, are you that Green Beret everybody's talking about here?'"

"Of course, the other inmates heard this," Stewart continued, "and (the guard) was like, 'Yeah, I read about you in the *Stars & Stripes*—you're that Green Beret.'"

A brief conversation about the guard's plans followed.

"That's how the word got out," Stewart said. Word soon spread about him being THAT Green Beret.

Unlike most prisoners at Fort Leavenworth whose sentences average at least 10 years, Stewart's was only eight.

"One can only speculate as to why they sent me to Fort Leavenworth," Stewart said. "It was a weird thing for everybody else, because everybody else there was looking at big numbers, and I'm in there with eight years."

Less than three months after Stewart's arrival at Fort Leavenworth, he received an email from his dad who wanted to know if he knew a woman by the name of Tamara Buehler.

After Stewart told his dad he didn't know her, his dad explained that Buehler was his accuser's roommate, employer and close friend of 11 years and said she had information proving Stewart's innocence but wanted to talk to a lawyer first.

That information included claims that, among other things, Heinrich had lied on the stand and had slept with several men since the night she spent with Stewart. In addition, it included news that Buehler's wedding, attended by some 250 people, was the one that Heinrich attended hours after she was supposedly savaged by Stewart.

**[Editor's note:** *Incredibly, none of the guests at Buehler's wedding were interviewed by German or American investigators to determine whether Heinrich had behaved unusually or showed signs of having been bruised or beaten only a few hours earlier.]*

More than anything, the message from his father gave prisoner #88175 another glimmer of hope.

"To this point, I had no faith. I just figured the world's gonna forget about me. I'm in prison," Stewart said.

Later, as Stewart's defense attorneys were submitting all of the necessary paperwork in an effort to get him a DuBay hearing during which new post-trial evidence could be considered by a military judge, government attorneys were putting up a fight.

"The prosecution," Stewart said, "was saying, 'No. Tamara is just lying. This person is lying. That's not true. Everybody's a liar, but my client isn't a liar.'"

# Request for Clemency

The outcome of Stewart's trial would not become official until the General Courts-Martial Convening Authority had signed off on it. That convening authority was Brigadier General Steven L. Salazar, commander of Headquarters 7th Army Joint Military Training Command, the parent unit of the International Special Training Center where Stewart had worked before his nightmare began. Attorneys from both sides would fight hard for 15 months before the general would issue a decision.

Officially, the fight began when a "Request for Clemency" package was submitted on Stewart's behalf December 2, 2009, by Captain Gleich.

The "GENERAL OVERVIEW" paragraph of the package summarized the soldier's case well:

"The bottom line up front is that SFC Stewart did not receive a fair trial. To rectify this injustice, the defense requests that you use your authority under Article 60, UCMJ and RCM 1107 and dismiss all charges and specifications for which SFC Stewart was found guilty. In support of this request, the defense will discus the following: (a) Facts — the defense will provide a brief overview of the facts; (b) New Evidence — the defense will provide an overview of the new evidence that has emerged since trial; (c) Setting Aside Findings of Guilt — the defense will explain reasons why this case was unjust and why you should dismiss all charges and specification; (d) Alternate Options — the defense will provide you with other options available to you to correct this injustice; (e) Clemency — the defense will argue for substantial clemency if you do not approve other options.

**At a minimum, the "FACTS" laid out in the same package appear to justify the claim made in the first sentence of the "GENERAL OVERVIEW" paragraph:**

On the night of 22/23 August 2008, Ms. Greta Heinrich voluntarily left a nightclub in Germany with the intention of having a one-night stand with SFC Kelly Anthony (Antonio) Stewart. On 5 November 2008, Ms. Heinrich had a telephone conversation with a friend whom she met while they were roommates together at a mental institution. Ms. Heinrich spoke to this friend about her night with SFC Stewart. Following that conversation, Ms. Heinrich reported that she had been raped and sodomized back in August.

Ms. Heinrich, the supposed victim, was institutionalized in a mental institution from October 2004 to February 2005. Despite describing in public the excruciating details of a purported brutal rape, this alleged victim chose to keep secret her psychiatric records from her time in the mental institution. She could have released those records but she refused. According to the alleged victim, her four month stay as an inpatient in a mental institution was simply for "burnout", because she worked too much. In response to a discovery request by defense, the prosecution tried to gain access to those records through the German government. The senior public prosecutor of Staatsanwaltschaft Stuttgart refused to provide those records.

During trial, the prosecution objected to the defense asking Ms. Heinrich why she refused to provide access to her psychiatric records, claiming that the information was not relevant. Furthermore, the government objected to the defense bringing up the fact that she met her friend, who motivated her to report the purported rape and sodomy, as roommates in the mental institution. The military judge sustained both objections. Consequently, the panel members were never made aware of these issues.

On 19 August 2009, SFC Stewart was found guilty of numerous offenses, including aggravated sexual assault, kidnapping, forcible sodomy, and assault and battery.

**In the "NEW EVIDENCE POST-TRIAL" section of the package, Stewart's defense attorneys highlighted two post-trial statements made by people familiar with Heinrich.**

**The first statement came from Tamara Buehler, Heinrich's former roommate, supervisor at her place of employment and close friend of 11 years:**

Statement of Tamara Buehler. On 15 November 2009, the defense first learned that a friend of the alleged victim had what was purported to be important information. While I was attending the annual fall Trial Defense conference, Ms. Tamara Buehler met with me and provided me with information which called into question the mental sanity of Ms. Heinrich. She faxed a statement to me the following week which was translated on 25 NOV 2009. In her statement, Ms. Buehler states that the alleged victim related to her that she was previously diagnosed with BPD (Borderline Personality Disorder). Ms. Buehler also related that in her "very close contact with Greta [the alleged victim] I very often noticed that her sense of perception is very warped at times. Situations that can be substantiated by facts are described by her from a totally different point of perception." Ms. Buehler also points out numerous incidents that directly contradict Ms. Heinrich's testimony:

A) Ms. Buehler reports receiving a text message from Ms. Heinrich on 23 August 2008 in which Ms. Heinrich described a lecherous night, where she "found my master." Ms. Buehler took this to mean that there was sex of the sadomasochist type and noted that there was no talk of something happening that Heinrich did not like.

Ms. Buehler states further that Ms. Heinrich claims that her encounter with SFC Stewart was "great SEX."

**CONTRAST** - Ms. Heinrich's text message and description of great sex directly contradicts her testimony at trial where she stated that she knew she was raped while she was still in the hotel room. As Ms. Heinrich put it, "I thought that he raped me. I felt it."

(B) Ms. Buehler states that "[u]pon leaving she [Ms. Heinrich] furthermore gave him her cell phone number; she was very eager to see whether he would call her."

**CONTRAST** - During trial, Ms. Heinrich gave the impression that she wrote down her cell phone number unwillingly and changed it because she was scared. In her testimony she claimed that SFC Stewart told her, "[y]ou will write down your cell phone number, and the right one; otherwise, you're not leaving". She went on to state that she wrote down the correct number because she would have done anything to get out of the room. In response to a question about what she did with her cell phone number, she stated that she had it changed so that no one could call her anymore. These statements are a far cry from Ms. Buehler's observations that she was eager to see whether SFC Stewart would call her.

(C) Testifying during the sentencing portion of trial, Ms. Heinrich stated that she is scared to be with people, scared to be with men, and scared to be with Soldiers. She went on to state that she has "no contact with men anymore." In answering a question posed by the prosecution regarding whether she engaged in any dating relationships with any men since the attack, Ms. Heinrich responded "no."

**CONTRAST** - In her statement, Ms. Buehler relates how Ms. Heinrich met with a teacher in the woods to have sex sometime between 13 to 15 July 2009, one month prior to the trial. Ms. Heinrich also had sex with another man sometime between 10 and 15 August 2009, shortly before the trial. She further describes how Ms. Heinrich had a crush on a friend between July and September and how she fell in love with a neighbor at the end of June. Each of these encounters prior to trial directly contradicts her testimony regarding her fear of men and her lack of relations with men since her encounter with SFC Stewart.

**The second statement came from Inge Queren, a 61-year-old native German whose past includes having been married to a U.S. service member. At the time of Stewart's court-martial, the 17-plus-year employee of the U.S. Army was serving as a victim/witness liaison for Heinrich. Her statement appears below:**

**Statement of Ms. Inge Queren.** At great risk to her career with the United States Military, Ms. Inge Queren, the victim/witness liaison, made a brave decision to come forward with her observations of Ms. Heinrich's erratic and bizarre behavior during trial. On 8 September 2009, Ms. Queren wrote an email to SFC Stewart's father. In that email, Ms. Queren states that "the victim's demeanor and her statements during the

> trial did not match at all. She described instances of Ms. Heinrich supposedly having nervous breakdowns for fear of SFC Stewart, and at the same time, walking close to SFC Stewart snapping that she was not afraid when Ms. Queren offered assistance. When Ms. Queren mentioned to Ms. Heinrich the possibility that the panel might think she was insane and not believe her because of her antics, Ms. Querent relates how the "nervous breakdowns" all of a sudden ceased. Having spoken with Ms. Queren after reading her e-mail, she wants to express her eagerness to discuss any matters with you personally regarding her observations of the alleged victim which led her to believe the verdict was wrong.

**It's important to note that, since she came forward with her observations about Heinrich, Queren has been demoted by her employer, costing her 414.21 Euros—approximately $500 per month—in income.**

**In the section of the package titled, "SETTING ASIDE FINDINGS OF GUILT," the defense offered several reasons to support the claim that Stewart should receive a new trial or, better yet, have his conviction and sentence tossed out. The first reason appears below:**

> **a. Overview:** Under Article 60, UCMJ and RCM 1107, you have the authority to set aside any findings of guilty and dismiss any specification and charge. In drafting the Uniform Code of Military Justice, the People of the United States of America, through their Senators and Representatives in Congress, have given you the discretion to exercise the power described above. The case of the United States v. Sergeant First Class Kelly A. Stewart represents the case for which you should exercise that authority entrusted to you by the People.

**b. SFC Kelly Anthony Stewart Was Unable to Receive a Fair Trial Because He was Unable to Compel Production of Ms. Heinrich's Psychiatric Records Under German Law.** This section will discuss SFC Stewart's constitutional right to have access to his accuser's psychiatric records, the importance of having access to his accuser's psychiatric records, the harm that was exacerbated by the Military Judge not even allowing the defense to mention the accuser's refusal to provide access to those records, and concluding remarks regarding this important issue.

**(i) Access to Psychiatric Records.** Under German Law, neither the defense nor the prosecution was able to compel the release of the alleged victims psychiatric records. In contrast to the German system, evidentiary rules in the UCMJ allow a military Judge to review psychiatric records to determine if they are relevant to a proceeding, thereby protecting the constitutional rights of the accused as well as the privacy rights of a potential victim.

In this case, because the alleged victim was a German civilian and her psychiatric records were located in Germany, the military Judge did not have the authority to order and in camera inspection of her records as he would be entitled to under M.R.E. 513. Had the trial occurred in the United States to an alleged victim who was American, the outcome may have been very different if the panel was able to know exactly why the alleged victim was institutionalized for four months not long before she made her allegations.

**(ii) Importance of Having Access to an Accuser's Psychiatric Records.** Having a Judge review the psychiatric records of a complaining witness is an integral part of any trial. The Court of Military

Appeals, in addressing a request for social service and mental health records for two complaining witnesses, declared that "[s]ome forms of emotional or mental defects have been held to 'have a high probative value on the issue of credibility....[A] conservative list of defects have to include...most or all of the neuroses,...alcoholism, drug addiction, and psychopathic personality.'" United States v. Reece, 25 M.J. 93, 95 (C.M.A. 1987). In Reece, the Court found the Judge abused his discretion in not even ordering an in camera inspection of the pertinent documents to determine if they contained information relevant to cross-examination or impeachment of the government witnesses. Reece, at 95.

**(iii) Specific Harm.** SFC Stewart has suffered a tremendous injustice from the German government's refusal to provide access to Ms. Heinrich's medical records. During trial, Ms. Heinrich was able to portray that she was in a mental institution for four months simply because of "burnout" from working too hard. The defense was not even able to inquire why she would not release her records. Thus, the military panel had no reason to suspect that Ms. Heinrich may have had a psychopathic personality of the kind that the Court in United States v. Reece found so probative on the issue of credibility.

The emergence of new evidence demonstrating Ms. Heinrich's erratic behavior and her previous diagnosis of Borderline Personality Disorder demonstrates why it is so important for a military Judge to be able to review psychiatric records. First, her being diagnosed with Borderline Personality Disorder (BPD) would have been highly relevant for the panel to determine here credibility. The

National Institute of Mental Health describes BPD as a "serious mental illness characterized by pervasive instability in moods, interpersonal relationships, self-image, and behavior. Second, evidence contained in her files may have explained why she would at best mistake consensual sex for rape because of her mental illness or at worst, fabricate a story of rape and forcible sodomy. Ms. Heinrich's refusal to provide access to her records and the German government's implicit acquiescence of her efforts at concealment have led to a conviction that is forever tainted by the military panel being kept in the dark with regard to Ms. Heinrich's sanity.

**(iv) SFC Stewart Must Not Bear the Full Burden of the German Government's Interest in Keeping Ms. Heinrich's Psychiatric Records Secret.** The German government chose not to exercise criminal jurisdiction in this case. The German government chose United States law to prosecute SFC Stewart. They did not, however, provide the United States with the tools necessary for a fair trial. They did not provide us with access to Ms. Heinrich's psychiatric records as is required by United States law. In the case Davis v. Alaska, 415 U.S. 308 (1974), the Supreme Court of the United States overturned a conviction because a law in Alaska forbid an accused from gaining access to a juvenile offender's records in a case where those records were extremely relevant. The court found:

> The State's policy interest in protecting the confidentiality of a juvenile offender's record cannot require yielding of so vital a constitutional right as the effective cross-examination for bias of an adverse witness. The State could have protected Green from exposure of his juvenile adjudication in these circumstances by refraining

from using him to make out its case; the State cannot, consistent with the right of confrontation, require the petitioner to bear the full burden of vindicating the State's interest in the secrecy of juvenile criminal records. Davis, at 320.

Just like in the case of United States v. Davis, SFC Stewart should not have to bear the full burden of the German government's interest in keeping Ms. Heinrich's psychiatric records a secret.

**(v) Conclusion.** As discussed, because a military Judge was unable to gain access to Ms. Heinrich's psychiatric records and because of the importance of attaining those records especially in light of the new evidence that has emerged since trial, the defense respectfully requests that you dismiss all charges and specifications to rectify this injustice.

**c. There Was Support for SFC Stewart on the Military Panel.** There are rules that prohibit panel members from discussing their votes in court-martial proceedings. While no panel member has violated that rule, SFC John A. Alam Sr., one of the panel members in the case, has written a letter in support of SFC Stewart. Furthermore, during trial, SFC Alam asked the following question of the military Judge during sentencing: "Suppose, hypothetically, I said - I was one of the voters to say, 'No. I don't think he was guilty.' Do I take that into consideration as I determine what his sentence should be or should I just determine that Sergeant First Class Stewart is charged—he's guilty and now I make the determination off of that?" As you can see from the attached letter, SFC Alam has not indicated his vote one way or another nor has he been asked by Defense which way he voted. Furthermore, during the trial, SFC Alam posed his referenced question as a hypothetical, thereby never indicating that he voted not guilty or that he was one of the voters who thought SFC Stewart was not guilty.

Despite being prevented from the Rules for Court Martial from finding out how each individual panel member voted, the defense submits that based on SFC Alam's hypothetical question and letter of support; there may have been support on the panel for SFC Stewart.

In the military Justice system, a conviction can be attained if at least two-thirds of the members present vote for a finding of guilty. In most other courts and jurisdictions in the United States of American, jury verdicts must be unanimous to convict someone of a crime. While it can never be known how the panel members voted in this case, the defense asks that when you make your determination in setting aside the findings of guilt, you factor SFC Alam's letter and hypothetical question together with the new information that has come to light after the verdict was announced.

**Perhaps the most important information contained in the package wasn't physical evidence, per se, but the observations of Heidi Livingston Klein, the wife of Command Sergeant Major Richard "Spike" Klein, about the fact that no women were detailed as members for the 10-member court-martial panel comprised of both enlisted members and officers.**

**The section, "d. No Women Were Detailed as Members for the Court-Martial," contained the following:**

While there is no requirement that women must be detailed as members for any particular court-martial, the verdict in this case is weakened by the lack of a female presence. Numerous women who are familiar with the facts of the case are particularly disturbed by some of the alleged victim's claims. Had even one woman been there to deliberate with the men on the panel, the alleged victim's story would have been seen in an entirely different light.

**Next, the defense cited a letter in which Klein shared observations about how a woman being detailed as a member of Stewart's court-martial may have affected the verdict:**

On top of the selective memory, there are also times when the accuser is clearly lying. She states that Kelly tried vaginal contact and briefly entered but could not get any further in as she was totally tightened and cramped up. As a woman, this is a ludicrous suggestion. It would be nice if "actual" rape victims could use this cramping technique so they could stop their attackers from entering further. This just physically does not happen. I would think that it would be much more difficult to forcibly sodomize her but he apparently did this while holding her hair with his left hand and holding her down with his right. Almost like a one-armed push-up with the ground resisting. Not only is this orifice much more difficult to enter, the angle at which he was supposedly doing it is, again, ludicrous. In a test, my husband, who is considerably stronger than Kelly, was physically unable to do this and I am almost 6 inches shorter than the accuser.

**Asked why she got involved in the case, Klein told this writer her biggest concern is that this case sets a precedent that allows a foreign national to make unfounded accusations at will against a U.S. service member serving abroad and, solely due to the military's need to be strict on crime, innocent people are found guilty.**

**"I felt the necessity to submit my observations, because it is simply in my nature to stand up for what is right," Klein explained. "I don't know how else to answer that question."**

**In addition to Klein's astute observations, the defense cited "Other Weaknesses With the Verdict" in section "e" of the document:**

> Sir, it is an unfortunate fact that people are falsely accused and falsely convicted of crimes they did not commit. Here we have a conviction where the alleged victim waited over two months before reporting the incident. She claims, "my entire body was covered in bruises, my right breast was so sore, infected, and swelled up..." Despite "injuries" to her entire body, these injuries were observed by no one else, including a doctor whom she saw for a bladder infection on the 27th of August, only four days following her encounter with SFC Stewart. Charges of kidnapping seem to be prosecution overreach when considering that the alleged victim freely left the club with SFC Stewart intending on a one night stand, voluntarily entered into the taxi with him, entered into his room, and did not leave or call for help even while the accused took a shower. Despite claims of screaming, there was no evidence of anyone hearing anything despite being in a crowded Marriott Hotel. Despite supposedly being "beaten," "kidnapped," "raped," and "forcibly sodomized," this alleged victim still gave SFC Stewart her telephone number before leaving the hotel. We now know that she remained excited about receiving a phone call from SFC Stewart after that day. Sir, in pointing out these weaknesses, the defense asks that you factor them in to your decision regarding setting aside findings of guilt in this case.

**In the final pages of the Request for Clemency package, Captain Gleich offered "ALTERNATIVE OPTIONS" for General Salazar's consideration. Excerpts of those options appear below:**

Rehearing. Under Article 60(e)(3), UCMJ, "[a] rehearing may be ordered by the convening authority . . . if he disapproves the findings and sentence and states the reasons for disapproval of the findings." Article 60(e)(3) also discusses the possibility of ordering a rehearing as to the sentence. The discussion section of R.C.M. 1107(e) states that "[a] rehearing may be appropriate when an error substantially affecting the findings or sentence is noticed by the convening authority." A rehearing would allow Sergeant Stewart the ability to present new evidence discovered post-trial of which the military panel was unaware. Given the lack of evidence in this case, even the smallest bits of evidence on the defense side would make a tremendous difference.

Post-Trial Article 39(a) Session. The other alternative is to order a post-trial article 39(a) session. Under R.C.M. 1101(d), "[t]he convening authority may direct post-trial session any time before the convening authority takes initial action on the case or at such later time as the convening authority is authorized to do so by a reviewing authority." A post-trial 39(a) session will allow the military Judge to take corrective action including reopening the hearing or granting a new trial.

For these reasons, if you decide not to set aside findings of guilt, the defense asks that you consider a rehearing. If a rehearing is not granted, the defense asks that you at least consider a rehearing on the sentencing. If neither of those two options are granted, the defense asks that you order a post-trial Article 39(a) session.

**The Request for Clemency package was sent to General Salazar's office where it would be handled by Lieutenant Colonel Francisco**

Villa, the 7th Army JMTC staff judge advocate who served as General Salazar's right-hand man on legal matters.

Because the Uniform Code of Military Justice requires only that the government respond to the request for a DuBay hearing in a "timely manner," the government took about ninety days to write a rebuttal in which they discounted all of the claims made by attorneys for Stewart. From the time the government submitted that rebuttal, according to the UCMJ, Stewart's lawyers had only 10 days to respond.

Though they never used the word, lying, Stewart's lawyers responded by saying, essentially, that the government was doing that in its rebuttal.

A month passed and, finally, the information from Stewart's lawyers reached the general and he ordered the government to bring accuser Heinrich in and ask her about the issues in dispute. When they questioned her, she admitted she had lied about some matters but also called Buehler a liar.

"Now, the prosecution knows that she lied," Stewart said, explaining that the prosecution then wrote a letter to the general recommending a DuBay hearing instead of overturning the outcome until a retrial could be held per his requests.

"The prosecution tells the general, 'Look, he's asking for all of these things here; let's just give him a post-trial 39(a),'" Stewart explained.

Craftily, prosecutors cited Heinrich's admission of lying during the sentencing period and asked the general to limit reviews to the sentencing portion only.

As a result, Stewart's attorneys were only able to talk about what Heinrich lied about during the sentencing portion, and not the trial portion during which she lied even more.

"We asked for a broader spectrum of the trial," Stewart said, explaining that the request was denied by the military judge, not the general.

Judge Kuhfahl said he wouldn't expand the scope of the hearing because the general didn't ask him to do that. In making such a decision, however, the military judge ignored the fact that the general didn't have the authority to expand the scope. Why? Because that authority rested with the military judge.

On April 7, 2010, more than four months after the Request for Clemency was submitted, General Salazar granted Stewart a post-trial Article 39(a) session during which his attorneys would be able to present new evidence in hopes of securing a new trial or some form of clemency. It was time for the prisoner to leave the prison—hopefully, for the last time—and ship all of his belongings home.

# Leaving Fort Leavenworth

It was mid-May 2010, and Stewart was about to leave the U.S. Military Disciplinary Barracks at Fort Leavenworth, Kansas, for Germany, where a hearing that might result in some form of clemency— or, perhaps, even a new trial—would soon take place.

"When I was out-processed out of Leavenworth, I had to ship all of my stuff home to the point that I thought I wasn't going back there, too," Stewart said, noting that both guards and long-time prisoners alike had told him they had never seen someone ship their stuff out and come back.

When he was picked up at the prison, he noticed immediately that this trip was going to be different than his last one.

"I am back to being Sergeant First Class Kelly Stewart," he explained. "I'm not Private Kelly Stewart, because this is kind of a jump back in time. It's weird about how the (Uniform Code of Military Justice) is.

"The convening authority hasn't signed off on me; therefore, I haven't really been reduced (in rank) yet," he said. "It's not official."

According to Army regulations, which were being followed this time, Stewart had to be picked up by soldiers from his unit who outranked him. Because only two Americans at the International Special Training Center—Command Sergeant Major Richard "Spike" Klein and Lieutenant Colonel David L. Grosso, his battalion commander—outranked him, the unit's parent, the 7th Joint Military Training Center, was tasked to provide escorts. They sent two E-8s and one E-5 as a driver. All were eleven-bravos (11B)—infantry guys.

The hospital gown and socks he wore on his way to Fort Leavenworth were replaced by civilian clothes—a set of blue Dickies pants, a blue polo shirt, a windbreaker and his own pair of civilian shoes—provided to him by his keepers at Fort Leavenworth. In addition, he traveled with a toiletry bag, a small book of photos and a handful of other small items.

"They showed up there and put a belly cuff on me and some handcuffs underneath my jacket so you couldn't see the cuffs, and it looked very professional," Stewart said, explaining that the entire trip—including obtaining rental cars, boarding aircraft in advance of other passengers and whisking through customs—was coordinated well. He even saw Paul Teutul Sr. and Paul Teutul Jr., the stars of the television show, "Orange County Choppers," while inside the Kansas City airport—a highlight for a guy who once owned a motorcycle.

Stewart attributed the change in treatment to the fact that, after he arrived at Fort Leavenworth in November 2009, both he and his father filed complaints with the Army Inspector General and other senior Army officials about the treatment he had received en route from Germany to the prison.

After noting that he was excited about being out of prison for the first time in a long while, Stewart said the story he told his new team of escorts about his life since meeting Heinrich was different than the one they had been told while being briefed about their latest assignment.

"They're all freaked out," he said, aware that his escorts were intimidated by the stories they had heard about the one-time SF soldier and combat veteran. "I told the guys, 'Hey, listen guys, I'm not here to give you any trouble. I'm going back, because the general thinks there were mistakes made and I've got an opportunity to overturn my case. I'm not gonna run from ya. I'm not gonna give you guys a hard time."

Stewart described the treatment he received on the way back to Mannheim as "real professional."

"They're not parading me around in there. They asked me if I needed coffee or something to drink for the drive. Real professional," Stewart explained. "On the way to the prison, they stop by McDonald's and let me get some food—a real nice treat, you know, after being in prison."

Stewart saw his treatment change dramatically after he was turned over to the folks at Mannheim. After all, they remembered him.

"At this point, I'm like a unicorn," Stewart explained, "because no one comes back from a max facility like Leavenworth all the way to Germany."

Despite Stewart's demands that he be treated professionally per Army regulations, he soon found out that (1) time had not healed any of the "wounds" from their time spent together nine months earlier and (2) except for his boots, all four of his uniform sets—the ones the folks at Mannheim had had in their possession since he entered their facility nine months earlier but did not let him wear when they transported him to Fort Leavenworth—were still there at Mannheim.

After the folks at Mannheim signed for Stewart and officially made him their prisoner again, they took him down and put him downstairs in the Special Housing Unit.

Legally, Stewart said, they couldn't keep him in the SHU, but they did anyway, because they didn't expect him to be there that long. Instead of releasing him from the SHU, they played "the prison game" of making him fill out and submit paperwork requests to be released from the 23/7 lockdown of the SHU.

Stewart's keepers at Mannheim weren't the only ones trying to ensure his treatment was less than pleasant.

Prior to Stewart's return to Germany, now-Major Bashore tried to make sure the SF veteran remained aware that he had been convicted nearly two years earlier. The trial counsel, who had been promoted from captain since the trial in August 2009, requested the following:

- That Stewart be shackled head to toe while in transit from his cell at Mannheim and during the course of the DuBay hearing;
- That Stewart appear in his Army Combat Uniform instead of the "Class A" uniform upon which his numerous medals and ribbons would be visible; and

- That two armed guards be posted in the courtroom during the hearing.

The military judge turned down the trial counsel's first two requests, resulting in Stewart showing up in handcuffs only and in his Class A uniform with numerous medals and ribbons visible. The request for two armed guards was approved.

Major Bashore also told the soldiers performing escort duty that Stewart would not be allowed to talk to his wife, Freija, or any other friends and family members who might appear at court that day. Order or not, they ignored the major's request.

Stewart said it was not only because the guard had read about his case at www.SaveThisSoldier.com, but also because he had served in the same unit as Master Sergeant John Hatley and Sergeant First Class Joseph Mayo, each of whom were sentenced to prison at Fort Leavenworth for killing enemy combatants. The guard told Stewart he was going to retire early due to being disgusted with the way the military justice system had treated so many soldiers.

The hearing would begin just after 11 a.m. May 19, 2010.

# The DuBay Hearing

While walking back to meet with civilian defense attorney Court, Stewart passed Judge Kuhfahl, the officer who had overseen his trial and would oversee the DuBay hearing during which new post-trial evidence would be considered. Stewart was nervous; after all, he had chosen not to show up for his sentencing, an act that could be regarded as disrespectful by the military judge.

"I was worried about how that was gonna go down," Stewart said. Perhaps, it was a good omen in advance of the hearing that would begin soon.

A not-so-good sign for what awaited him that day was the arrival of Major Bashore.

Throughout the day on May 19, 2010, the trial counsel would repeatedly refer to Stewart as "Private Stewart" despite the fact that he was standing there for all the world to see in his Class A uniform, complete with all of the accouterments—including rank insignia, patches, badges and a chest full of ribbons—indicative of a stellar SF career.

"He did everything he could in there to tear me down," Stewart said, referring to the trial counsel who had also instructed the soldier's escorts to "Stop referring to him as Sergeant Stewart!" during transport.

"Now, I'm sitting in court and this whole courtroom is full," Stewart said. "I've got both sides of this little-bitty courtroom full of people. I was embarrassed in one aspect, because the details of this are getting ready to come out." He also worried about women and children in the room hearing them.

"I'm nervous," he said. "My wife's in there, and this is gonna be the first time she sees the woman I cheated on her with.

"I was embarrassed, because I put myself in a situation like this," he said for at least the fourth time during my interview.

Stewart noted that the wife of one of his buddies took his daughters for the day so they wouldn't have to be exposed to what went on during the hearing.

All of the attorneys who had participated in Stewart's court-martial nine months earlier were present. Before any witnesses were called, however, attorneys from both sides met with Judge Kuhfahl to discuss pre-hearing considerations. Chief among them was the subject of whether or not German citizens who would be called to testify would be read their rights under German law—or, in effect, be required to swear to tell the truth.

Incredibly, Judge Kuhfahl decided they would not and, according to the Record of Trial, said, "I am not concerned about those issues," leaving observers of the case to wonder whether or not any of the German witnesses would feel compelled to tell the truth.

With Stewart not knowing the full details about who was going to testify and what they might say, the Post-Trial Article 39(a) session began at 11:09 a.m., called to order by Judge Kuhfahl.

The first government witness called during the session was accuser Heinrich. The transcript of this German citizen's exchange with the assistant trial counsel is brief and reminds one of President Bill Clinton's definition of the word "is." The text of that exchange appears below as taken from the Record of Trial:

**Greta Heinrich, civilian, was called as a witness for the prosecution, was sworn, and testified through the interpreter as follows:**

**DIRECT EXAMINATION**
**Questions by the assistant trial counsel:**

Q. You are Greta Heinrich of Boeblingen, Germany?

A. Yes, correct.

Q. Did you have a sexual encounter with a man prior to August of 2009?

A. Yes, correct.

Q. During your pre-sentencing testimony in the case of US v Stewart you stated, and I quote, "I have no contacts to men anymore," when I asked you how the accused's conviction affected you regarding men. Please explain what you meant by "no contacts."

A. I did not have a relationship to a male. I did not have a partnership with another man since 2007.

Q. And please explain what you mean by this partnership or relationship.

A. Partnership means to me that I share the life with somebody else and I create my life with that person--together with that person.

Q. Did you consider your one sexual encounter with a man prior to August 2009 to be a dating relationship or partnership?

A. No. It was one evening, a one-night stand, and it was not a date.

Q. Was it not a relationship?

A. No. It was not a relationship, just a one-night stand.

ATC: No further questions, Your Honor.

## CROSS-EXAMINATION

**Questions by the civilian defense counsel:**

Q. Ms. Heinrich, you said you had a single sexual encounter with a man prior to August of 2009; is that your testimony?

A. Yes, correct.

Q. And just so we're all clear, we're talking in the time period between August 2008 and 2009. We are not talking ancient history, correct?

INT: I'm sorry.

Q. We're talking--when we say before 2000 and--August 2009--we are putting the limit of August 2008 to August 2009.

A. Yes, correct.

Q. When in this time period did you have the one sexual encounter you're talking about?

A. July 2009.

Q. And without going into any great detail, can you tell us who this person is? I don't mean a name, but what he was.

A. Yes. It was just in a guest house. He was a teacher, and he was there for visiting purposes.

Q. And "sexual encounter" is a generic phrase. Did it include sexual intimacy?

A. Yes, correct. There was sexual intercourse.

Q. And it is your testimony that that is the only sexual contact of that sort that you had between August 2008 and August 2009.

A. Yes, correct.

Q. Did you also, in the previous sentencing hearing, make the statement, "I have no contacts to men anymore"?

A. What do you mean by "contacts"?

Q. The question is did you say that, not what you meant by it. Did you say that?

A. If I meant by it no partnership, then yes, that's correct.

Q. Do you remember being asked, "How has this affected you regarding men"?

A. Yes.

Q. Do you remember answering at page 630, line 5, "I have no contacts to men anymore"?

A. I do not recall exactly, but I do recall that I was asked how this has affected me in regards to men.

Q. The rest is argument.

Do you remember in the testimony indicating that your social life changed as a result of the incident?

A. Yes, correct.

Q. Do you remember saying that you used to be with people a lot but that's not the way anymore, now you spend a lot of time alone?

A. Yes, correct.

Q. And do you remember being asked, "Why do you spend so much time alone"?

A. No, I don't recall.

Q. So you don't remember answering that it was at home where you feel safe?

A. I don't recall, but it would only make sense that I said that.

Q. Do you remember also stating that most of the time you can't bear it if men look at you?

A. Yes, correct.

Q. Between June of 2009 and August of--and the trial in August of 2009 where were you working and living?

A. I lived in the Allgaeu and I worked in a pension.

*[**Editor's Note:** "Pension" is German for bed and breakfast.]*

Q. And who was there--for whom did you work?

A. For an old co-worker of mine whom I had met during my training, my apprenticeship; and during that apprenticeship we struck up a friendship.

Q. Okay. In the hearing in August of 2009 did you indicate that you were scared of American soldiers?

ATC: Objection, Your Honor, relevance.

MJ: Overruled.

Q. In the hearing in August of 2009 did you indicate that you were scared of American soldiers?

A. Yes, correct, and it is not changed ever since.

**[Pause.]**

Q. Did you in the hearing of August 2009 indicate that you were scared to be with people?

**[The interpreter translated the question in German.]**

CDC: The question is whether she was afraid to be with them, not whether she was afraid of them.

A. Yes, that's correct. I had tremendous problems being among other people.

Q. You testified in the hearing that you cut your hair as a result of this incident, correct?

A. Correct, yes.

Q. Isn't it true though that throughout the previous 10 years or so you would always have long hair and then cut it back to short hair and then have long hair--I mean, it was a habit of yours to do that, correct?

ATC: Objection, relevance.

MJ: Overruled.

A. No, that is not correct. My hair has been long for two years.

Q. But previous to that it had been short.

INT: Huh?

Q. But previous to those two years it had been short.

A. No, it is longer than two years. It was at the beginning of my apprenticeship in 2001, but I don't really recall for sure.

CDC: Excuse me, Your Honor.

**[The civilian defense counsel conferred with the defense counsel.]**

Q. Do you remember being asked, "How do you feel when a man looks at you with interest"?

A. Yes, I do remember that question.

Q. And you answered--do you remember answering, "Most of the time I can't bear it if men look at me"?

INT: I couldn't hear.

Q. And do you remember answering, "Most of the time I can't bear it if men look at me"?

A. Yes, correct.

Q. Have all of--this may be outside the scope, Your Honor, and if so, please cut me off. Have all of these problems continued to the present day?

ATC: Objection.

MJ: Basis?

A. Relevance, Your Honor. It doesn't matter what she is right now after the trial almost a year later. It mattered how she was in August 2009.

MJ: Defense?

CDC: Your Honor, we believe that there will be evidence that what she has said about August 2008 to August 2009 is not accurate and that it continues to be inaccurate, which is a factor related to the willfulness of any false statement.

MJ: Well, the point of the hearing is to determine whether she lied in August of 2009----

CDC: Yes, sir.

MJ: ----so I'm going to sustain the government objection.

CDC: One moment, Your Honor.

**[Pause.]**

CDC: Thank you, Your Honor. No further questions.

MJ: Any redirect, Government?

ATC: No, Your Honor.

**EXAMINATION BY THE COURT-MARTIAL**
**Questions by the military judge:**

Q. Okay. Ms. Heinrich, I have a few questions for you. Okay. I believe you said that you do remember being asked, "How has this affected you regarding men?"

A. Yes, correct.

Q. Okay. I am telling you that you did, in fact, testify, "I have no contacts to men anymore." Do you remember making or giving that response?

A. If that is written down as such, then I did say that.

Q. Okay. When asked why you have no contacts with men you said, "I couldn't bear it if something like that happened to me again."

A. Correct.

Q. Do you remember making that response?

A. Yes, I do remember.

Q. Now, the incident that you testified to related to Sergeant Stewart, that was a one-night stand, correct?

INT: I'm sorry, sir.

Q. The incident that you testified to regarding Sergeant Stewart was also a one-night stand.

A. Yes, correct.

Q. And the incident you testified to earlier about the teacher was a one-night stand.

A. Yes, from my point it was a one-night stand, but the teacher wanted a relationship. I didn't.

Q. But you only had sex with him on one occasion.

A. Yes, correct, one time.

Q. And that was about a month prior to your testimony in August.

A. Yes, correct, it was in July.

Q. Did you not consider what had occurred with the teacher as contact with men?

A. We didn't see each other for a longer period of time and it was not a relationship or partnership with this person.

Q. So when you said, "I have no contact to men," are you saying you were defining "contact" as "relationship"?

A. I understood it to be relationship because during the daily course of life I always have contact with other men.

Q. You stated at the previous hearing that you had not engaged in any dating relationships since the attack.

A. Yes.

Q. Was that true?

A. Yes, that's correct.

**[Pause.]**

A. I did tell the teacher at the time what had happened to me because the teacher wanted a relationship with me and I did try to restart my life again and so I tried it, but I just couldn't.

Q. Prior to the trial in August, did anybody ever ask you whether you had had sexual intercourse with someone after the attack?

INT: I'm sorry, sir. Can you repeat the question again?

Q. Prior to testifying in August 2009, did anyone associated with the trial ask you if you had had sexual intercourse since the attack?

A. I don't recall that anybody had asked me that. It would have been after and not before.

Q. Did you ever voluntarily disclose to anyone associated with the trial that you had had sex with this teacher prior to the hearing?

INT: Prior to?

Q. Prior to the hearing in August of 2009.

A. Yes. I told Mrs. Buehler.

Q. She was your employer?

A. Well, yes, but she was foremost my friend. We have known each other for at least 11 years.

MJ: Any questions based on mine?

ATC: Yes, Your Honor.

## REDIRECT EXAMINATION

**Questions by the assistant trial counsel:**

Q. Frau Heinrich, how long had you known the teacher before you engaged in sexual intercourse with him?

A. I believe he had been a guest in that pension for two weeks.

Q. Okay. Did you spend time with him socializing or interacting with him during that two-week stay at the pension?

A. No, I--I was working. I did not have any--any--I did not meet with him. I did not have any dates in that time period with him either. It was only that one time when we had sex.

**[The assistant trial counsel conferred with the trial counsel.]**

ATC: No further questions, Your Honor.

**RECROSS-EXAMINATION**

**Questions by the civilian defense counsel:**

Q. Was Frau Buehler the only person you told of the sex with the teacher?

A. Yes, correct.

Q. Do you remember a guest in the hotel--in the pension--Donna Leyden, an older British--Canadian woman?

INT: I'm sorry, sir. An old British?

Q. Do you remember a guest in the pension Donna Leyden, a 70-year-old Canadian woman?

A. Yes, but I don't really know her.

Q. Did you tell her that you had lured the teacher to a romantic picnic on the river nearby and later had great sex in the teacher's room the night before?

ATC: Objection, relevance, Your Honor.

MJ: Overruled.

[The interpreter began to translate the question. The witness moved the microphone away from the interpreter.]

CDC: Excuse me, it was too long a question. Let me break it down.

MJ: Let me stop you for a second. Ms. Heinrich, can you turn the mic back to the interpreter so we can hear her?

**[The witness did as directed.]**

MJ: That's fine. Thank you.

Q. Did you tell Mrs. Leyden how you lured the teacher to a romantic picnic on the Tobol, which is a nearby river, and that you later had great sex in the teacher's room the night before?

A. So the question is that I told Donna Leyden those things that you just mentioned----

Q. That's the question.

A. ----to me. No. This is not correct.

Q. Do you remember previously telling Donna Leyden that there was a teacher you were interested in and you wanted to get to know him better?

A. No, that's not correct.

CDC: No further questions at this time, Your Honor. Thank you.

ATC: No further questions, Your Honor.

**EXAMINATION BY THE COURT-MARTIAL**
**Questions by the military judge:**

Q. Ms. Heinrich, I'm sorry. I have a few more. Did you think that the jury would think poorly of you if they knew you had sexual intercourse a month before the trial?

A. Yes, correct.

Q. Why did you think that?

A. Because that day of the incident that was a--I had a one-night stand and I was trying to have a relationship and I was trying to try it with the teacher--to have a relationship with that teacher. It was an attempt on my own to get back into life.

Q. So did you think that the jury would not believe you about the attack if they knew that you had engaged in another one-night stand?

A. I just don't know. I was just so, so afraid that nobody would believe me--nobody would believe me what happened to me.

**[Pause.]**

A. I did not lie. I took an oath, and I said the truth, and I did not lie.

Q. When you were asked a question about not having contact--or excuse me, when you made the statement that you had no contact with men anymore, did the incident with the teacher run through your mind?

A. Yes.

Q. Did you intentionally not mention that because you didn't want the jury to think poorly of you?

A. No, I did not intentionally suppress that. I just was afraid that nobody would believe me.

Q. What do you mean you're afraid nobody would believe you?

A. I mean by that I was afraid that nothing would happen to that man after he had done those things to me. I was so afraid that nobody would respect what I had to go through the entire year--nobody would understand what had happened to me.

Q. So you were afraid that the jury would not punish Sergeant Stewart if they knew about the sex with the teacher?

A. Well, the situation was very, very difficult for me. I don't really know exactly what I thought in detail at the time, but the whole situation was very, very difficult for me.

MJ: Thank you, Ms. Heinrich. Any questions based on mine?

ATC: No, Your Honor.

CDC: Just one for clarification, Your Honor.

**RECROSS-EXAMINATION**
**Questions by the civilian defense counsel:**

Q. Ms. Heinrich, did you also have sexual contact with a very tall black guest at your pension?

ATC: Objection, Your Honor.

MJ: Overruled. It seems to go to your direct examination as to how often and with how many because she did say only one--overruled.

A. No, not correct.

CDC: Thank you, Your Honor, no further questions.

MJ: Temporary?

**ATC: Temporary excusal, Your Honor.**

**[The witness was temporarily excused, duly warned, and withdrew from the courtroom.]**

Heinrich's testimony would be called into question later during the session.

Following her testimony, the defense called Donna Leyden, a 71-year-old Canadian woman living in Baden-Baden, Germany, at the time of the trial, to testify via phone.

When the government cited no notice in objecting to the witness being allowed to testify, defense attorneys countered by telling Judge Kuhfahl they had learned of her name only 30 minutes earlier. The judge overruled the government's objection and the questioning began.

After confirming that she had met Heinrich at the Heubethof, a bed and breakfast type of lodge in Allgaeu where Heinrich worked during the summer of 2009, Leyden recounted how Heinrich had described to her an encounter she had had with a teacher who was also staying at the inn.

"Yes. I remember quite clearly because, as I said before, I am 71 years old and she told me that there was a school class there," she explained, "and that they had a teacher that was really quite handsome and she would like to maybe get him to perhaps go to bed with her.

"And she said that she had plans and that she would see what happens. And I thought it was kind of weird her telling me this stuff," Leyden continued. "And then—this was on a Wednesday. I had brought the wedding gown up to the lodge, and on the Friday night I came back again for the wedding ceremony. And (Heinrich) came to me very excited and said that it worked out last night—that could have been Thursday, I guess—and said that she had made a nice romantic picnic and gone on the Tobol river and then they came back and had sex...I thought it was weird that she told me the story."

Asked whether Heinrich had indicated anything about whether she wanted to have a longer-term relationship with this teacher, Leyden replied.

"Oh, no, I think that she thought it was just a one-night stand."

In summary, Leyden testified that Heinrich had confided in her that she had had a one-night stand with a man despite having told the military court during Stewart's trial that she was "afraid to go—be with people."

The next defense witness was Tamara Buehler, Heinrich's roommate for six months during 2009, close friend for 11 years and owner-supervisor at her place of employment.

Asked if, during the time Heinrich lived with her, Heinrich ever told her that she had intimate sexual contact with any man, Buehler said she had—with at least two different men!

"On the first occasion, it was in July and it happened with a teacher with whom she had a picnic and—on a Thursday evening," Buehler said. "And the next day, which was Friday morning, she came to me and told me that she had sex with him."

Asked about the second occasion, she provided many details.

"The second occasion was we had—we had a drama group from the Senegal at our place, and there was one guy who was two meters and seven centimeters tall and 145 kilograms in weight," she explained. "His name is Pub."

Buehler went on to explain what Heinrich told her the next morning about her evening with Pub.

"(S)he came back being very happy and told me that they had sexual intercourse, that she gave him a blow job, and that she wanted him to do the same for her, but he did not do that."

Asked if that was the only time Heinrich had told her that she had sexual intercourse with the African, Buehler said it was not. Heinrich and Pub had sex again August 14, 2009.

Again, contrary to what Heinrich told the court while under oath during the Stewart's trial, Buehler said Heinrich did not appear to be scared to be with people.

"She appeared to be happy to be with others, and she always had been the center of attention," Buehler told the court.

On cross-examination by the trial counsel, Buehler was asked if, prior to testifying, she had reviewed a November 2009 letter she had written to Captain Gleich. She said she had.

Asked why she didn't tell Heinrich about the letter she wrote to Captain Gleich, Buehler's answer was shocking.

"I was afraid of her reaction," Buehler explained. "Prior to her vacation, she had bought herself a book about serial murderers, and I just did not know how she would react if I had told her."

Asked what caused her to want to do something (i.e., speak out) in November 2009, more than two months after the trial, Buehler said she wanted "the truth to come to light."

"I learned of some things," she explained further. "And the most important thing was that on Halloween I found out—I heard from her that she went to a party, met a man there, went to his place, and had sex, and I was just shocked about that. She didn't know the man. She met him there. She didn't even know him--."

A short while later, while Buehler was still on the witness stand, Judge Kuhfahl asked her if Heinrich had specifically said "sexual intercourse and not just sexual activity?"

"Yes. And she said that he wanted to have anal intercourse while she was bent over the radio, and she didn't want that," Buehler continued. "And she also told me that on that incident she was not using a condom—I'm sorry, she was using a condom because usually she would not use a condom, and that's really a topic usually that we quarrel about because we have different opinions on that."

"And you were told all of this prior to the original court-martial?" the military judge asked.

Buehler said she was.

Before she finished answering a few other questions from Judge Kuhfahl, Buehler made sure he heard something else she learned from Heinrich.

"She wanted to meet Pub again after the court-martial," Buehler said.

Apparently catching the military judge by surprise, he asked her to repeat what she had said.

"She wanted to meet Pub again after the court-martial."

The statement stunned Stewart.

"I was sitting there like, 'Holy shit, this is the greatest day in such a long time, probably since the birth of my youngest daughter,'" Stewart said. He was feeling vindication upon hearing others say the things he had been saying for so long.

"People I don't even know are saying it. I'm just sitting there thinking, 'There's no way I'm not going home.' That was the first time I felt like, 'Hey, I'm gonna walk out of prison.'

"To me, it felt like I was convicted of murder with a knife that had my DNA on it (and) now I have a forensic specialist saying there's no way that could be my DNA," Stewart said. "It's not even the same nationality or person and then they've got a red-light picture of me in a different place that proves I wasn't even there.

"That's how I felt right then: truly vindicated."

"I'm thinking, man, this is great. I just have to hold on a little longer. There's gonna be some more valleys. Gotta hold it together here."

During the lunch break, Stewart explained, his wife, Freija, made a statement—one he will never forget—to lighten the mood among those in his group of supporters.

"My wife is right behind me and she says, 'You know, I might just say that it was alcohol and it was dark, but, man, am I disappointed in the person that you chose to sleep with,'" she said, according to her husband. "Everybody started laughing. It really showed the strength and resolve of my wife."

Stewart's accuser was out of the courtroom when the statement was made, he said, so she didn't hear it.

After his wife made that statement, Stewart thanked all of his supporters—including those people who he had not even met who came to testify on his behalf—and, in front of them, apologized to his wife and everyone else for putting himself ahead of his family and getting himself into the situation he was in. He also promised her that nothing like it would ever happen again.

"I wanted my wife to know, in front of everybody else... no matter what happens today, my time in Special Forces is done and my (priority) is my wife and my kids," he said.

"It was a difficult time for me, just because who wants to admit to letting people down," he continued. "Who wants to acknowledge that they failed people? Who wants to admit that they let people down? But I did it."

Heinrich returned to the witness stand one more time as the last witness of the day for the government. Though she denied that she had had sexual encounters with two men, she did not deny having had sex with one man—the teacher—in direct contradiction to her earlier statement, "I have no contacts to men anymore."

The hearing ended and everyone in the courtroom expected Judge Kuhfahl to make his recommendation in a process that would probably take about 10 days. Once made, that recommendation would be forwarded to the convening authority for a decision within about two weeks.

As with many aspects of Stewart's case, things didn't work out as expected. He remained in the Special Housing Unit at Mannheim until late August. At the prison, he questioned the commandant about why he was being held in the SHU against regulations, and the commandant told him, "You know, you shouldn't really poke the bear in the eye when he's the one who's got the keys... and the authority to allow you to come up to the general population."

# Good News, Not Great News

**On August 26, 2010, Stewart was still a prisoner at the U.S. military prison in Mannheim, Germany, when he received word about a decision being made by Brigadier General Steven L. Salazar, the General Courts-Martial Convening Authority over his case.**

**General Salazar disagreed with the opinion of Lieutenant Colonel Francisco Villa, his staff judge advocate, who said that "there is no legal error; therefore, no corrective action is warranted" and his recommendation that the sentence issued by the court August 20, 2009, be approved. The exact wording of the general's decision appears below:**

**ACTION BY THE CONVENING AUTHORITY:**

After having considered this memorandum and all 27 enclosures, I disagree with the recommendation of the Staff Judge Advocate. I hereby disapprove the findings of Guilty of Specification 1 of Charge II and Charge II and dismiss Specification 1 of Charge II. In reassessing the sentence I have applied the principles of United States v. Reed, 33 M.J. 98, 99-100 (CMA 1991); the United States v. Sales, 22 M.J. 305, and United States v. Moffeit, 63 M.J. 40 and have determined that a two (2) year reduction of the sentence to confinement is warranted. I have further determined that clemency shall be given in the form of an additional 3 year reduction of the sentence to confinement and a reduction of the adjudged Dishonorable Discharge to a Bad-Conduct Discharge. I therefore approve only so much of the sentence as provides for confinement for three (3) years and a Bad-Conduct Discharge.

**Below is further clarification of the general's decision:**

• First, the general reduced the length of Stewart's sentence from eight years (with one year already served) to three years, making him eligible for parole immediately;

• Second, he dismissed the charge of inveigling (i.e., using flatter to accomplish an objective;

• Third, he changed Stewart's discharge condition from "dishonorable" to "bad conduct"; and

• Finally, he waived the automatic forfeiture of all of Stewart's pay and allowances for a period of six months and directed that the funds go to Stewart's wife, Freija.

In the end, however, Stewart did not get the retrial he had wanted.

"When those orders were signed, a lot of the other guards—old guards that had been doing prison (duty) for a long time—were excited," Stewart said. "I mean, real excited.

"They're like, 'Kelly, look man, this is good for ya,' because they'd never seen someone get three-quarters of their sentence taken away and all these other things" plus they'd seen him become eligible for parole, have visitation with his wife and kids, etc.

"Finally, the guys in there had some respect for me," Stewart said, adding, "I felt like shit, because that's not what I wanted. I just wanted a retrial and, at that point, I knew I was going back to prison or somewhere else and I was gonna be a convicted felon." That was something he had hoped was never going to happen.

Soon, Stewart was headed back to Fort Leavenworth, given "very professional" treatment like that he received en route to Mannheim, this time accompanied by two guards—one male and one female.

Upon returning to Fort Leavenworth, the prison was in serious turmoil following a riot that reportedly resulted from some prisoners feeling like the guards had treated them badly.

"That's what I went back to, which was a very difficult time."

Amidst his many difficulties, Stewart faced many questions from his fellow prisoners.

"Everyone's like, 'What the hell are you doing back? You've been gone for like 90 days, almost four months,'" he said. "Everyone thought I was out. Even the guards. I told 'em the whole thing, and they were even more pissed off."

They were confused, too, by the fact that Stewart, now with only a three-year sentence and up for parole, was back in a max facility.

"I think, ultimately, it's because I had been in a max facility and they weren't going to put me in a Level 2 facility," Stewart said, though the reasoning behind that decision remains unclear both to him and to the director of prisoner services with whom he talked about the matter.

About returning to Leavenworth a second time, Stewart said he actually preferred it to the prospect of having to adjust to a new prison. He was, as odd as it might sound, "comfortable there."

While at Fort Leavenworth, Stewart worked in the prison laundry and was involved with one of the three charitable organizations run by prisoners of the facility. Along with more than 400 of his fellow inmates earning no more than 15 cents an hour doing jobs around the prison, he helped raised as much as $5,000 per year to donate to worthwhile causes outside of the prison.

He also enjoyed teaching classes to fellow inmates, got involved in the prison ministry programs and tried to be "the voice of the inmates to the prison establishment."

Those activities would keep him busy for another seven months.

# Parole Packet

Having just won a small legal battle in the war for his freedom, Stewart now had to win another—convincing members of the Army Clemency and Parole Board that he should be released from confinement.

"My parole packet was actually 570 pages long," he said. "My mindset, when I put it together, was... 'I'm not just a name on a memo or a registration number; I'm actually a human being.

"I wanted them to see, 'Hey, here I am. You've got this female saying all of these things about me and (she's) the only person to this date... that's ever come forward and said that I was a piece of shit,'" he said, adding that, rather than being cocky or bragging, he just wanted them to know the truth.

"All these people are coming forward that know her and say that she's lying—and not only lying about my situation but, you know, she's had all these issues."

Included among the 570 pages was a list of Stewart's awards, decorations and achievements as well as dozens of letters written by family members, friends and fellow soldiers. The goal: to provide panel members a better understanding of who Stewart is as they considered his sentence.

To read some of the letters and other documents included in Stewart's parole packet, visit http://ThreeDaysInAugust.com.

# Leaving Fort Leavenworth Again

It was a day Stewart had looked forward to with both excitement and trepidation. On one hand, he was getting out of prison. On the other, it was humiliating for him to think about his parents having to come to the prison to pick up their son.

On March 31, 2011, Stewart was released from the U.S. Military Disciplinary Barracks at Fort Leavenworth, Kansas.

Stewart's wife, Freija, would have been there to pick him up that day, but the legal battle had drained their finances so much that they decided it would be best for all involved if she and their children waited until the fall—while they were en route to her next Army assignment in Colorado—to see him. Instead, his parents met him outside the prison gates at around 11 o'clock that morning.

Living outside of prison as a "free man" required Stewart to make several adjustments, one of which involved doors.

Stewart said he waited for his dad to open the door of the truck for him. Why?

"Because, in prison, we don't open our doors," he explained. "(The guards) open the doors for us and they close them behind us."

As soon as he got into the truck, Stewart spent time several minutes on the phone with his wife and a few other people.

After that, his dad drove him to a convenience store so he could buy a pair of sunglasses to replace the ones he forgot in his cell amidst the excitement of leaving prison.

"I actually had cash in my hands that I had just gotten five minutes earlier," he explained. "I hadn't seen cash in several years. Now, I've got a couple twenties and some change in my hand. Loose change. I hadn't seen change in several years."

At the convenience store, Stewart felt like everybody knew he had just gotten out of prison.

"I felt like everybody was staring at me," he said.

He went on to describe the thoughts swimming through his mind as he grabbed a bottle of water, some sunflower seeds and other items.

"I actually wanted to buy up like 50 things in there, but I was trying to pace myself," he said, describing himself as being like the proverbial "kid in a candy store."

"You've been eating the same bland food for two years," he continued, comparing prison food to what it might be like to eat nothing but the 12 different types of meals on a McDonald's menu for two years straight.

Stewart said he was tempted to eat some of every kind of food imaginable, but soon learned—thanks, in part, to a headache and a "sugar rush"—that doing so was dangerous for someone coming off a bland prison diet.

In addition to dietary concerns, Stewart talked about having to make other adjustments to life outside prison.

"I'd be lying to say I haven't had to make some adjustments," he said, before explaining that he found out that your face gets sore if you laugh and smile a lot for the first time in a long time.

"I spent the first 30 or 40 minutes when we were driving trying to look at so many different things," he said, "because I'd been living in the same gray area where the farthest distance you could see was maybe 150 meters."

He went on to describe the jubilation of being able to see colors, things and people he hadn't seen in a while.

Asked if his experience was similar to the scene played out in so many movies when a man leaves prison and is struck by how green the grass is or how blue the sky is, he said it was and then elaborated on life inside the walls.

"Only in prison do you see a plane fly overhead and actually try to dream about what it would be like to be on that plane," he said, explaining that such effort serves to provide you with an escape from where you are.

"After several months in prison, you don't dream outside the walls," Stewart said, "because the reality is you don't know what it's gonna be like outside the walls."

For Stewart, his first few days of life outside of Fort Leavenworth involved driving to Kentucky, where one of his dad's brothers would give him a Dodge truck to drive while out of prison, and then on to Virginia, where another of his dad's brothers would give him a steady job and a place to stay while on parole. Their generosity was much appreciated.

Once in Virginia, Stewart would have to incorporate more serious adjustments into his life.

Being on parole meant that he would have to report to a parole officer on a regular basis, informing him of his activities. The biggest adjustment of all, however, involving having to carry the "sex offender" label and register as a sex offender with law enforcement authorities wherever he lived and traveled for the rest of his life—unless, that is, he could get his verdict overturned.

Today, Stewart lives in rural Virginia inside a 31-ft trailer equipped with a working kitchen, stove, bathroom, toilet, 19-inch television and microwave oven. He communicates with his wife and children via Skype, using the new MacBook Pro his father purchased for him.

Though he's earning money while working for his uncle, Stewart has a long and costly road ahead of him. In addition to the costs of continuing his fight for a new trial and, hopefully, getting his conviction overturned, he has other costs weighing on him.

One week before he arrived at Fort Leavenworth the first time, the Army informed him that he had to pay back the $20,000 bonus he received in 2006. Because he received it while serving in a combat zone, Stewart believes it should have been tax-free. The Army thinks otherwise.

In addition, the Army says Stewart owes $3,478.27 for breaking his lease in Germany before it was up, despite the fact that the Soldiers and Sailors Relief Act says that one can get out of a lease if he is deployed or has a change in duty assignment—such as being reassigned to Fort Leavenworth. That made the total the Army says Stewart owes $23,478.27.

# The Last Mission in Iraq

U.S. Army Sergeant First Class Kelly A. Stewart deployed to Iraq several times during his seven-year career as a Special Forces professional and built a reputation as a stand-up guy who would do anything for his country, according to Neal Riley, a man who served with Stewart during his last mission in Iraq. For eight months in 2006, both were members of a Special Operations Task Force Operations Detachment Alpha (a.k.a., "A-Team"). On May 14, 2010, I spoke with Riley about the time he spent with his brother in arms.

Riley recalled the time he spent with Stewart as one during which he "got a new brother".

"My team was assigned to work with an Iraqi Special Operations force," Riley explained, "and our job was to, basically, go after high-value targets and, that's when I began working with Kelly" who was on a different team.

"I would say Kelly struck me right away as someone who really has an aptitude for Special Operations type of work and, especially, the type of work we were doing.

"And the reason is, I think a lot of people get into Special Forces for various reasons, but Kelly's family background kind of went to that. His father was Special Operations and served in Vietnam on the Air Force side."

Riley came from the same background. His father was in Special Forces, and he counts that experience as one which gave him "a real good understanding of how Special Operations works."

"Technically, Kelly struck me as somebody who was very proficient and very good at his job," he continued. "And that wasn't just my impression, that was the impression of my entire team."

Stewart, at that time, was working a little bit more on the intelligence side, whereas Riley and his team were working on the operations side.

"We were the guys that were headed out of the Green Zone, the safe zone, and going out into Sadr City to carry out the missions that were assigned to us," Riley said.

During these types of missions, he said, survivability relies solely on intelligence and on the kind of information soldiers get before they go in there.

"That will determine your success or failure of your mission and whether or not your guys are gonna come back alive," he concluded.

"Right away, Kelly built up a huge reputation with my team (and became) the go-to guy for us.

"Because he had such knowledge on where we were headed and the kinds of people we were up against, we began asking him if he wanted to come with us.

Riley went on to explain that, though the intel side does not normally mix with the operations side, things were different when it came to Stewart. Not only did he jump at any chance he could get to work with the operators, but the operators came to believe that if they "had a vacant slot, a seat that needed to be filled, an extra gun with us, (Stewart) was going to be that guy."

Considering that their missions almost always involved firefights and run-ins with Improvised Explosive Devices, Riley said Stewart's eagerness to serve set him apart.

"Not everybody was jumping at the opportunity to go with us," Riley explained. "Kelly was an individual who, anytime we needed somebody, he was going to be there. But we always wanted to choose him as well, because he had the knowledge, the specialized knowledge, that would help us plan the mission better—and he also was technically proficient as a gunslinger too, to put it bluntly. (He was) always welcome, for those reasons.

On numerous occasions, Riley had the opportunity to see Stewart perform on the battlefield.

"(On) a lot of the missions, we would meet heavy resistance," Riley said. "That would come in the form of Mahdi Militia or any type of militia force that would be on a rooftop—maybe a four- or five-story building—and they would be armed with anything from AK-47 to an RPG rocket.

"There were early warnings systems in place in these areas in Sadr City," he continued. "Someone would trip or pull a fuse and take out the power for a whole city grid and that would be a warning that the Americans were coming and these guys would be alerted and there would be a heavy firefight. So that's the environment we worked in.

"If we had it our way, we would go in just like a SWAT team here in America would go in—no shots fired, you arrest your individual you were looking for, you bring him back, collect some evidence, take some pictures, bring the individual back to an Iraqi court, turn him over to an Iraqi judge, present the evidence, and you're done. That's the perfect mission.

"Typically," he said, "it didn't end that way. Typically, it would end in a firefight.

It was during such firefights that Riley got to see Stewart in action.

"There were countless times—and I think it was pretty typical of our missions and the people we were working with that—during any given mission, somebody would save your life and you would save their life, countless times, just by the nature of what we were doing.

"Whether it was on the operations side where Kelly contributed to a high degree or on the planning side where he contributed to a high degree, if you were able to gather intelligence on whether there was an IED planted on a certain route and you were able to avoid that route, then you can see how that could be incredibly important. (It) really drives those statistics with low casualty rates.

"On the personal side," Riley said, "you only have to do that a couple times for somebody, where you're relying on them like that and they're coming through for you before suddenly you've got a new brother. That's pretty much how that went down. So we operated for about eight months like that."

On their last mission in Iraq, Riley and Stewart saw a comrade critically wounded, shot through the chest.

"Basically, my role switched from being a combat leader to a medic that quick, and Kelly took up the slack," said Riley, who was serving dual roles as both a troop leader and medic. "(Kelly) went from being just an 'extra gun' to taking up my position as a troop leader—of Iraqi troops, not American.

"I had to put down my gun in order to treat this casualty, but there were still bullets flying around—buzzing around our heads like bees, quite literally," he said. "So that was hard for me to do, but he reassured me that he had me covered.

"Kelly stood over the top of me and the casualty pretty much the whole time on the way back out of Sadr City," he continued, "and it was under intense fire."

In addition to being their last mission together, Riley said it was also the most significant.

"It sticks out in my mind the most, because it was such a good example of how you really do rely on, and quite literally put your life in, somebody else's hands.

Riley went on to describe the battle scenario.

"One of the things about Sadr City is that, if you ever heard the descriptions of Mogadishu—how a city suddenly erupted with fighters, they just come out of the woodwork—Sadr City was quite a bit like that," he explained. "People would just surface with weapons, and they were ready to fight.

"(They had) a determination and tenacity that shocked me, just absolutely shocked me," he said, adding that it was either a strong belief in martyrdom or just a real determination to crush the Americans.

"I'm not sure which," he said, "but whatever it was, I was really impressed by it; I was shocked."

Something that hasn't impressed Riley since returning from Iraq is the military justice system and the impact misconceptions appear to have had on the court-martial of his brother in arms, Stewart.

Riley believes misconceptions, fueled by German media reports and based on Hollywood movie scripts and intra-service rivalries, played a significant role in the court-martial panel reaching a verdict that called for his brother in arms to spend eight years behind bars at the U.S. Military Disciplinary Barracks at Fort Leavenworth, Kansas.

Further, Riley believes Stewart deserves the benefit of the doubt and should be granted a new trial.

"Special Forces has always been at a disadvantage with conventional troops because, by its nature, it's elite," Riley said. "The question is always, 'What makes you so special?'"

He went on to explain that there are a lot of answers to that question, but the fact that someone feels the need to ask it gives an indication of how that makes conventional forces feel sometimes.

"The whole Hollywood culture of what a Special Forces guy—a 'loose cannon' or 'rogue' soldier—can do (and) what kind of damage he can do on the run" combines with media buildup to create some serious problems in the minds of people.

In the case of Stewart, Riley was referring to the fact that German news media accounts sensationally painted his friend as a Rambo-like character loose in the Bavarian Forest, a fugitive from justice who must have been guilty because he fled his court-martial proceedings.

"I don't think that was the situation at all," Riley said emphatically.

"Like Kelly's father points out, Kelly never meant to hurt anybody. He never meant to engage. Had he decided to do any of those things, I'm convinced he could have succeeded at either one. You're talking about someone who trained people to operate in secret, underground cells.

"Could Kelly have escaped and gotten away and found himself far away from his trouble?" Riley asked rhetorically. "Yeah, I think he well could have done that.

"Could he have killed a lot of police or military who were trying to locate him? Yeah. Absolutely. I saw his effectiveness in combat.

"He chose not to do either one of those," Riley reasoned. "I don't think either even entered his mind.

"All you've got to do to understand his motivation is to understand his commitment to Special Forces and to his brothers in the Special Forces, but also to his family—to his mother, his father, and certainly to his kids and his wife.

"I define any kind of suggestion that he would have done any of those things as absolutely ludicrous.

"I think it also probably speaks to his character in regards to the crime that he was accused of as well."

Riley believes it's important for the average reader looking at Stewart's story to understand that what's at stake "is bigger than just the soldier, just Kelly, because I think that every Special Operations soldier—or any soldier—is at risk for these kinds of outcomes.

"When you look at the effect that it has, not just on him—I mean, the poor guy is sitting in Leavenworth without any, at this point, without any real hope for a change.

"You obviously can see what it does to his family. Not only just draining their finances, but putting on incredible stress. Everyday, they wake up to face this situation.

"Man, it's gut-wrenching," he continued. "It just rips my heart out."

Riley went on to note that there are so many other soldiers who face battles similar to the one faced by Stewart.

"Look at the (Navy) SEAL who just got vindicated. Guess what? He's a fighter!" Riley said, referring to SO2 Matthew V. McCabe, one of the three U.S. Navy SEALs who opted to face court-martial rather than have an unwarranted stain on his record.

"This guy wanted to go to trial so he could beat this thing," Riley said.

McCabe was one of three SEALS who was offered administrative punishment after an Iraqi insurgent alleged that he was punched in the stomach during his apprehension for his alleged involvement in the murder and mutilation of the bodies of four Blackwater contractors in Fallujah, Iraq, in March 2004. All three

SEALs were acquitted during court-martial proceedings in April and May 2010.

"I guarantee you, this scared him more than anything he every faced in combat," Riley said. "Every soldier's scared of this kind of scenario way more than any ever facing the bullets of an enemy.

"You always hope that somebody's got your back."

Riley has Stewart's back.

"I got to know him pretty well because of the circumstances we were in," Riley explained. "Just from the outset, because he's somebody that I know and I trusted him with my life, I don't think the charges are true.

"At the same time, for a lot of reasons—mostly because of my medical training, I think—I'm able to pull back and look at some things a little more objectively.

"In other words, if I remove my emotional response to that and I look at the evidence that I've been able to see—and I'm a layman as far as the law is concerned, but I still think my perspective is valid—if I'm able to look at the evidence without any emotion, I can see there are some serious inconsistencies and that there seems to be a blatant disregard for not only the facts that are available, but a complete... no one has investigated any further to uncover anything.

According to Riley, any reasonable individual looking at the case would conclude, at a minimum, that it warrants a retrial or some sort of submission of new evidence or review.

"So far, it seems that the opposite is happening," he said. "Somebody, or a group of people, for whatever reason, are blocking any kind of moves in that direction.

"I think, if we owe our veterans anything, it's an opportunity to present all the facts and to have a review that seems to be thorough—and this one, so far, reeks of injustice. Complete injustice."

He went on to say that he thinks our society is gonna have a lot of veterans entering into the justice system just by the nature of the effects of war, and that he thinks our country has to give every veteran the benefit of the doubt.

"(Kelly's) is just one case, just the tip of the iceberg, I think, for what our society has to deal with," he said. "Certainly, Kelly deserves the benefit of the doubt and he deserves the fair trial, and I don't think he got (it)."

# AFTERWORD

"I'll assume all responsibility and all punishment," said Stewart. "You know, if they came to me right now and said, 'You know what? We're gonna drop all these charges but find you guilty of adultery and you're gonna have to retire.' You know what? I'll wear that, because that I am guilty of. I did do that, and I admitted to that in court and that story's never changed."

After encouraging me to look through the Record of Trial and the content of my interviews with him, he said his story has never changed, it's never varied, and then he spoke about his accuser.

"If you look at (Greta Heinrich's) story, as time goes on, her story gets more detailed and better," he explained. "It becomes more theatrical, and there's not one person that's come forward to this date and said, 'That's the kind of person Kelly is. He's guilty.'"

Stewart added that he's put everything about his case out on the internet at SaveThisSoldier.com so that anyone can email him or his dad and say, "Bullshit."

"To date, no one has done that," he concluded, while noting that many people have come forward about his accuser.

Government attorneys have fought so hard against a retrial, Stewart said, because the Uniform Code of Military Justice prohibits them from introducing any new evidence into such a proceeding.

"They didn't want a retrial, because they know they didn't have a strong case to begin with, and, if this goes in there with a different set of jurors and we're able to add all this new evidence and all these new people in there, they know they're screwed. That's their motivation."

As for Brigadier General Steven L. Salazar, Stewart believes that, while taking 15 months to take action instead of the typical review time of 120 days, "He did the most that he could for me."

Stewart said his civilian defense counsel told him his case is the only one he's seen during 35 years of practicing law that any convening authority has ever taken that long to take action.

"If it was such an easy decision, why didn't the general do it earlier?" Stewart asked.

Stewart's case is not unique. He was reminded of that fact in mid-March when he received a call from someone who pointed him to a newspaper article (See Top Special Forces Command NCO under investigation, FayObserver.com, May 6, 2011), about Command Sergeant Major Mario Vigil, the former top enlisted soldier in Army Special Forces Command at Fort Bragg, North Carolina.

The senior noncommissioned officer was, according to the article, "removed from his position while commanders investigate allegations that he had an extramarital relationship" and the woman making the allegations said in court documents that she was pregnant with Vigil's child. Both parties had, according to the article, accused each other of domestic violence.

Aside from the pregnancy aspect, Stewart said, the story was no different than his own and could have escalated to something more.

Fortunately for Command Sergeant Major Vigil, he was allowed to retire from the Army without the case going to a court-martial. The case, however, is not without irony when seen side by side with Stewart's case.

Command Sergeant Major Vigil is the same man who, along with Stewart's commander at the time, was one of the approving authorities responsible for the revocation of his SF tab years earlier—before Stewart's appeals process was over. As the right-hand man to the Special Forces Command commander, he recommended Stewart's SF tab—something special for which he had worked so hard—be revoked before the soldier's appeals process had ended.

"He's the guy who took my tab away," said Stewart who, at the same time he was careful to say he wasn't judging the senior noncommissioned officer, said he would have never taken someone else's SF tab before his appeals process was finished.

"He had the ability to say, 'No, don't take his tab,'" Stewart continued, but he didn't.

Conversely, Command Sergeant Major Richard "Spike" Klein, the senior enlisted person at the International Special Training Center where Stewart worked at the time of his court-martial, refused to sign the tab revocation paperwork.

In the end, Stewart said he believes in the system and doesn't want what happened to him to happen to anyone else. Despite the fact that filters are in place to ensure justice, problems occur with investigators, prosecutors and others involved.

"When those people think that you're guilty, it's difficult for the people on the outside that have the authority—like General Salazar—to go against that grain," Stewart explained. "I truly believe that General Salazar thinks I'm innocent, but I don't think that he's willing to risk his career for me.

"I don't think, as a one-star (general), he was willing to just let me out of prison and take the hard right over the easy left," he said.

Stewart went on to cite what he described as examples that prove decisions like the one made by General Salazar happen all the time.

"Four-star generals—McChrystal and all these other people—wouldn't do it for Pat Tillman," he said. "So why would they do it for me when they've seen the fallout that happens when you stand up for one person?

"The system is kind of slighted in that aspect," he continued. "In order for you to be court-martialed, this is the sequence of events that has to happen: A company commander or a captain has to say, 'Yeah, there's enough stuff here for this to get pushed forward.'

"It goes to a battalion commander who's a major. That battalion commander looks at it and says, 'Yeah, this should go to a court-martial.'

"It goes to a brigade commander who's a colonel. That brigade commander says, 'Yes, this is what's going on. I need to proffer charges against this soldier.' He makes an Article 32 (investigation) happen.

"Now, three officers have already said that this should go forward," Stewart continued, explaining that a major is in charge of the Article 32 investigation and fact-finding to determine whether a trial should happen.

Citing the fact that three officers have already said it's worth prosecuting, Stewart said, "Do you think this one guy is gonna say it's not?"

At court-martial, Stewart said, he found himself facing a jury of his so-called "peers" who know already about the numerous "filters" the case had to pass through to reach the court-martial phase. Who could blame them for thinking the accused is guilty?

Stewart pointed out another "filter" that apparently failed him early in the process.

"When CID comes to that first commander, they should have already done all of their investigation work (to the point) where they felt like this was a chargeable thing," Stewart said, adding that the evidence collection, interviewing of witnesses and getting witnesses other than the accuser herself to corroborate what she was saying should have taken place before a court-martial.

But those things did not happen.

* * *

To learn more about Kelly A. Stewart and/or to help his family pay legal and other costs related to his battle for military justice, please visit: www.SaveThisSoldier.com.

* * *

For information, news and updates related to the book, visit www.ThreeDaysInAugust.com.

# ACKNOWLEDGMENTS

Many thanks to Kelly A. Stewart and his parents, John and Renate Stewart, for their efforts in helping me tell this story. Thanks also to Neal Riley for sharing firsthand knowledge of the man whose life is the focus of this book. And thanks to the numerous others—you know who you are—who helped me tell this story.

Most of all, thanks to my wife and boys who put up with me even as I spent what sometimes seemed like 25 hours a day writing and researching this book.

# ABOUT THE AUTHOR

A native of Enid, Oklahoma, Bob McCarty graduated from Oklahoma State University with a degree in journalism in 1984. During the next two decades, he served stints as an Air Force public affairs officer, a political campaign manager, a technology sales consultant and a public relations professional.

In October 2006, Bob began writing full time at BobMcCarty.com. Since then, his work has been published regularly at Andrew Breitbart's BigGovernment.com, BigHollywood.com, BigJournalism.com and BigPeace.com and occasionally at other new media sites, including PajamasMedia.com.

Bob's writing efforts have received mentions in several major media outlets, including Fox News Channel, *Chicago Sun-Times and St. Louis Post-Dispatch.* In addition, they've been cited and/or republished by several top new media outlets, including American Spectator, American Thinker, CNET News, The Drudge Report, Hot Air, Hugh Hewitt, Michelle Malkin, The Corner at National Review and World Net Daily among others.

Bob has appeared on several popular radio programs, including those hosted by Bob Grant, Curtis Sliwa, Dana Loesch, Jan Michelson, Erich "Mancow" Muller and Peter Boyles, to name a few, as well as on numerous online radio programs across the United States and abroad.

In 2010, Bob was nominated for the Hewitt Award by *The Atlantic* magazine blogger Andrew Sullivan. The short list of others who've been nominated for the award includes conservative radio talk radio legend Rush Limbaugh, so he's in good company.

Bob is married, the father of three boys, and lives near St. Louis.

# CONNECT ONLINE

Twitter = http://twitter.com/@3DaysInAugust
Facebook = https://www.facebook.com/pages/Bob-McCarty/289259524420018
For news, information and updates about the book, visit www.ThreeDaysInAugust.com

Made in the USA
Lexington, KY
14 March 2012